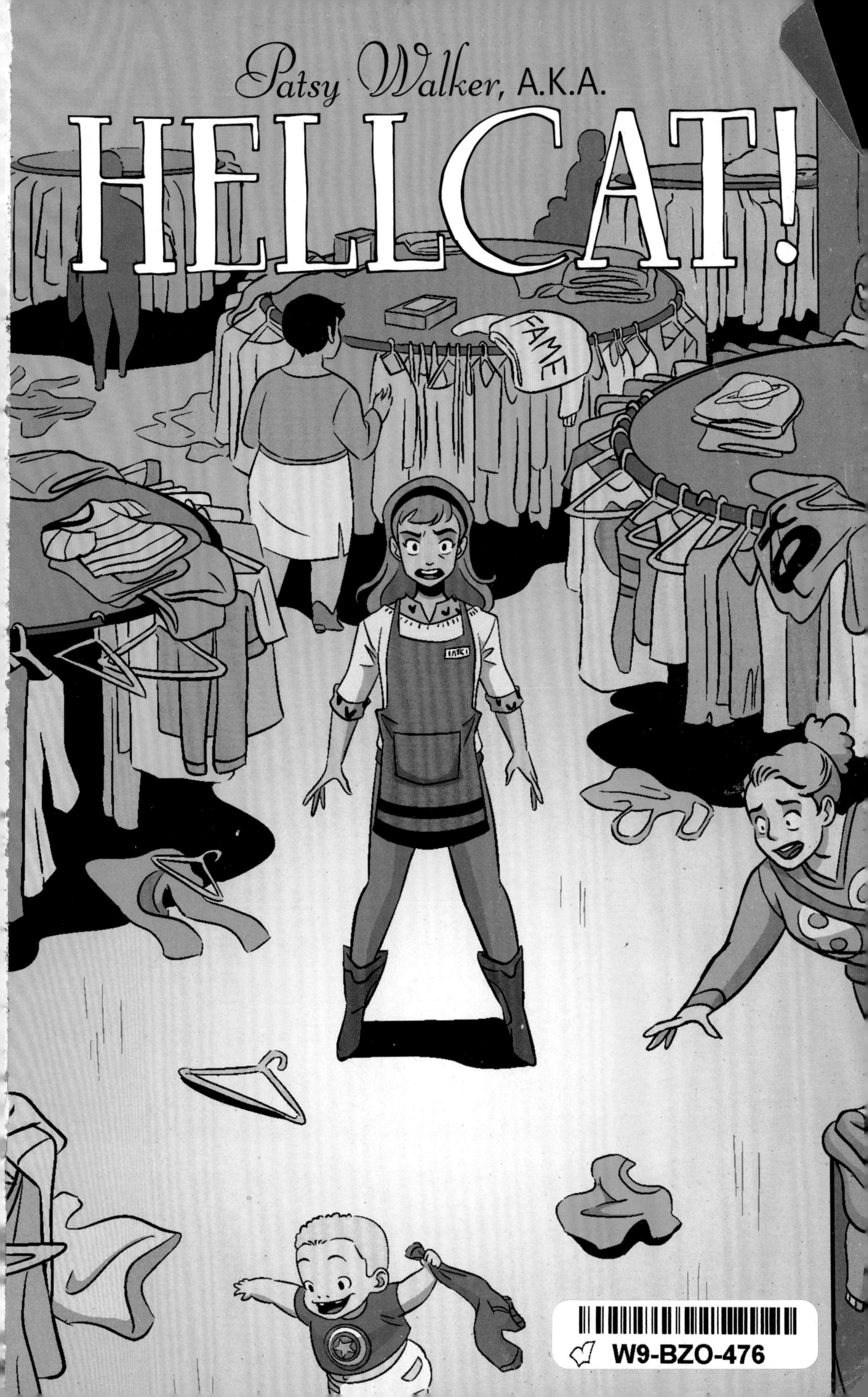
Patsy Walker, A.K.A.
HELLCAT!
FAME

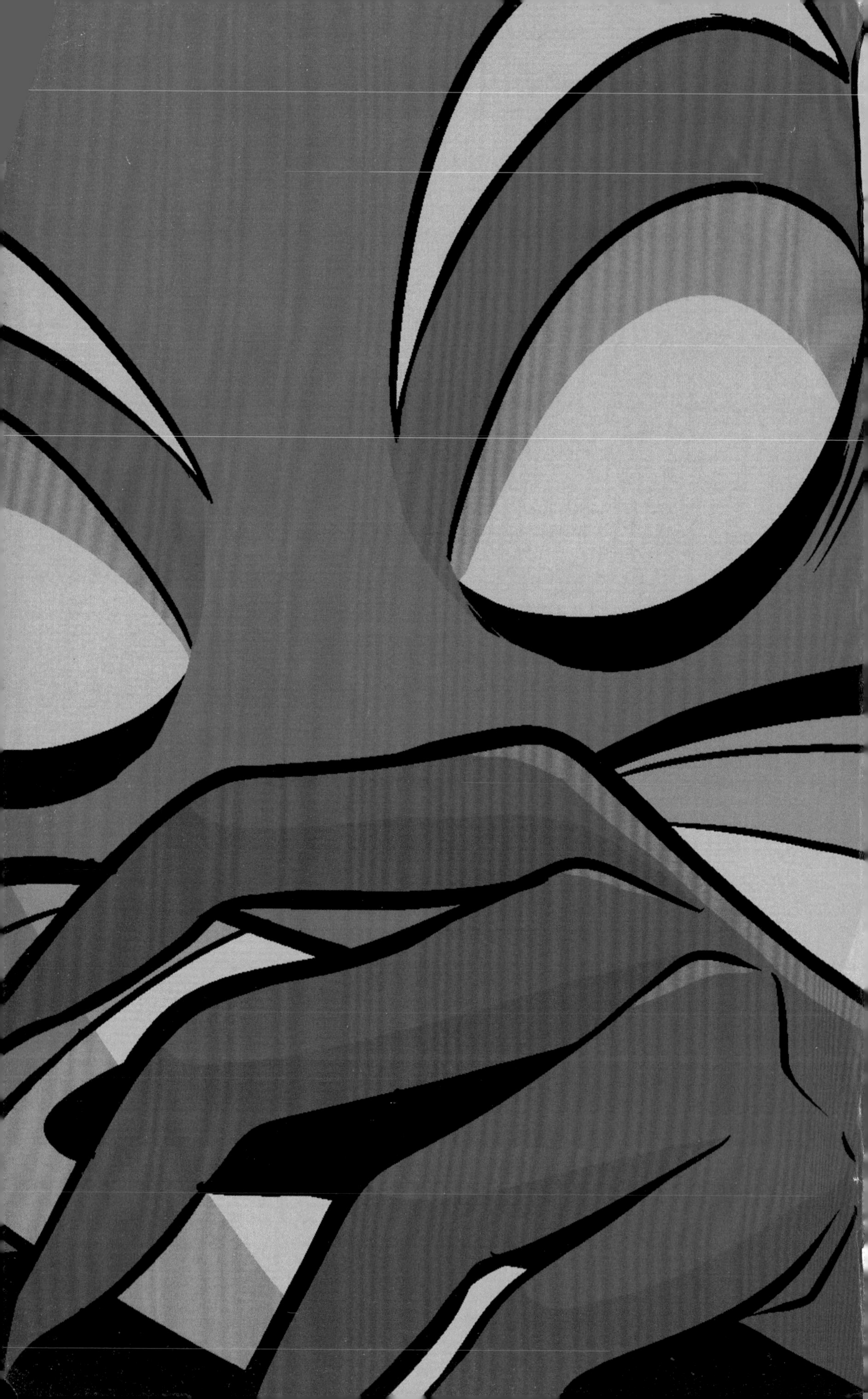

Patsy Walker, A.K.A.

HELLCAT!

Hooked on a Feline

Kate Leth
WRITER

Brittney L. Williams (#1-5)
& Natasha Allegri (#6)
ARTISTS

Megan Wilson (#1-5)
& Natasha Allegri (#6)
COLOR ARTISTS

VC's Clayton Cowles
with **Joe Sabino** (#1)
LETTERERS

Chris Robinson
ASSISTANT EDITOR

Wil Moss
EDITOR

Jennifer Grünwald
COLLECTION EDITOR

Sarah Brunstad
ASSOCIATE EDITOR

Alex Starbuck
ASSOCIATE MANAGING EDITOR

Mark D. Beazley
EDITOR, SPECIAL PROJECTS

Jeff Youngquist
VP, PRODUCTION & SPECIAL PROJECTS

David Gabriel
SVP PRINT, SALES & MARKETING

Jay Bowen
BOOK DESIGNER

Axel Alonso
EDITOR IN CHIEF

Joe Quesada
CHIEF CREATIVE OFFICER

Dan Buckley
PUBLISHER

Alan Fine
EXECUTIVE PRODUCER

PATSY WALKER, A.K.A. HELLCAT! VOL. 1: HOOKED ON A FELINE. Contains material originally published in magazine form as PATSY WALKER, A.K.A. HELLCAT! #1-6. First printing 2016. ISBN# 978-1-302-90035-9. Published by MARVEL WORLDWIDE, INC., a subsidiary of MARVEL ENTERTAINMENT, LLC. OFFICE OF PUBLICATION: 135 West 50th Street, New York, NY 10020. Copyright © 2016 MARVEL. No similarity between any of the names, characters, persons, and/or institutions in this magazine with those of any living or dead person or institution is intended, and any such similarity which may exist is purely coincidental. **Printed in Canada.** ALAN FINE, President, Marvel Entertainment; DAN BUCKLEY, President, TV, Publishing & Brand Management; JOE QUESADA, Chief Creative Officer; TOM BREVOORT, SVP of Publishing; DAVID BOGART, SVP of Business Affairs & Operations, Publishing & Partnership; C.B. CEBULSKI, VP of Brand Management & Development, Asia; DAVID GABRIEL, SVP of Sales & Marketing, Publishing; JEFF YOUNGQUIST, VP of Production & Special Projects; DAN CARR, Executive Director of Publishing Technology; ALEX MORALES, Director of Publishing Operations; SUSAN CRESPI, Production Manager; STAN LEE, Chairman Emeritus. For information regarding advertising in Marvel Comics or on Marvel.com, please contact Vit DeBellis, Integrated Sales Manager, at vdebellis@marvel.com. For Marvel subscription inquiries, please call 888-511-5480. **Manufactured between 4/22/2016 and 5/30/2016 by SOLISCO PRINTERS, SCOTT, QC, CANADA.**

10 9 8 7 6 5 4 3 2 1

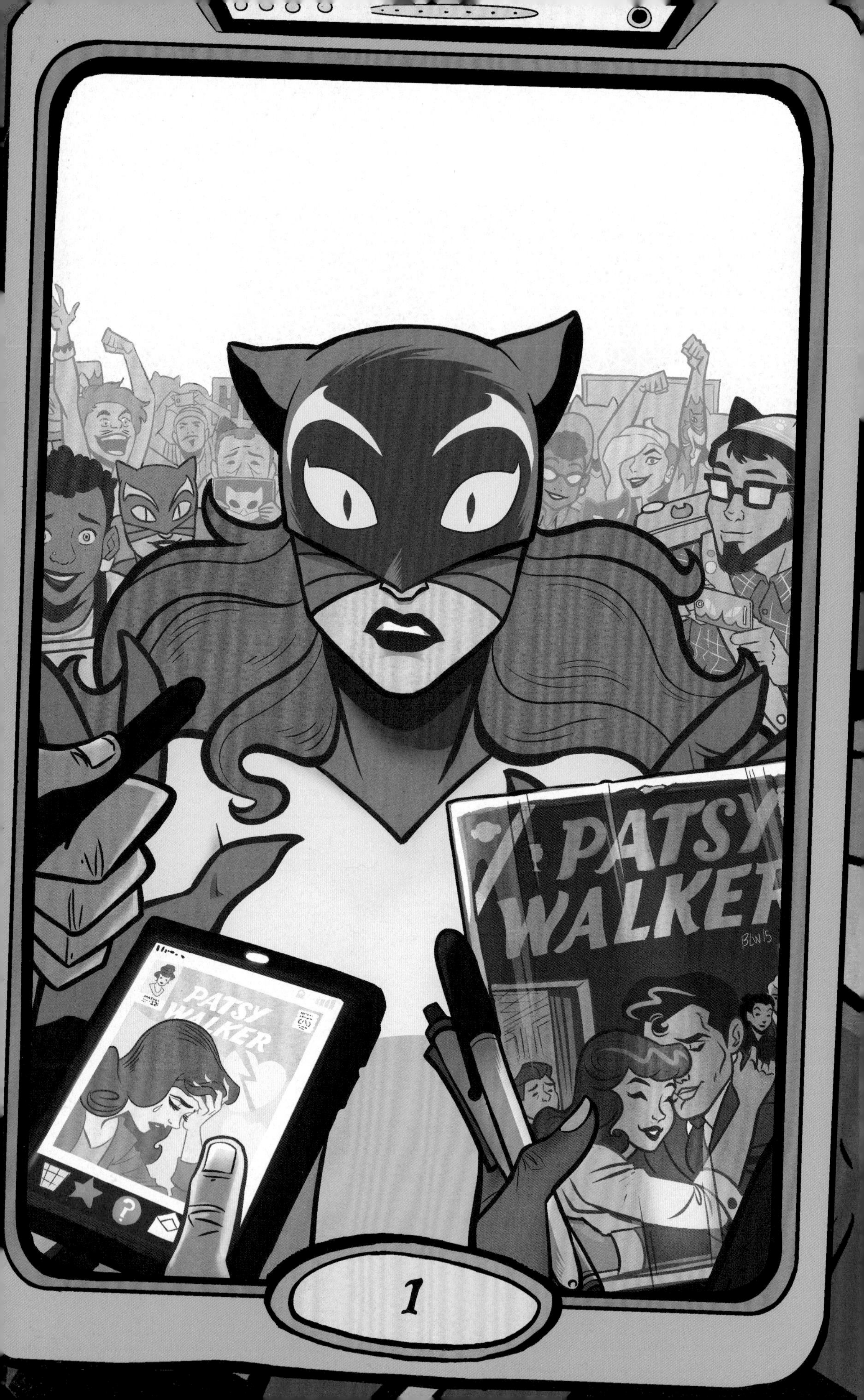
PATSY WALKER
PATSY WALKER
BLW'15
1

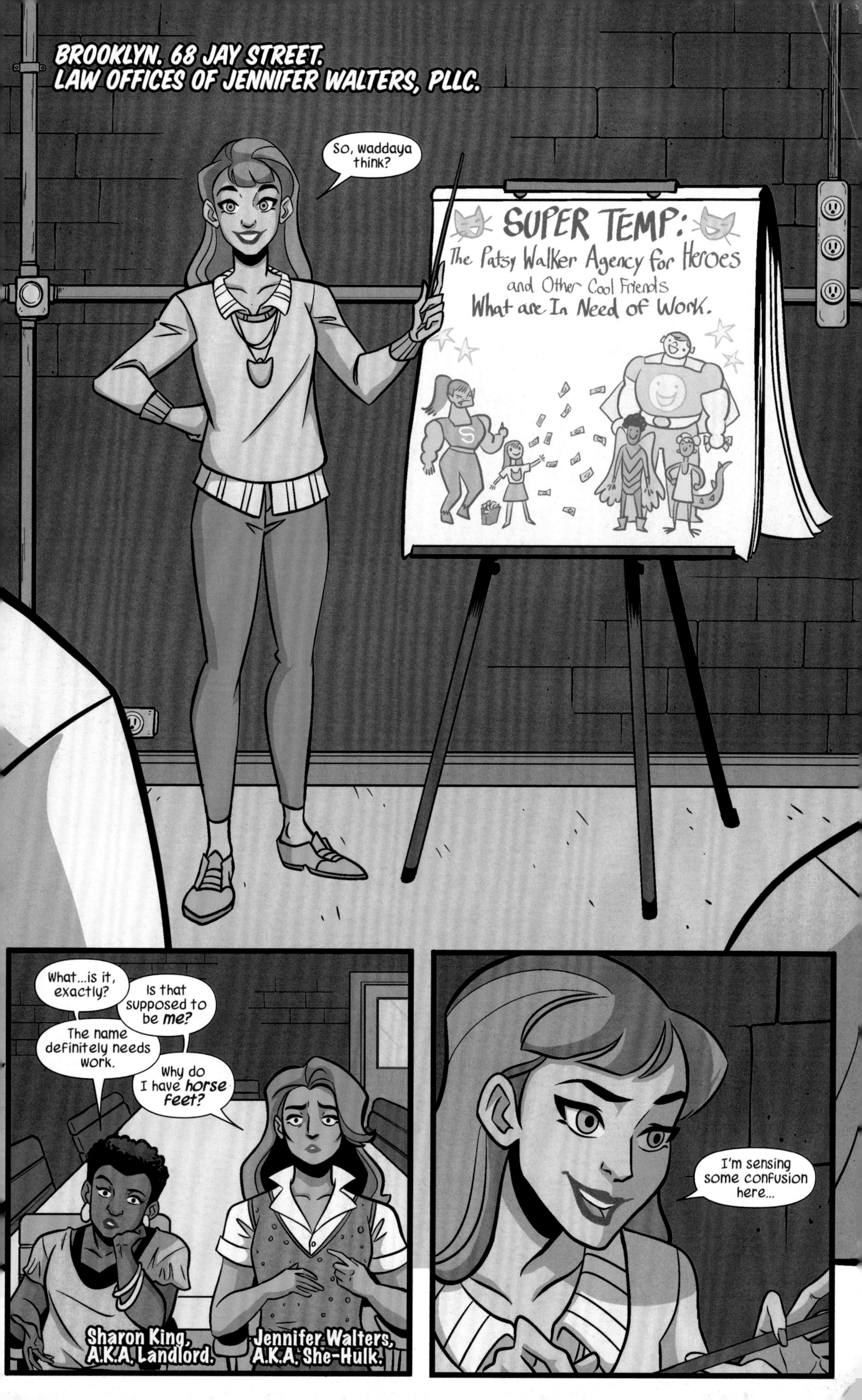
BROOKLYN. 68 JAY STREET.
LAW OFFICES OF JENNIFER WALTERS, PLLC.
So, waddaya think?
SUPER TEMP:
The Patsy Walker Agency for Heroes
and Other Cool Friends
What are In Need of Work.
What...is it, exactly?
Is that supposed to be me?
The name definitely needs work.
Why do I have horse feet?
Sharon King, A.K.A. Landlord.
Jennifer Walters, A.K.A. She-Hulk.
I'm sensing some confusion here...

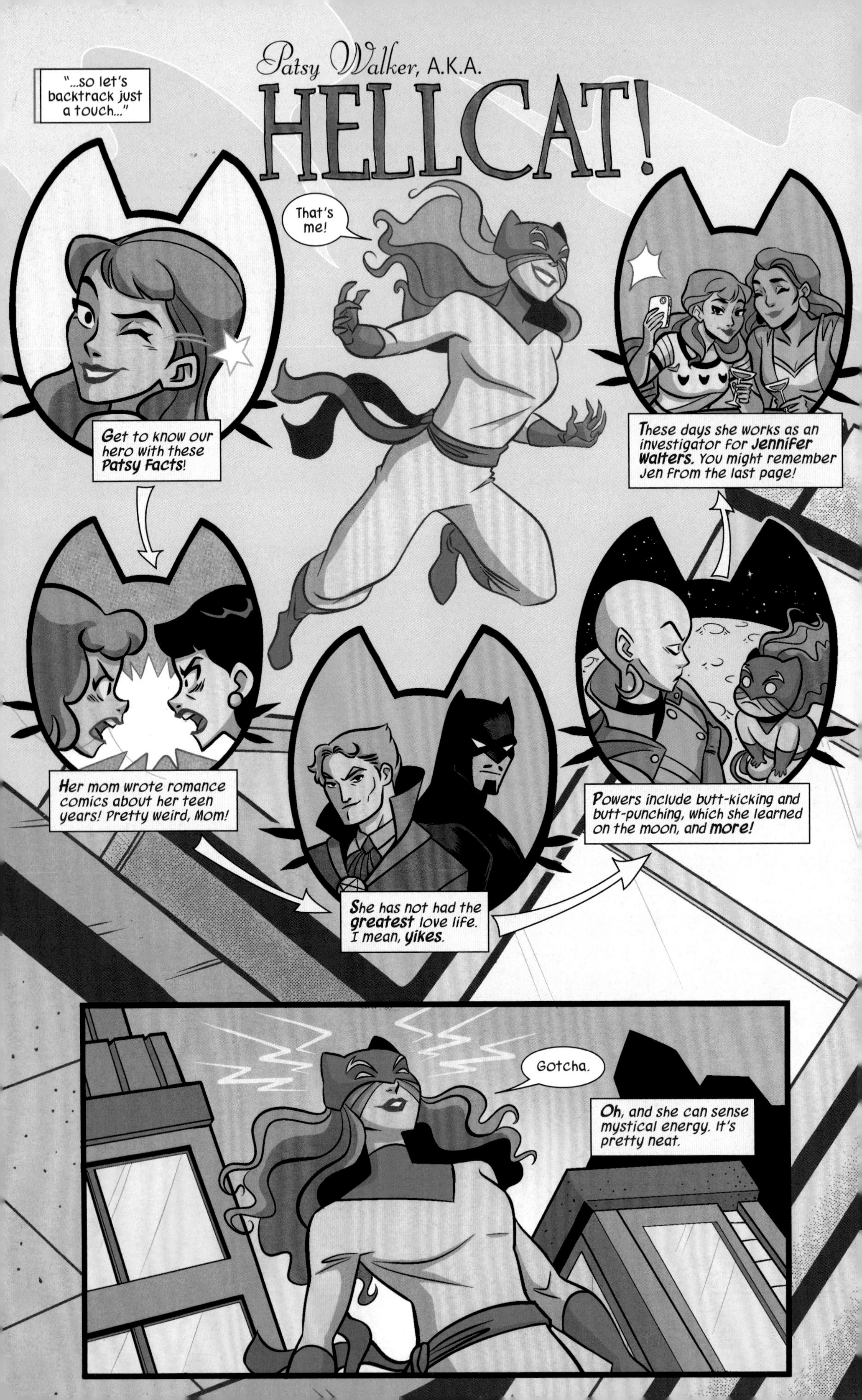
Patsy Walker, A.K.A.
HELLCAT!
"...so let's backtrack just a touch..."
That's me!
Get to know our hero with these Patsy Facts!
Her mom wrote romance comics about her teen years! Pretty weird, Mom!
She has not had the greatest love life. I mean, yikes.
Powers include butt-kicking and butt-punching, which she learned on the moon, and more!
These days she works as an investigator for Jennifer Walters. You might remember Jen from the last page!
Gotcha.
Oh, and she can sense mystical energy. It's pretty neat.

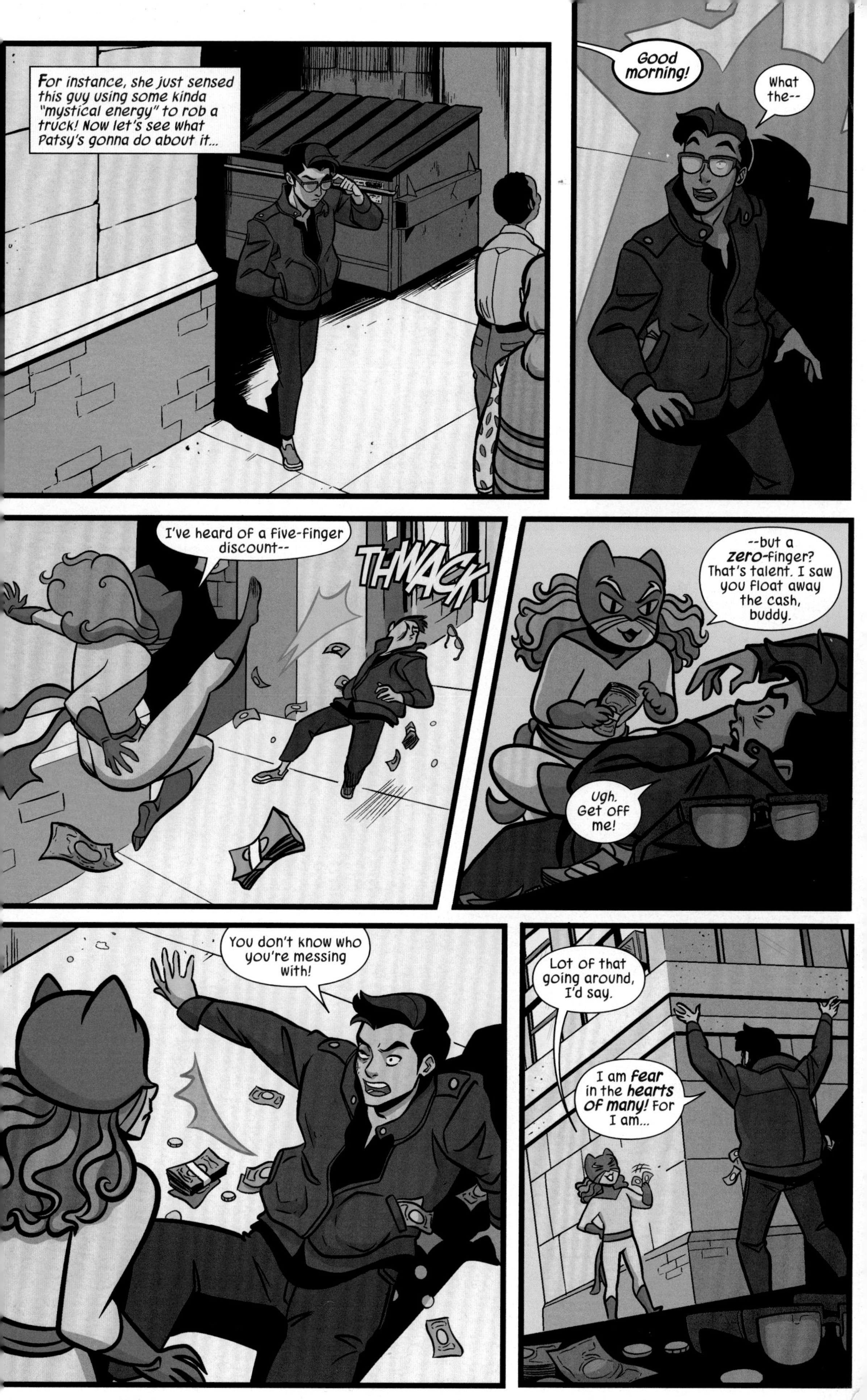
For instance, she just sensed this guy using some kinda "mystical energy" to rob a truck! Now let's see what Patsy's gonna do about it...
Good morning!
What the--
I've heard of a five-finger discount--
THWACK
--but a zero-finger? That's talent. I saw you float away the cash, buddy.
Ugh. Get off me!
You don't know who you're messing with!
Lot of that going around, I'd say.
I am fear in the hearts of many! For I am...

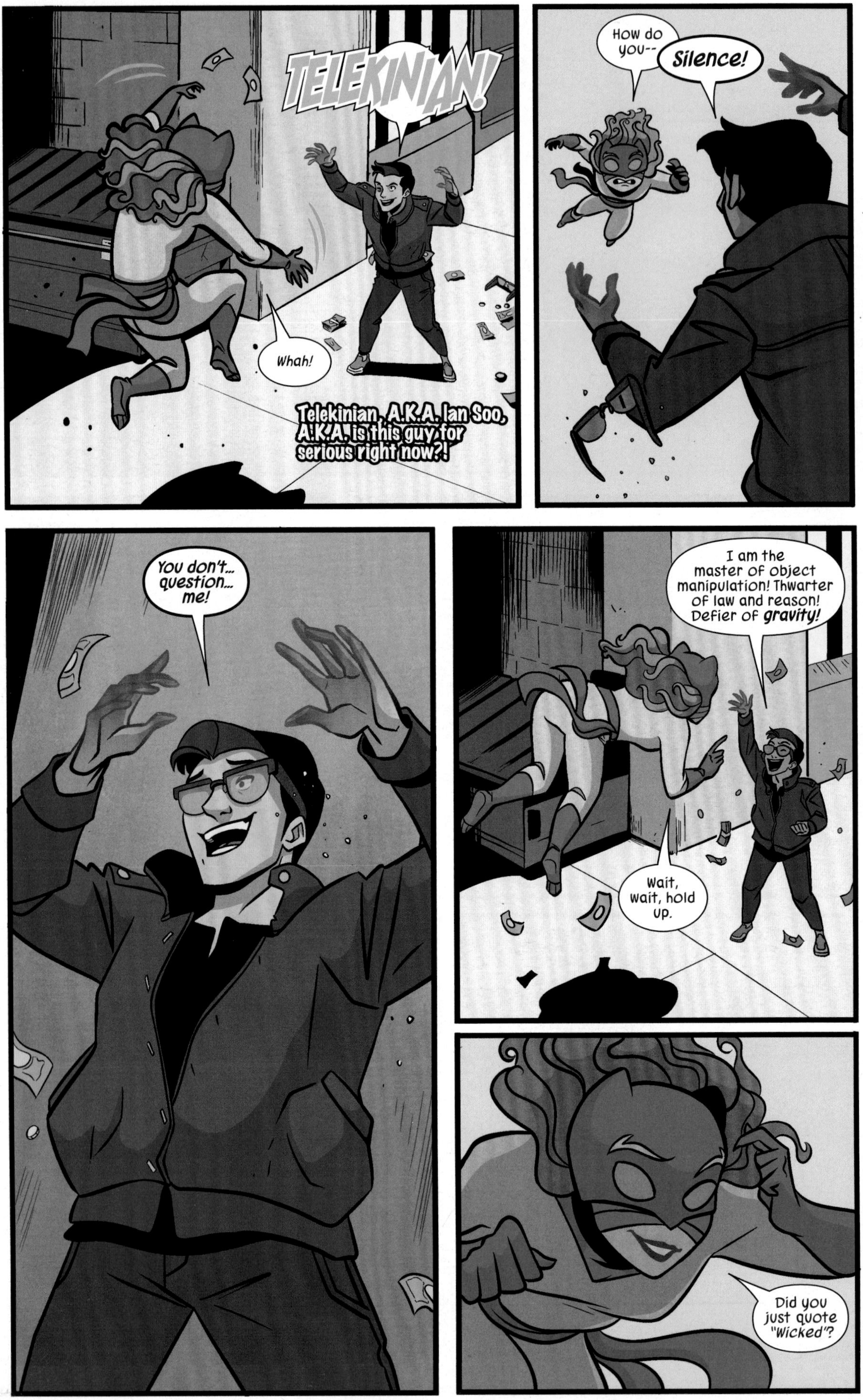
TELEKINIAN!
Whah!
Telekinian, A.K.A. Ian Soo, A.K.A. is this guy for serious right now?!
How do you--
Silence!
You don't... question... me!
I am the master of object manipulation! Thwarter of law and reason! Defier of gravity!
Wait, wait, hold up.
Did you just quote "Wicked"?

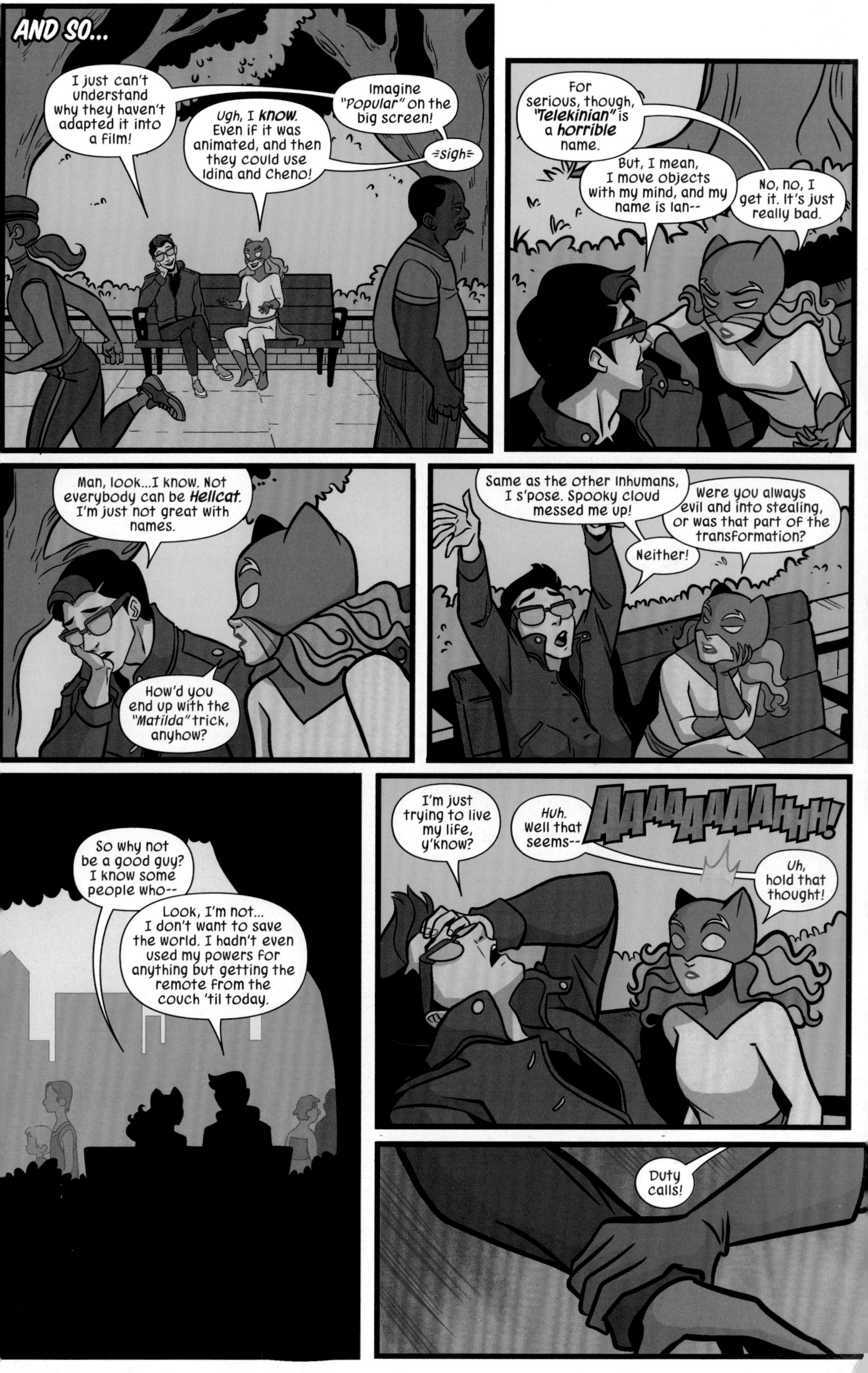
AND SO...
I just can't understand why they haven't adapted it into a film!
Ugh, I KNOW. Even if it was animated, and then they could use Idina and Cheno!
Imagine "Popular" on the big screen!
=sigh=
For serious, though, "Telekinian" is a horrible name.
But, I mean, I move objects with my mind, and my name is Ian--
No, no, I get it. It's just really bad.
Man, look...I know. Not everybody can be Hellcat. I'm just not great with names.
How'd you end up with the "Matilda" trick, anyhow?
Same as the other Inhumans, I s'pose. Spooky cloud messed me up!
Were you always evil and into stealing, or was that part of the transformation?
Neither!
So why not be a good guy? I know some people who--
Look, I'm not... I don't want to save the world. I hadn't even used my powers for anything but getting the remote from the couch 'til today.
I'm just trying to live my life, y'know?
Huh. Well that seems--
AAAAAAAAHHH!
Uh, hold that thought!
Duty calls!

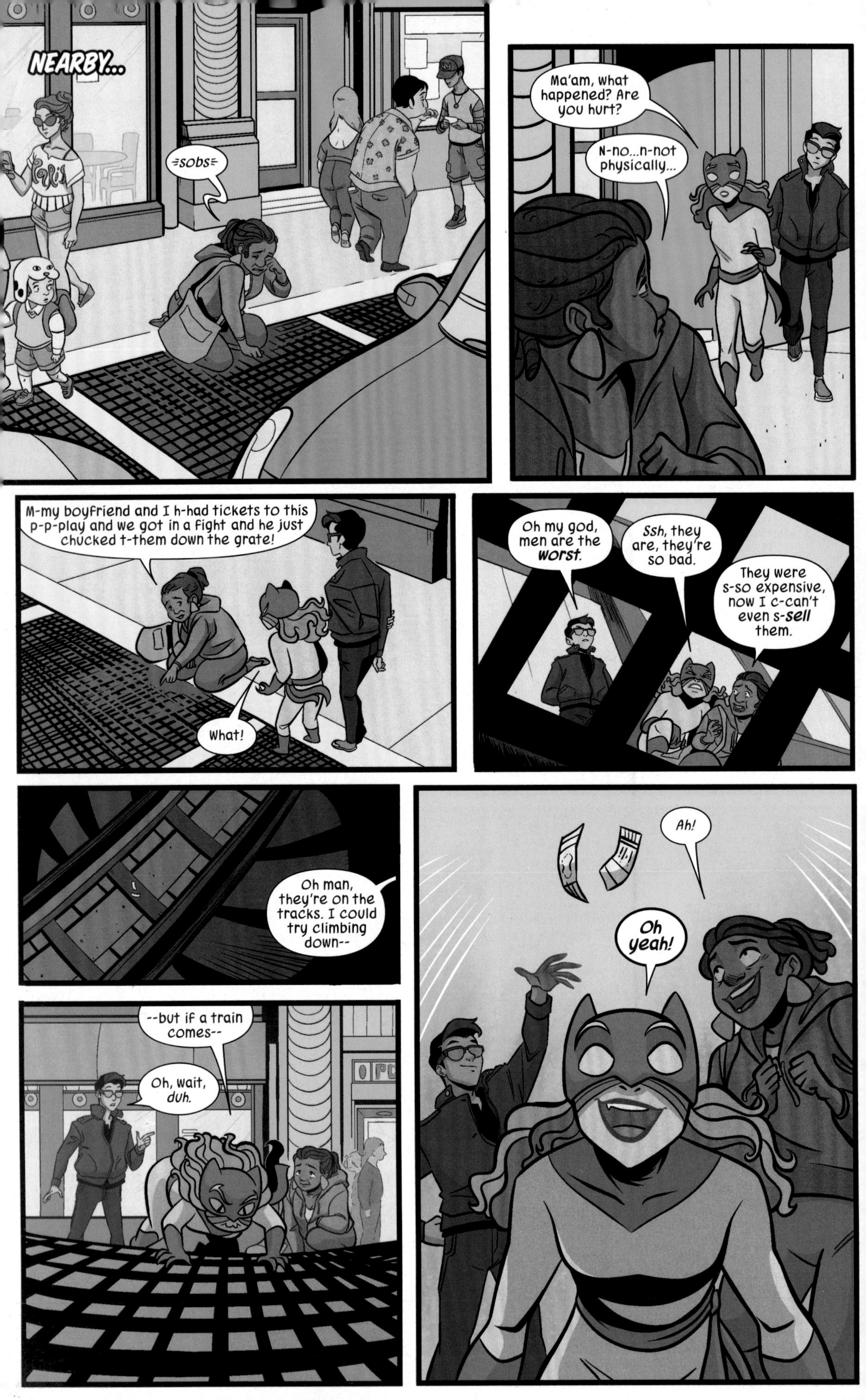
NEARBY...
=sobs=
Ma'am, what happened? Are you hurt?
N-no...n-not physically...
M-my boyfriend and I h-had tickets to this p-p-play and we got in a fight and he just chucked t-them down the grate!
What!
Oh my god, men are the *worst*.
Ssh, they are, they're so bad.
They were s-so expensive, now I c-can't even s-*sell* them.
Oh man, they're on the tracks. I could try climbing down--
--but if a train comes--
Oh, wait, duh.
Ah!
Oh yeah!

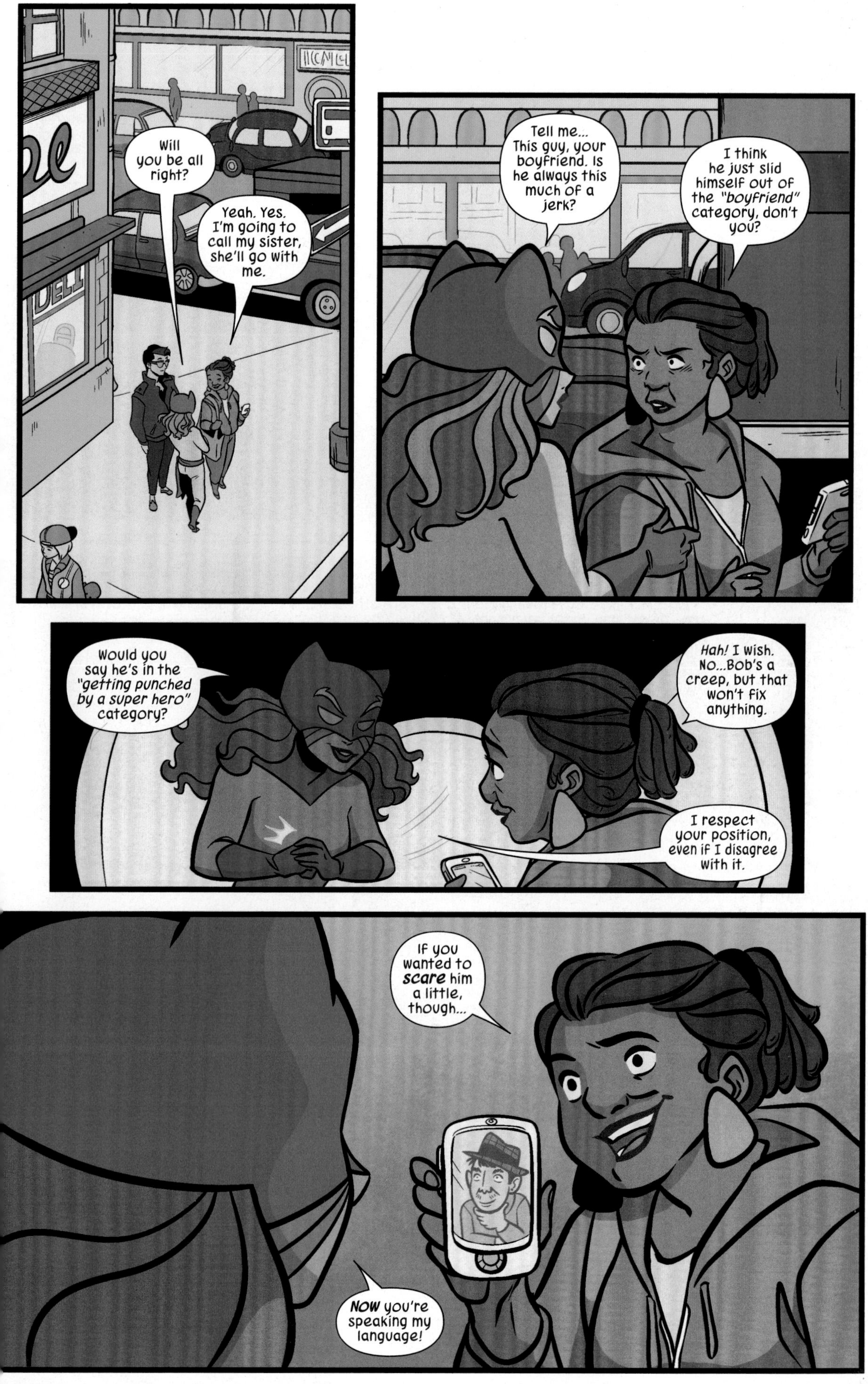

Will you be all right?
Yeah. Yes. I'm going to call my sister, she'll go with me.
Tell me... This guy, your boyfriend. Is he always this much of a jerk?
I think he just slid himself out of the "boyfriend" category, don't you?
Would you say he's in the "getting punched by a super hero" category?
Hah! I wish. No...Bob's a creep, but that won't fix anything.
I respect your position, even if I disagree with it.
If you wanted to scare him a little, though...
NOW you're speaking my language!

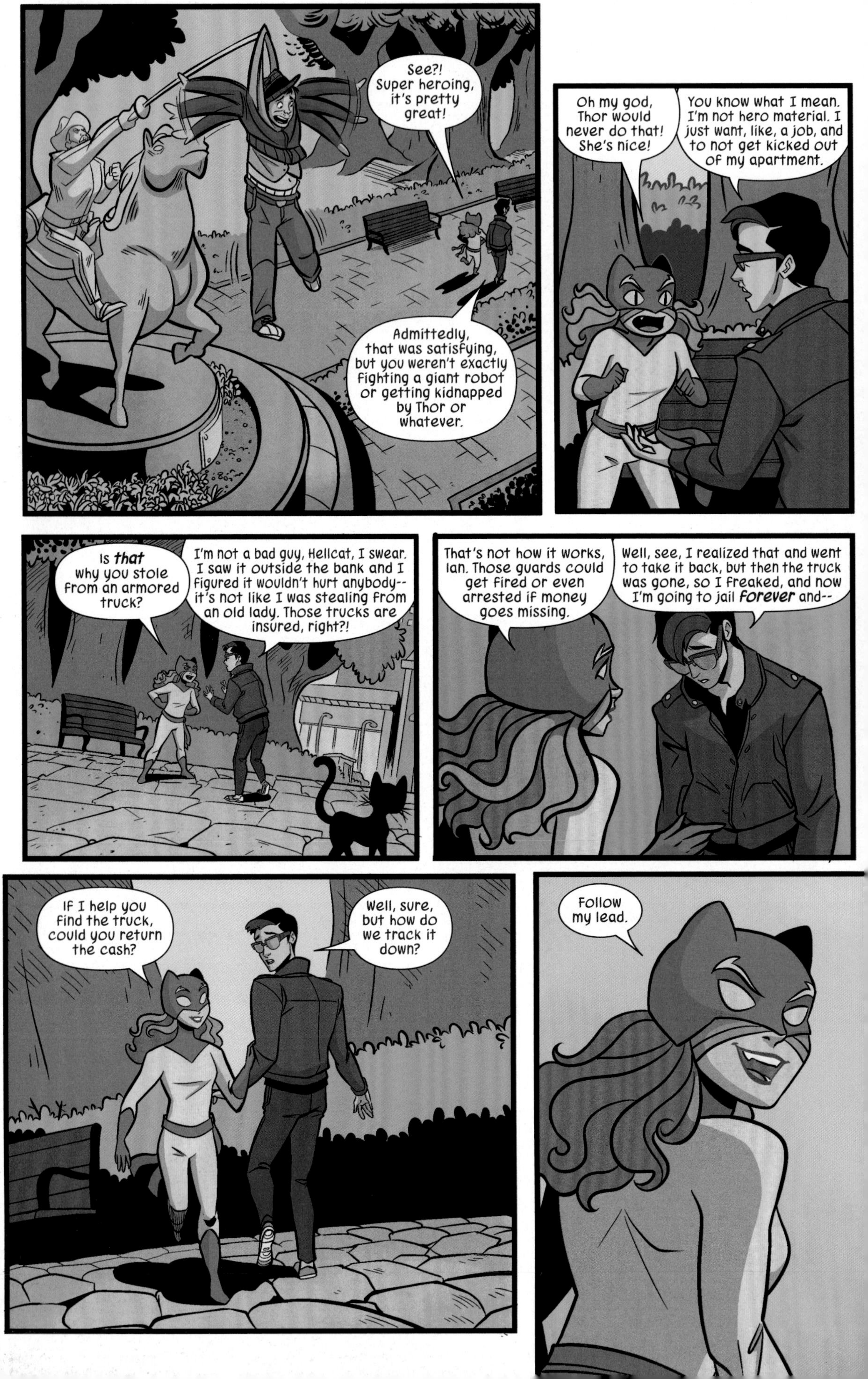

See?! Super heroing, it's pretty great!
Admittedly, that was satisfying, but you weren't exactly fighting a giant robot or getting kidnapped by Thor or whatever.
Oh my god, Thor would never do that! She's nice!
You know what I mean. I'm not hero material. I just want, like, a job, and to not get kicked out of my apartment.
Is *that* why you stole from an armored truck?
I'm not a bad guy, Hellcat, I swear. I saw it outside the bank and I figured it wouldn't hurt anybody--it's not like I was stealing from an old lady. Those trucks are insured, right?!
That's not how it works, Ian. Those guards could get fired or even arrested if money goes missing.
Well, see, I realized that and went to take it back, but then the truck was gone, so I freaked, and now I'm going to jail *forever* and--
If I help you find the truck, could you return the cash?
Well, sure, but how do we track it down?
Follow my lead.

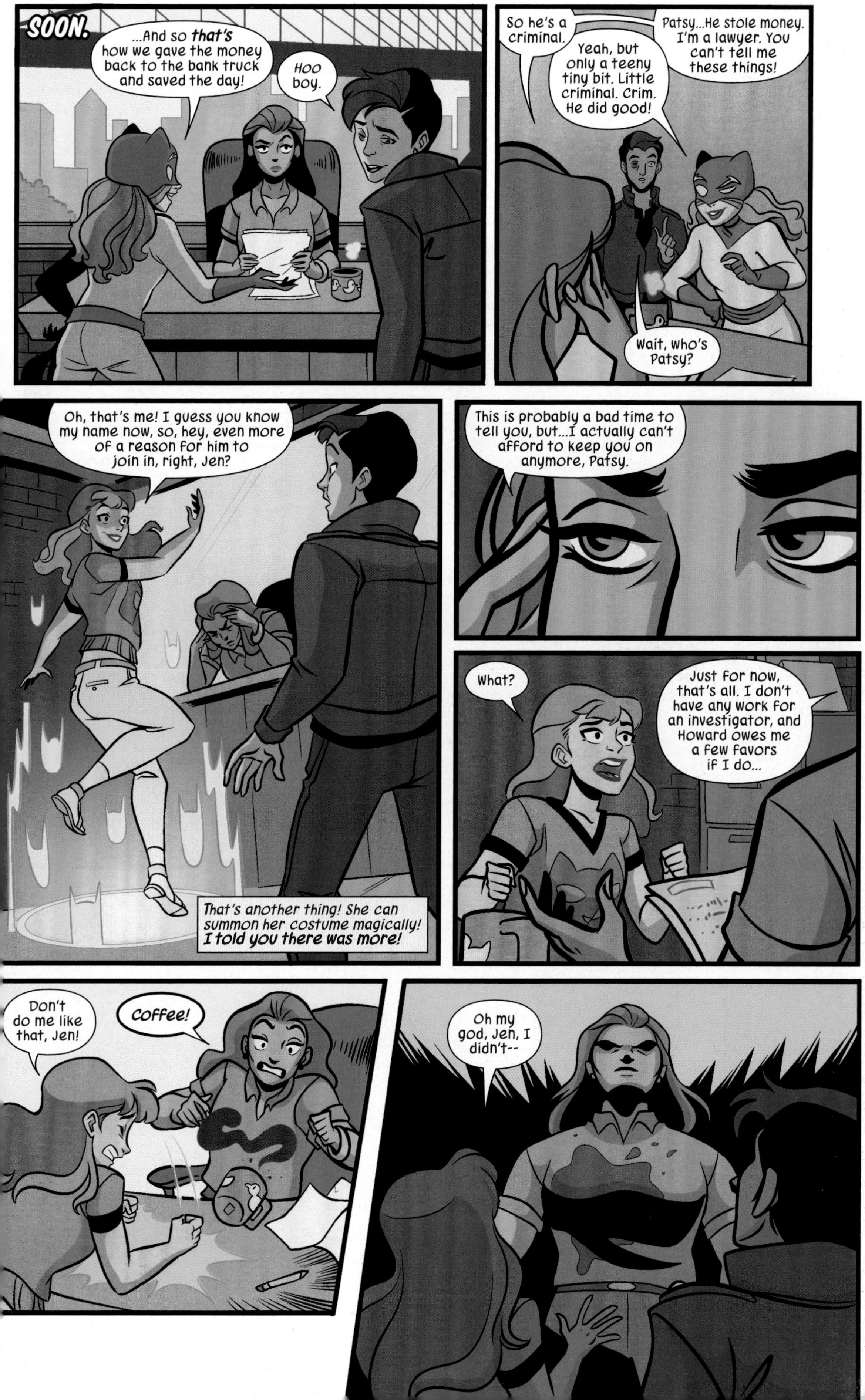
SOON.
...And so that's how we gave the money back to the bank truck and saved the day!
Hoo boy.
So he's a criminal.
Patsy...He stole money. I'm a lawyer. You can't tell me these things!
Yeah, but only a teeny tiny bit. Little criminal. Crim. He did good!
Wait, who's Patsy?
Oh, that's me! I guess you know my name now, so, hey, even more of a reason for him to join in, right, Jen?
That's another thing! She can summon her costume magically! I told you there was more!
This is probably a bad time to tell you, but...I actually can't afford to keep you on anymore, Patsy.
What?
Just for now, that's all. I don't have any work for an investigator, and Howard owes me a few favors if I do...
Don't do me like that, Jen!
Coffee!
Oh my god, Jen, I didn't--

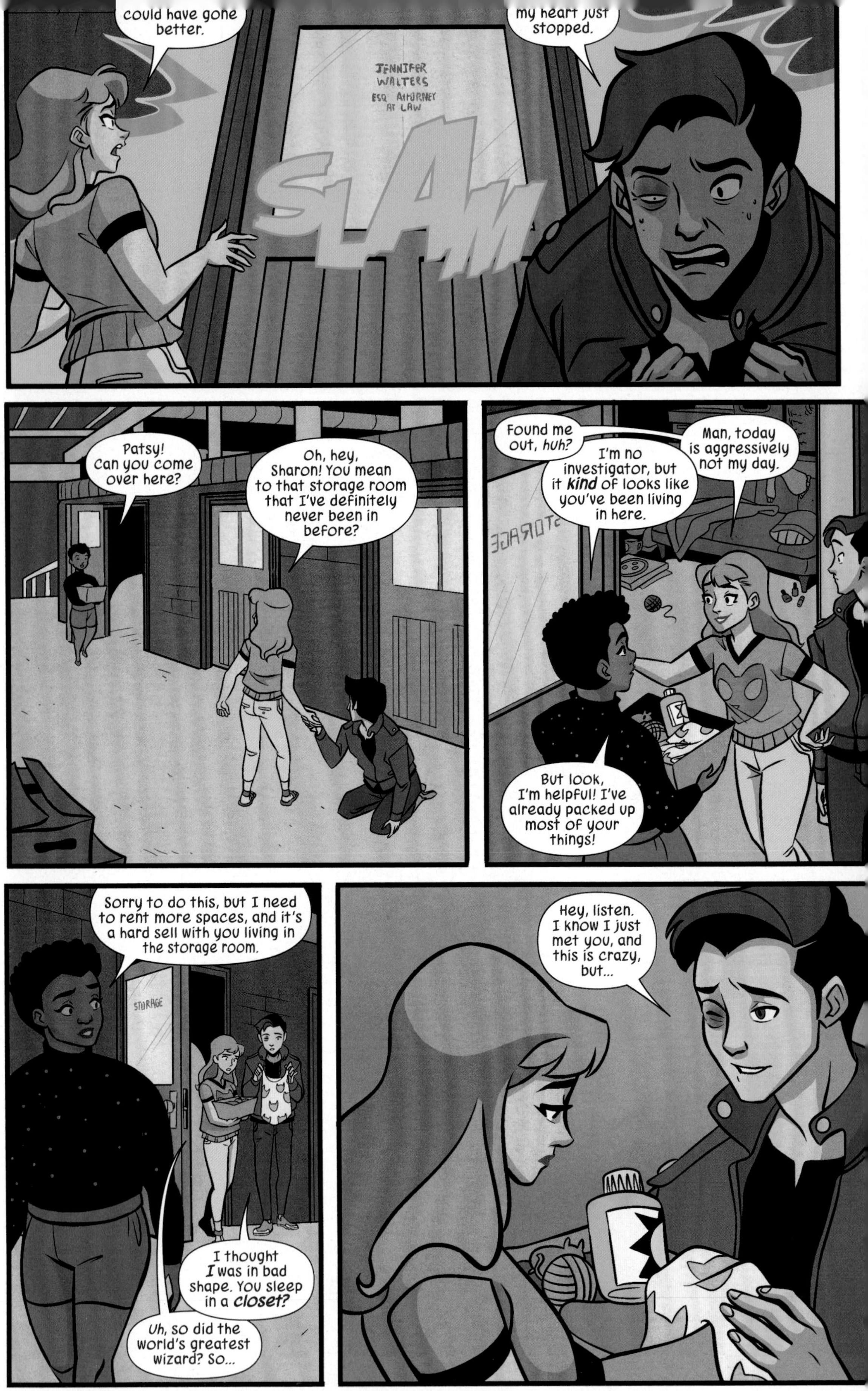

could have gone better.
my heart just stopped.
JENNIFER WALTERS ESQ ATTORNEY AT LAW
SLAM
Patsy! Can you come over here?
Oh, hey, Sharon! You mean to that storage room that I've definitely never been in before?
Found me out, huh?
I'm no investigator, but it kind of looks like you've been living in here.
Man, today is aggressively not my day.
STORAGE
But look, I'm helpful! I've already packed up most of your things!
Sorry to do this, but I need to rent more spaces, and it's a hard sell with you living in the storage room.
STORAGE
I thought I was in bad shape. You sleep in a closet?
Uh, so did the world's greatest wizard? So...
Hey, listen. I know I just met you, and this is crazy, but...

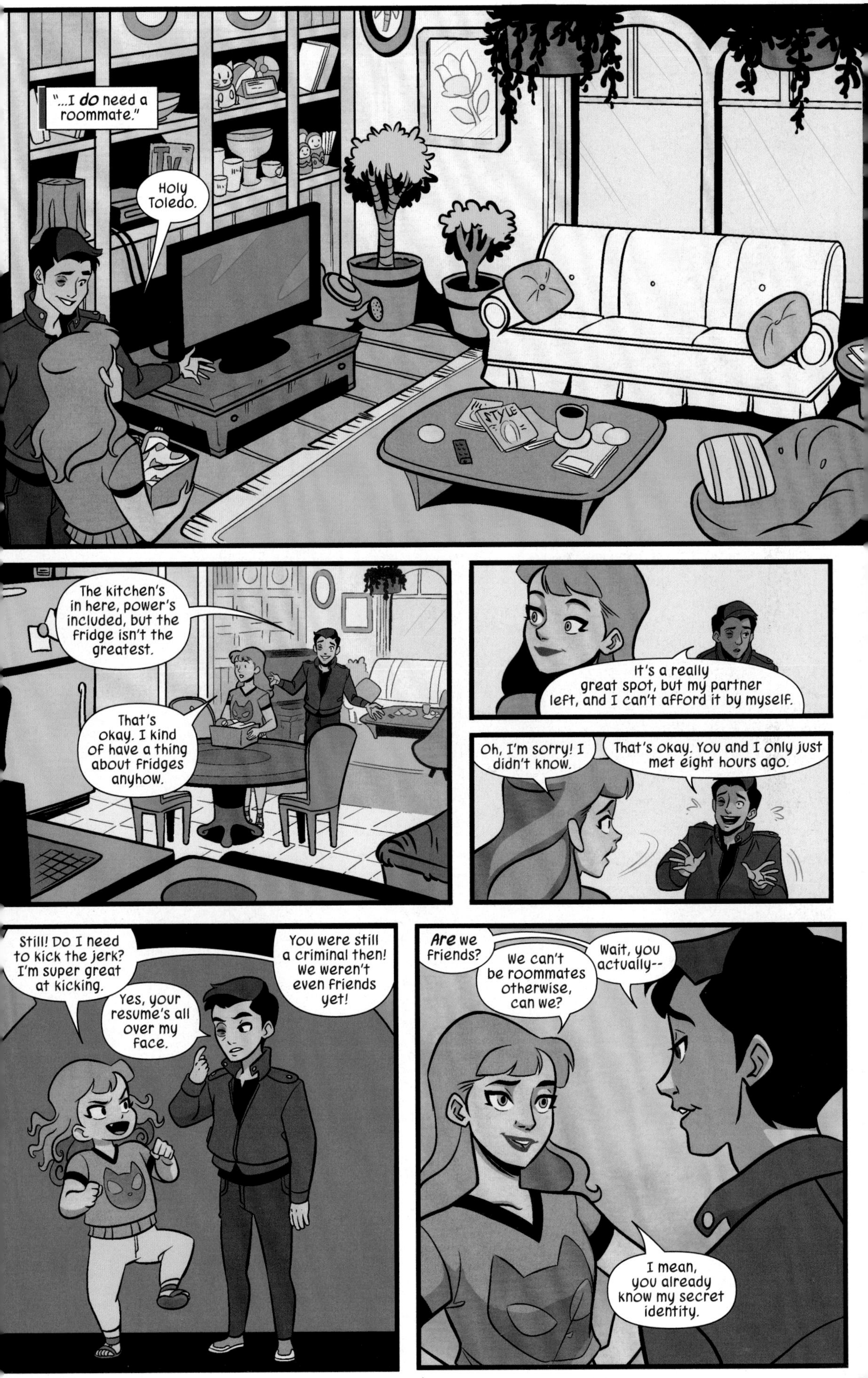
"...I *do* need a roommate."
Holy Toledo.
The kitchen's in here, power's included, but the fridge isn't the greatest.
That's okay. I kind of have a thing about fridges anyhow.
It's a really great spot, but my partner left, and I can't afford it by myself.
Oh, I'm sorry! I didn't know.
That's okay. You and I only just met eight hours ago.
Still! Do I need to kick the jerk? I'm super great at kicking.
Yes, your resume's all over my face.
You were still a criminal then! We weren't even friends yet!
Are we friends?
We can't be roommates otherwise, can we?
Wait, you actually--
I mean, you already know my secret identity.

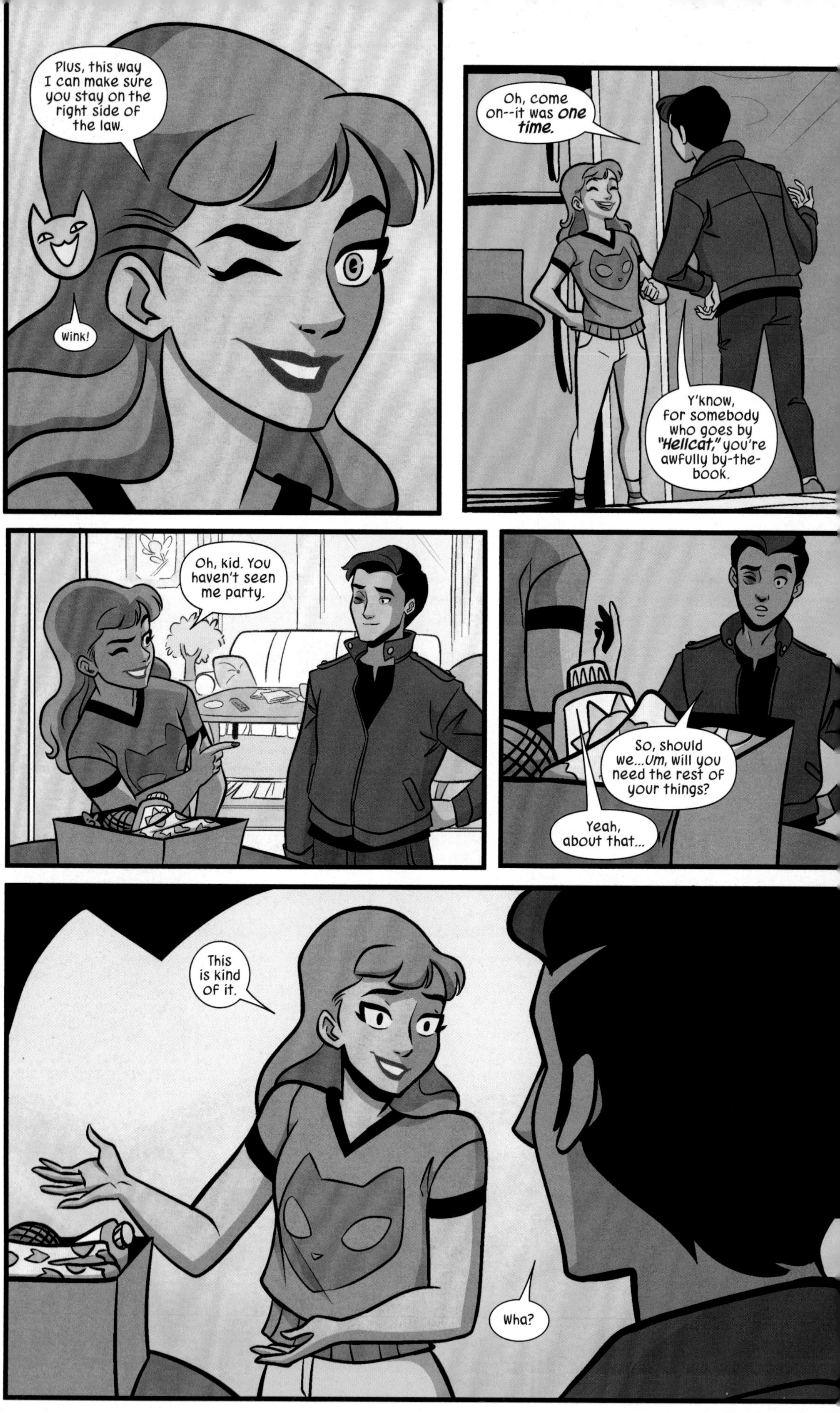
Plus, this way I can make sure you stay on the right side of the law.
Wink!
Oh, come on--it was *one time.*
Y'know, for somebody who goes by *"Hellcat,"* you're awfully by-the-book.
Oh, kid. You haven't seen me party.
So, should we...*Um,* will you need the rest of your things?
Yeah, about that...
This is kind of it.
Wha?

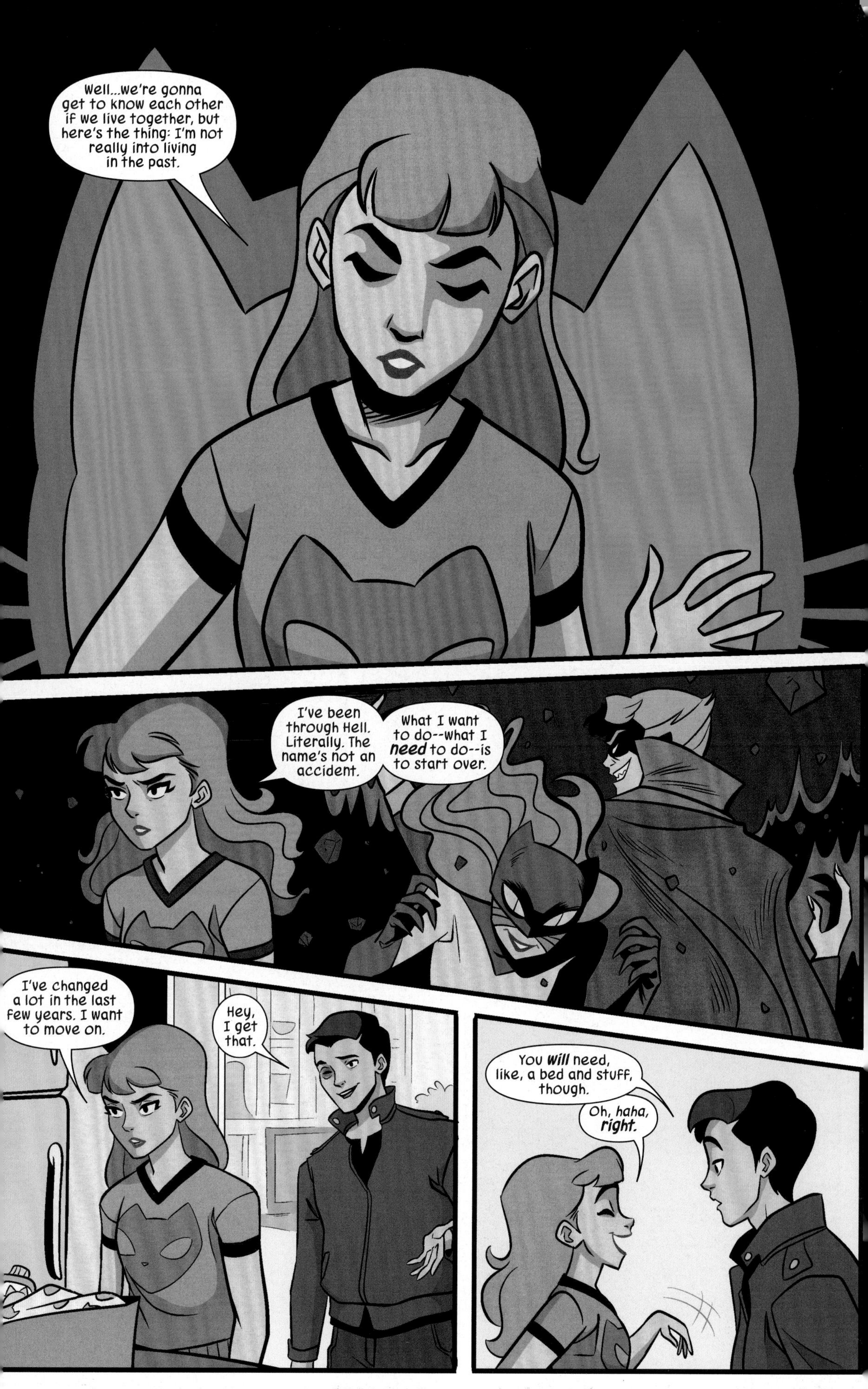
Well...we're gonna get to know each other if we live together, but here's the thing: I'm not really into living in the past.
I've been through Hell. Literally. The name's not an accident.
What I want to do--what I *need* to do--is to start over.
I've changed a lot in the last few years. I want to move on.
Hey, I get that.
You *will* need, like, a bed and stuff, though.
Oh, haha, right.

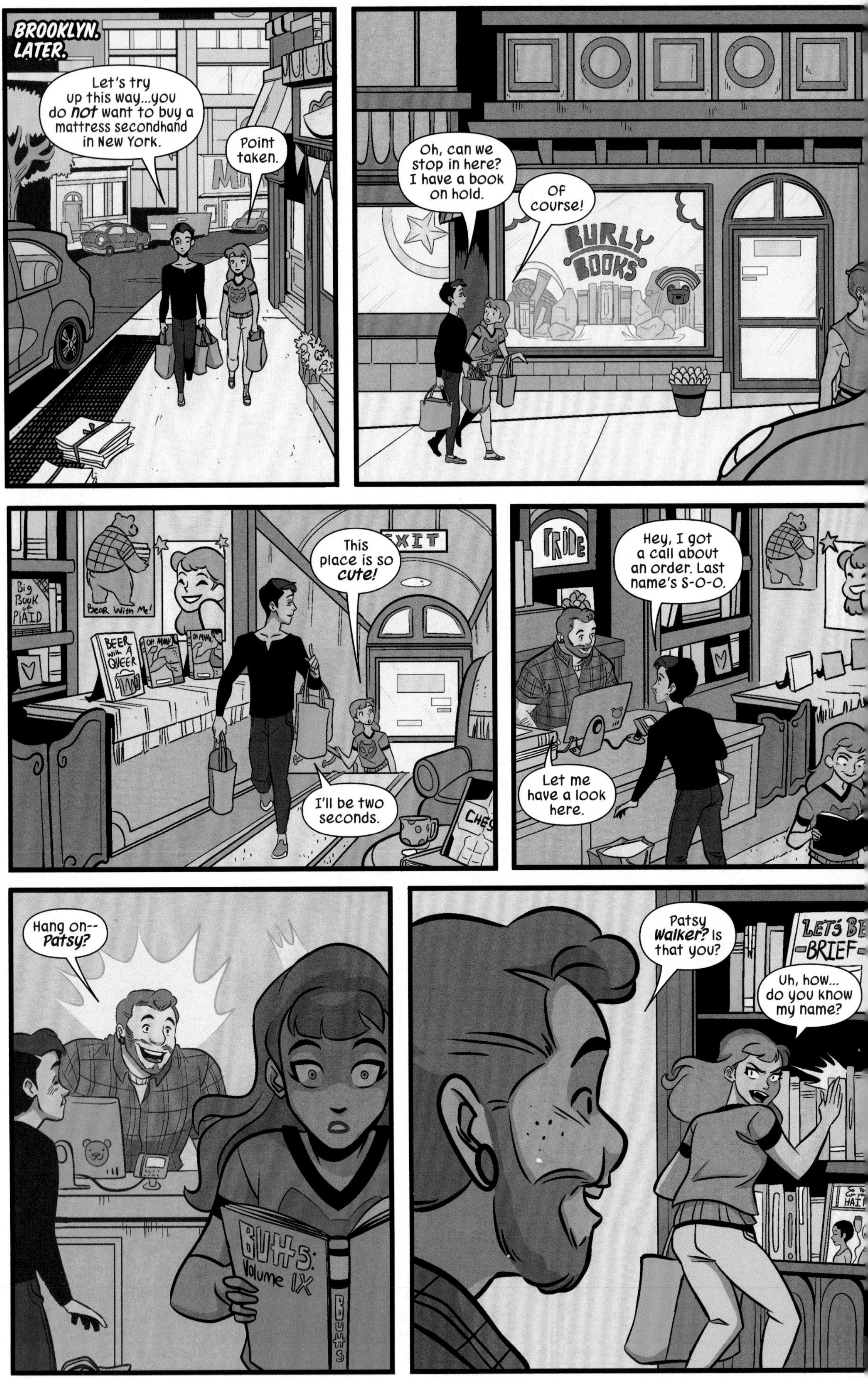

BROOKLYN. LATER.
Let's try up this way...you do *not* want to buy a mattress secondhand in New York.
Point taken.
Oh, can we stop in here? I have a book on hold.
Of course!
BURLY BOOKS
This place is so *cute!*
EXIT
Bear With Me!
Big Book of PLAID
BEER with a QUEER
I'll be two seconds.
PRIDE
Hey, I got a call about an order. Last name's S-O-O.
Let me have a look here.
Hang on-- *Patsy?*
BUHS: Volume IX
Patsy *Walker?* Is that you?
LET'S BE BRIEF
Uh, how... do you know my name?

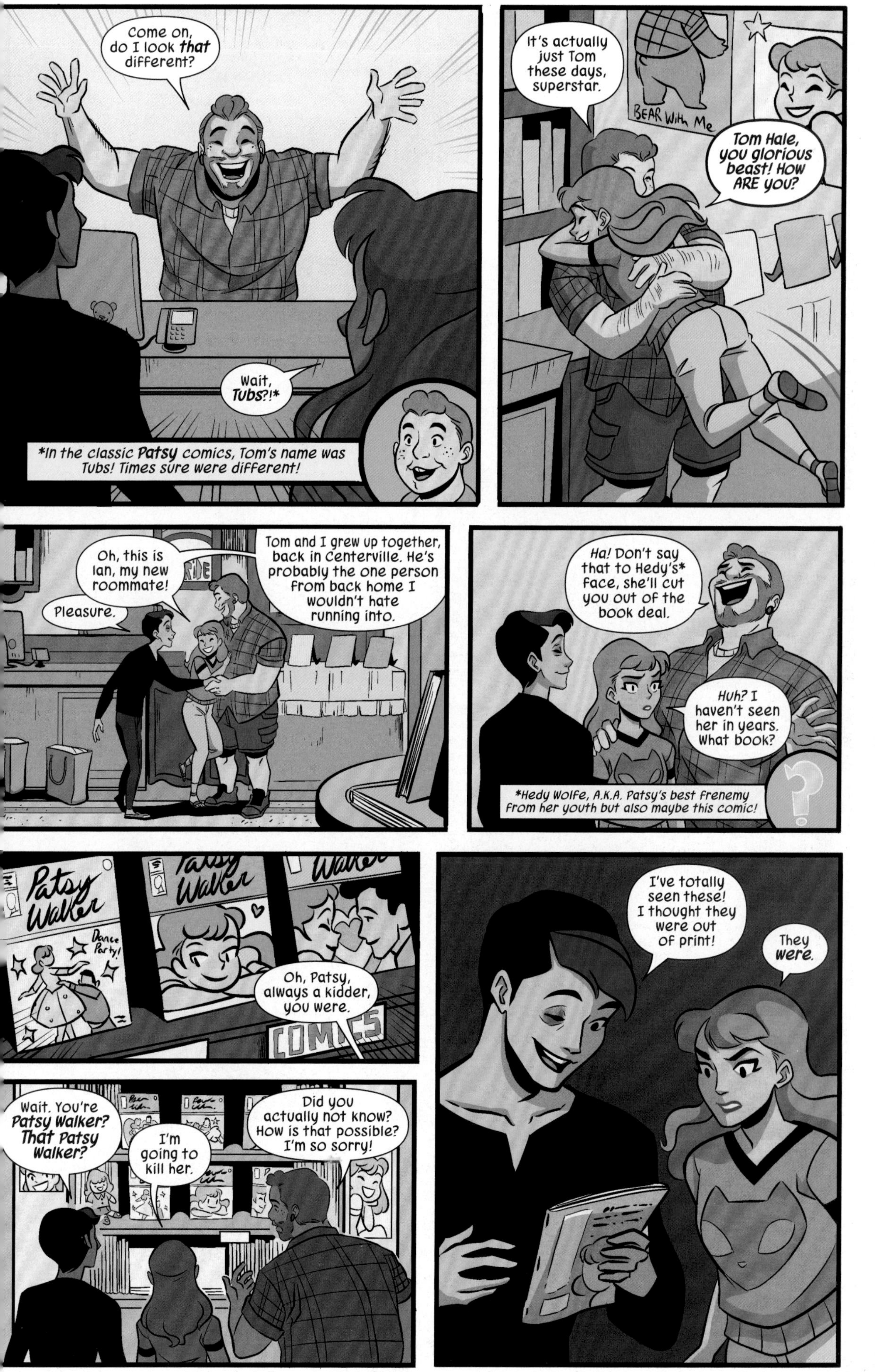
Come on, do I look *that* different?
Wait, *Tubs*?!*
*In the classic *Patsy* comics, Tom's name was Tubs! Times sure were different!
It's actually just Tom these days, superstar.
BEAR With Me
Tom Hale, you glorious beast! How ARE you?
Oh, this is Ian, my new roommate!
Pleasure.
Tom and I grew up together, back in Centerville. He's probably the one person from back home I wouldn't hate running into.
Ha! Don't say that to Hedy's* face, she'll cut you out of the book deal.
Huh? I haven't seen her in years. What book?
*Hedy Wolfe, A.K.A. Patsy's best frenemy from her youth but also maybe this comic!
Patsy Walker
Dance Party!
Oh, Patsy, always a kidder, you were.
Wait. You're *Patsy Walker*? *That Patsy Walker*?
I'm going to kill her.
Did you actually not know? How is that possible? I'm so sorry!
I've totally seen these! I thought they were out of print!
They *were*.

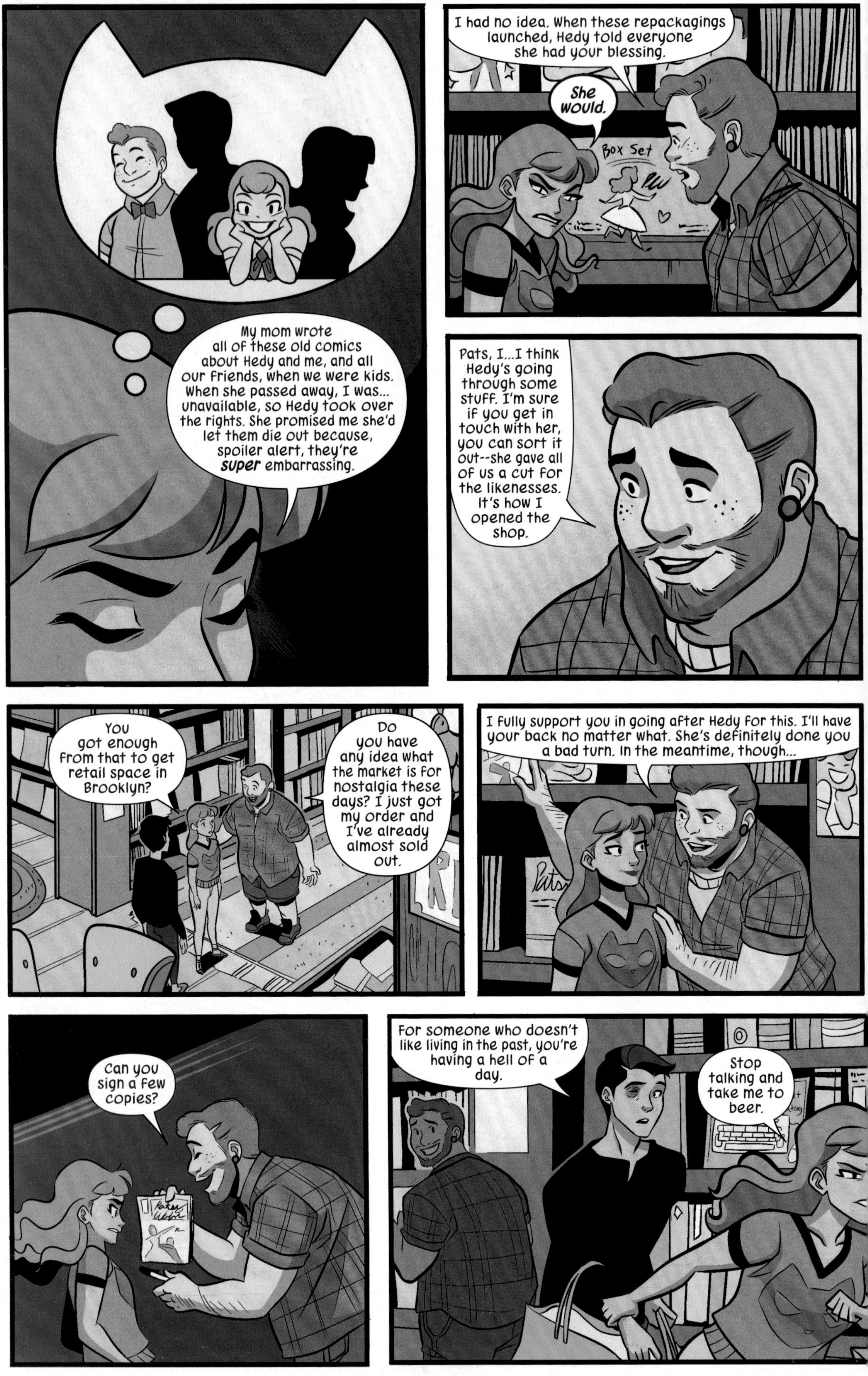
My mom wrote all of these old comics about Hedy and me, and all our friends, when we were kids. When she passed away, I was... unavailable, so Hedy took over the rights. She promised me she'd let them die out because, spoiler alert, they're super embarrassing.
I had no idea. When these repackagings launched, Hedy told everyone she had your blessing.
She would.
Box Set
Pats, I...I think Hedy's going through some stuff. I'm sure if you get in touch with her, you can sort it out--she gave all of us a cut for the likenesses. It's how I opened the shop.
You got enough from that to get retail space in Brooklyn?
Do you have any idea what the market is for nostalgia these days? I just got my order and I've already almost sold out.
I fully support you in going after Hedy for this. I'll have your back no matter what. She's definitely done you a bad turn. In the meantime, though...
Can you sign a few copies?
For someone who doesn't like living in the past, you're having a hell of a day.
Stop talking and take me to beer.

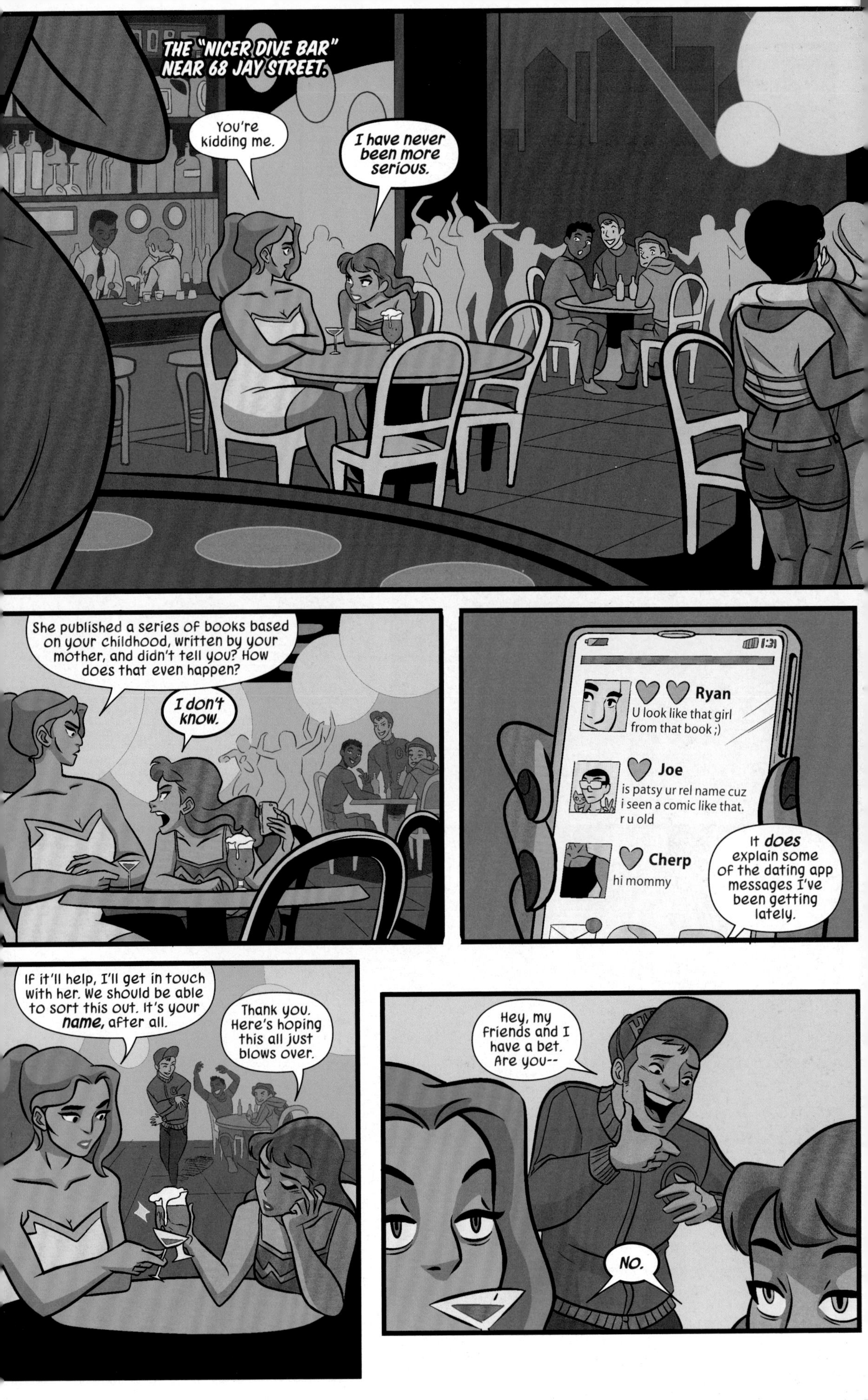
THE "NICER DIVE BAR" NEAR 68 JAY STREET.
You're kidding me.
I have never been more serious.
She published a series of books based on your childhood, written by your mother, and didn't tell you? How does that even happen?
I don't know.
Ryan
U look like that girl from that book ;)
Joe
is patsy ur rel name cuz i seen a comic like that. r u old
Cherp
hi mommy
It does explain some of the dating app messages I've been getting lately.
If it'll help, I'll get in touch with her. We should be able to sort this out. It's your name, after all.
Thank you. Here's hoping this all just blows over.
Hey, my friends and I have a bet. Are you--
NO.

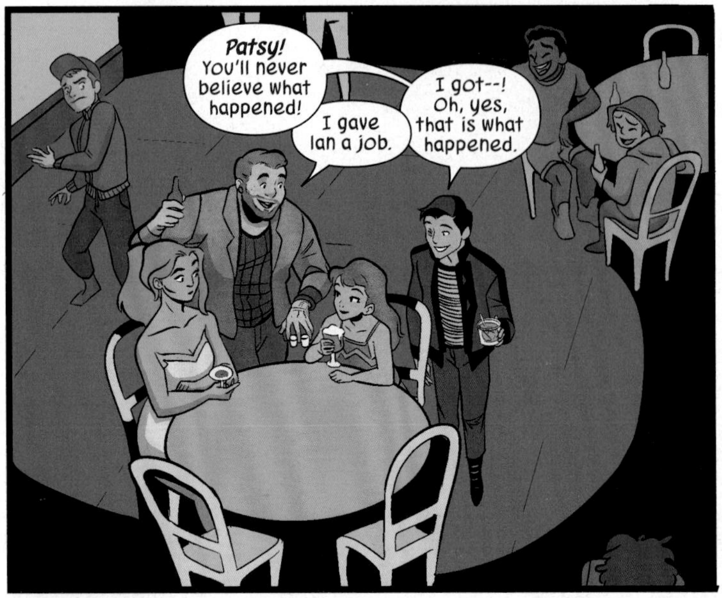
Patsy! You'll never believe what happened!
I gave Ian a job.
I got--! Oh, yes, that is what happened.

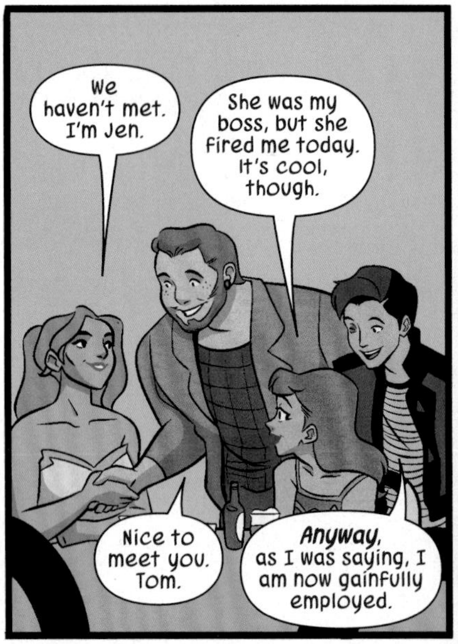
We haven't met. I'm Jen.
She was my boss, but she fired me today. It's cool, though.
Nice to meet you. Tom.
Anyway, as I was saying, I am now gainfully employed.

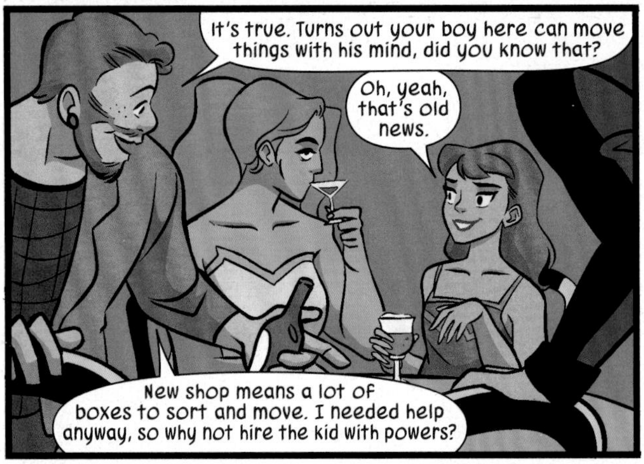
It's true. Turns out your boy here can move things with his mind, did you know that?
Oh, yeah, that's old news.
New shop means a lot of boxes to sort and move. I needed help anyway, so why not hire the kid with powers?

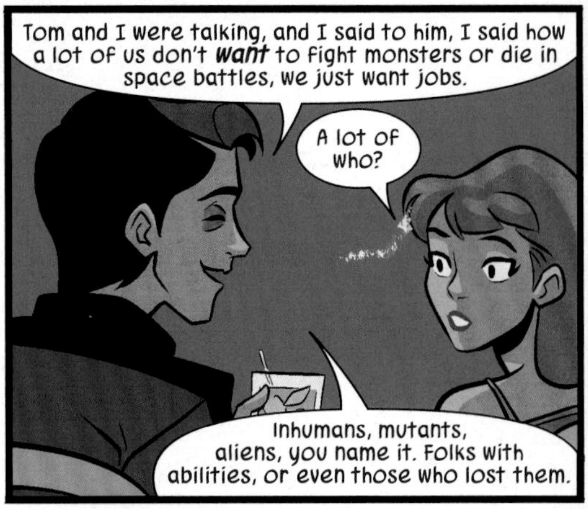
Tom and I were talking, and I said to him, I said how a lot of us don't want to fight monsters or die in space battles, we just want jobs.
A lot of who?
Inhumans, mutants, aliens, you name it. Folks with abilities, or even those who lost them.

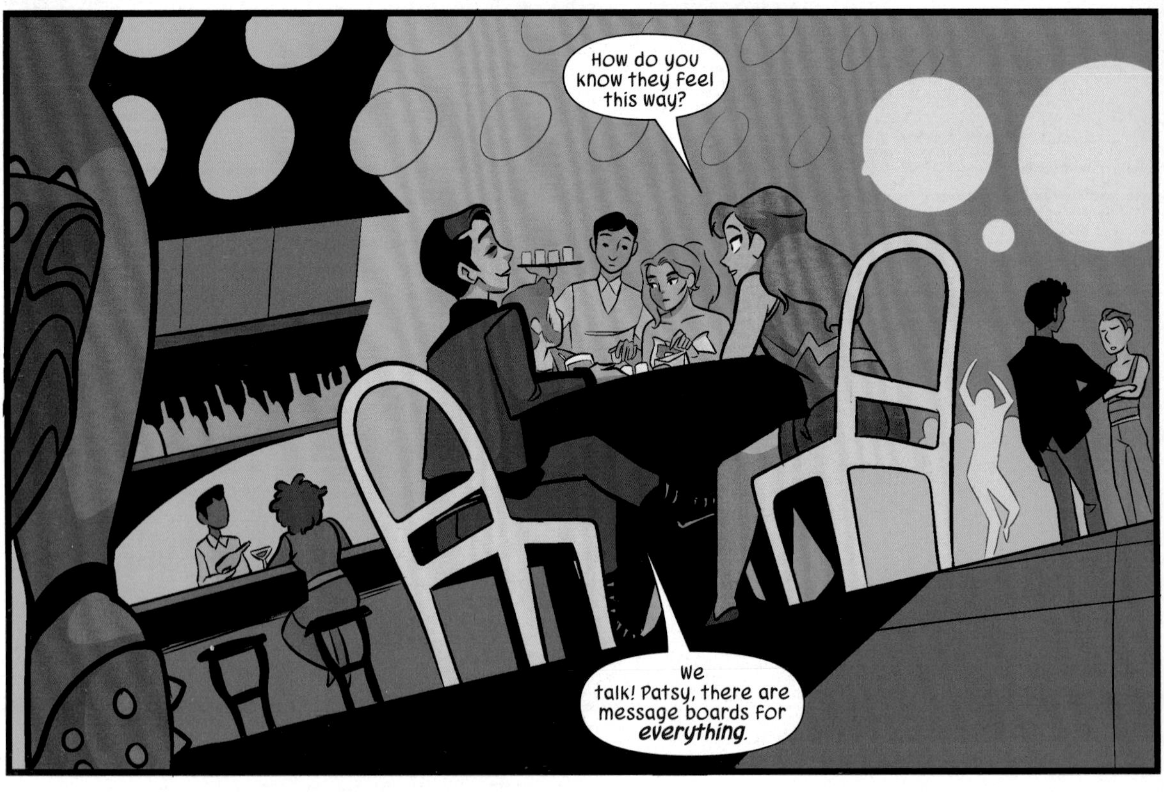
How do you know they feel this way?
We talk! Patsy, there are message boards for everything.

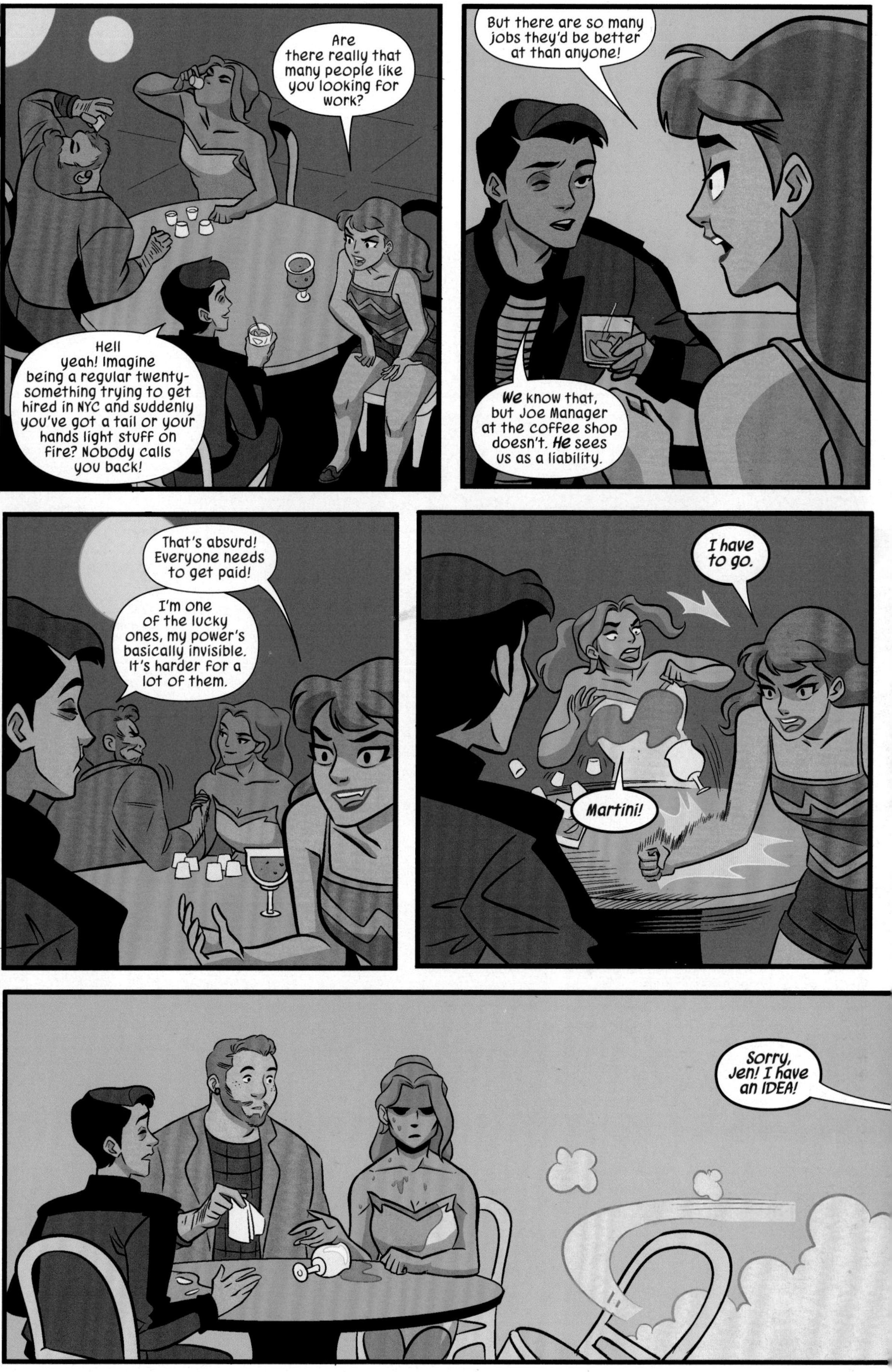
Are there really that many people like you looking for work?
Hell yeah! Imagine being a regular twenty-something trying to get hired in NYC and suddenly you've got a tail or your hands light stuff on fire? Nobody calls you back!
But there are so many jobs they'd be better at than anyone!
We know that, but Joe Manager at the coffee shop doesn't. He sees us as a liability.
That's absurd! Everyone needs to get paid!
I'm one of the lucky ones, my power's basically invisible. It's harder for a lot of them.
I have to go.
Martini!
Sorry, Jen! I have an IDEA!

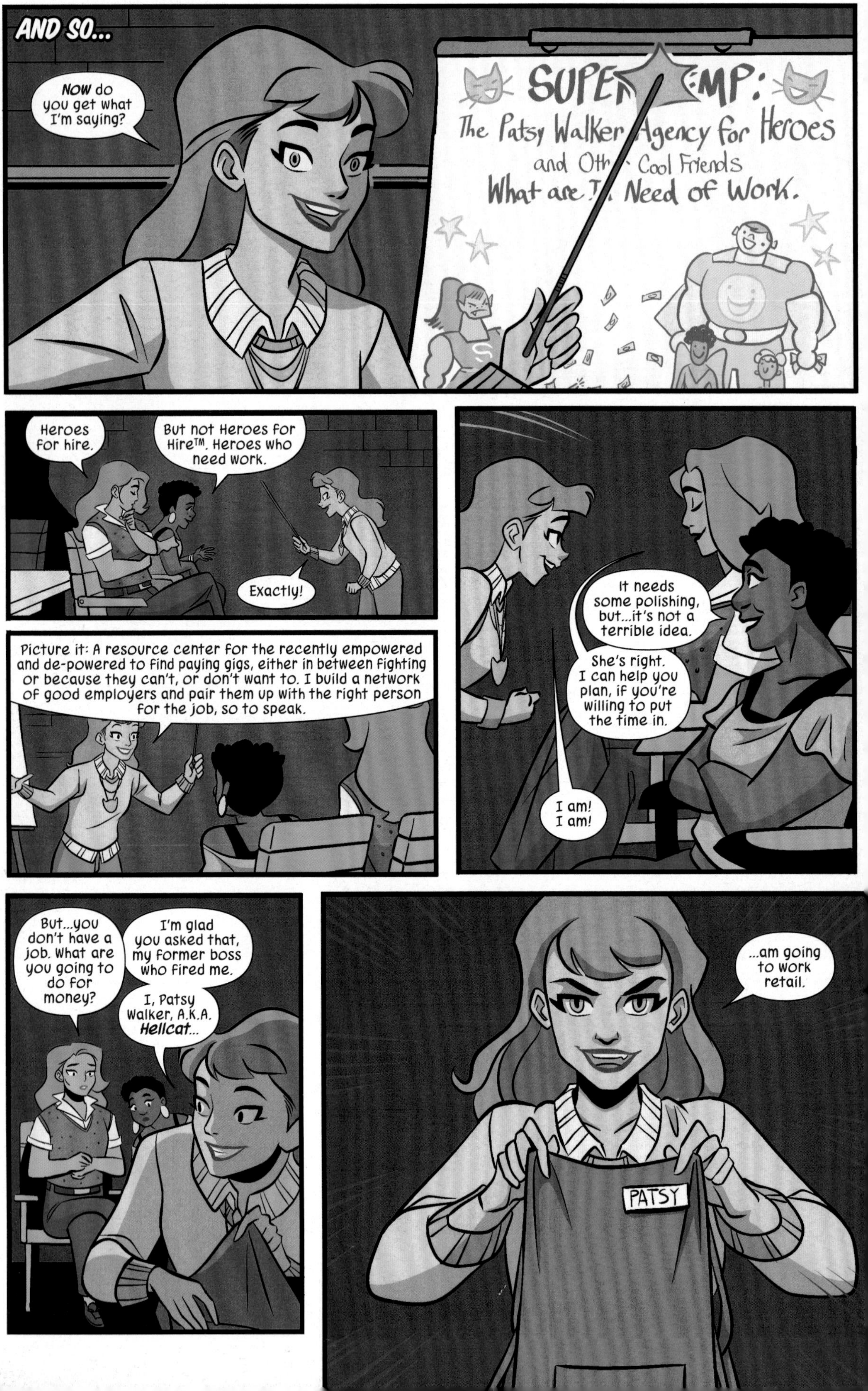
AND SO...
NOW do you get what I'm saying?
SUPE MP:
The Patsy Walker Agency for Heroes
and Oth Cool Friends
What are I Need of Work.
Heroes for hire.
But not Heroes for Hire™. Heroes who need work.
Exactly!
Picture it: A resource center for the recently empowered and de-powered to find paying gigs, either in between fighting or because they can't, or don't want to. I build a network of good employers and pair them up with the right person for the job, so to speak.
It needs some polishing, but...it's not a terrible idea.
She's right. I can help you plan, if you're willing to put the time in.
I am! I am!
But...you don't have a job. What are you going to do for money?
I'm glad you asked that, my former boss who fired me.
I, Patsy Walker, A.K.A. Hellcat...
...am going to work retail.
PATSY

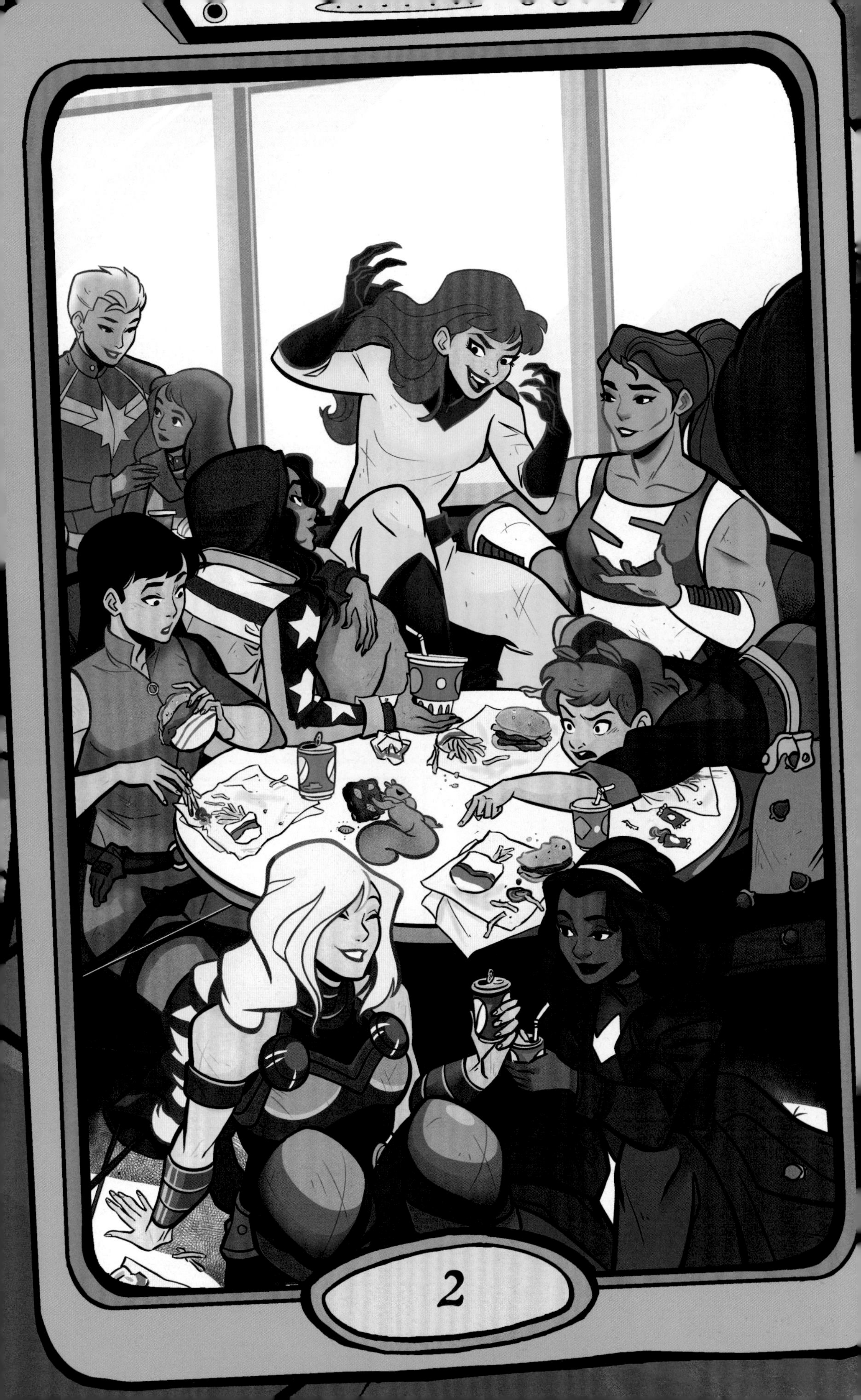
2

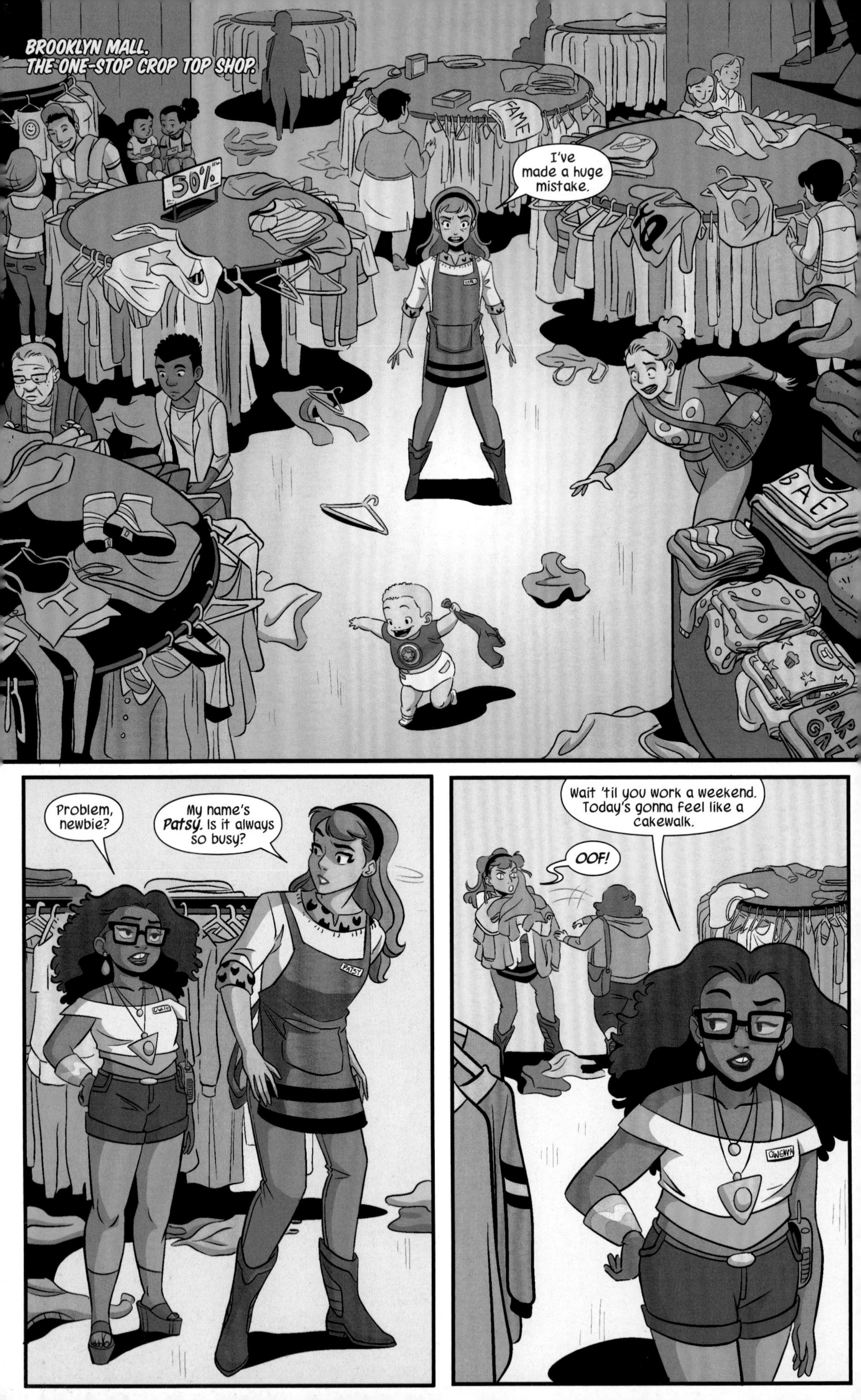
BROOKLYN MALL.
THE ONE-STOP CROP TOP SHOP.
FAME
50%
I've made a huge mistake.
BAE
Problem, newbie?
My name's Patsy. Is it always so busy?
PATSY
Wait 'til you work a weekend. Today's gonna feel like a cakewalk.
OOF!
GWENYN

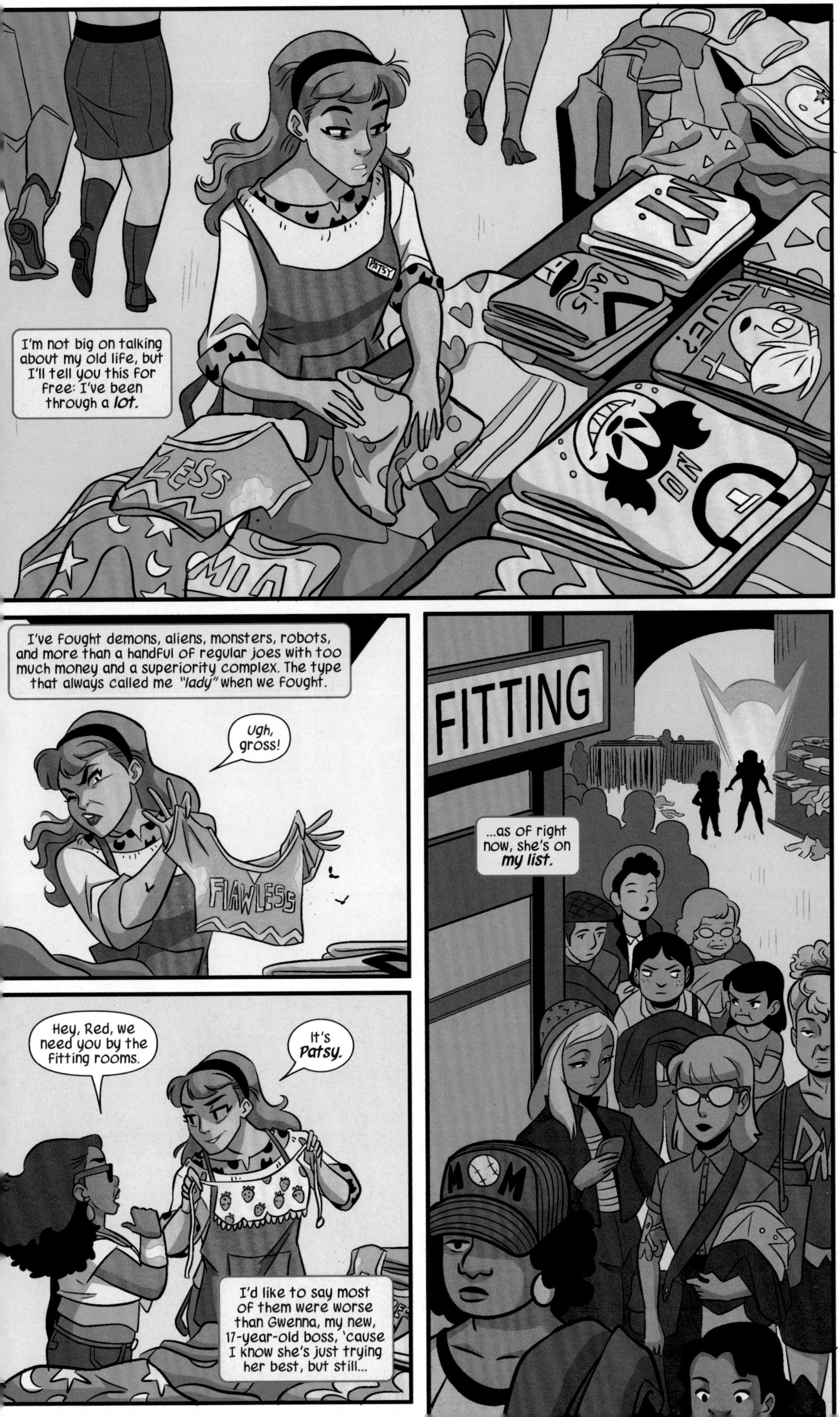
I'm not big on talking about my old life, but I'll tell you this for free: I've been through a *lot.*
I've fought demons, aliens, monsters, robots, and more than a handful of regular joes with too much money and a superiority complex. The type that always called me *"lady"* when we fought.
Ugh, gross!
Hey, Red, we need you by the fitting rooms.
It's *Patsy.*
I'd like to say most of them were worse than Gwenna, my new, 17-year-old boss, 'cause I know she's just trying her best, but still...
FITTING
...as of right now, she's on *my list.*

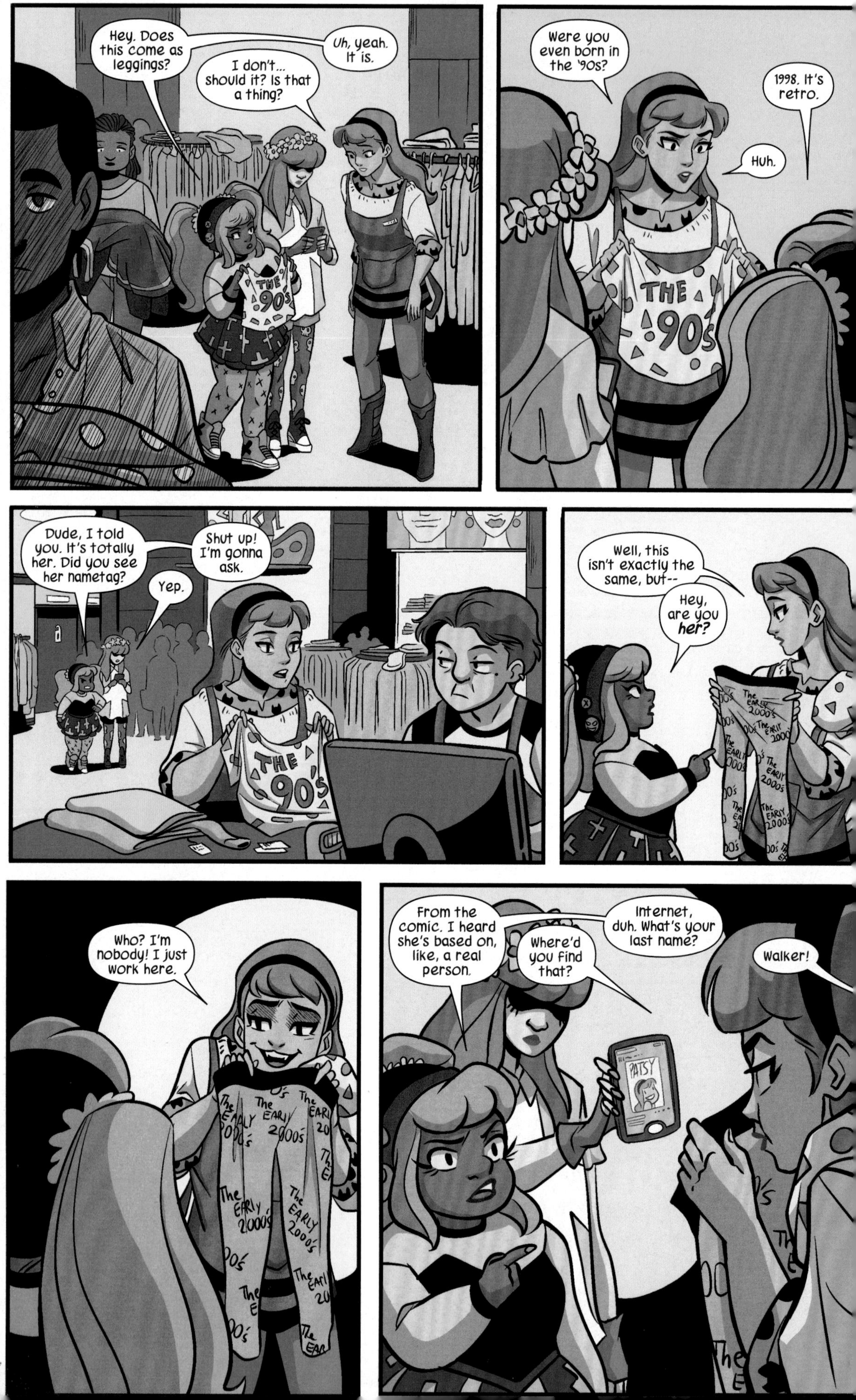
Hey. Does this come as leggings?
I don't... should it? Is that a thing?
Uh, yeah. It is.
THE 90'S
Were you even born in the '90s?
Huh.
1998. It's retro.
THE 90'S
Dude, I told you. It's totally her. Did you see her nametag?
Yep.
Shut up! I'm gonna ask.
THE 90'S
Well, this isn't exactly the same, but--
Hey, are you *her?*
Who? I'm nobody! I just work here.
From the comic. I heard she's based on, like, a real person.
Where'd you find that?
Internet, duh. What's your last name?
PATSY
Walker!

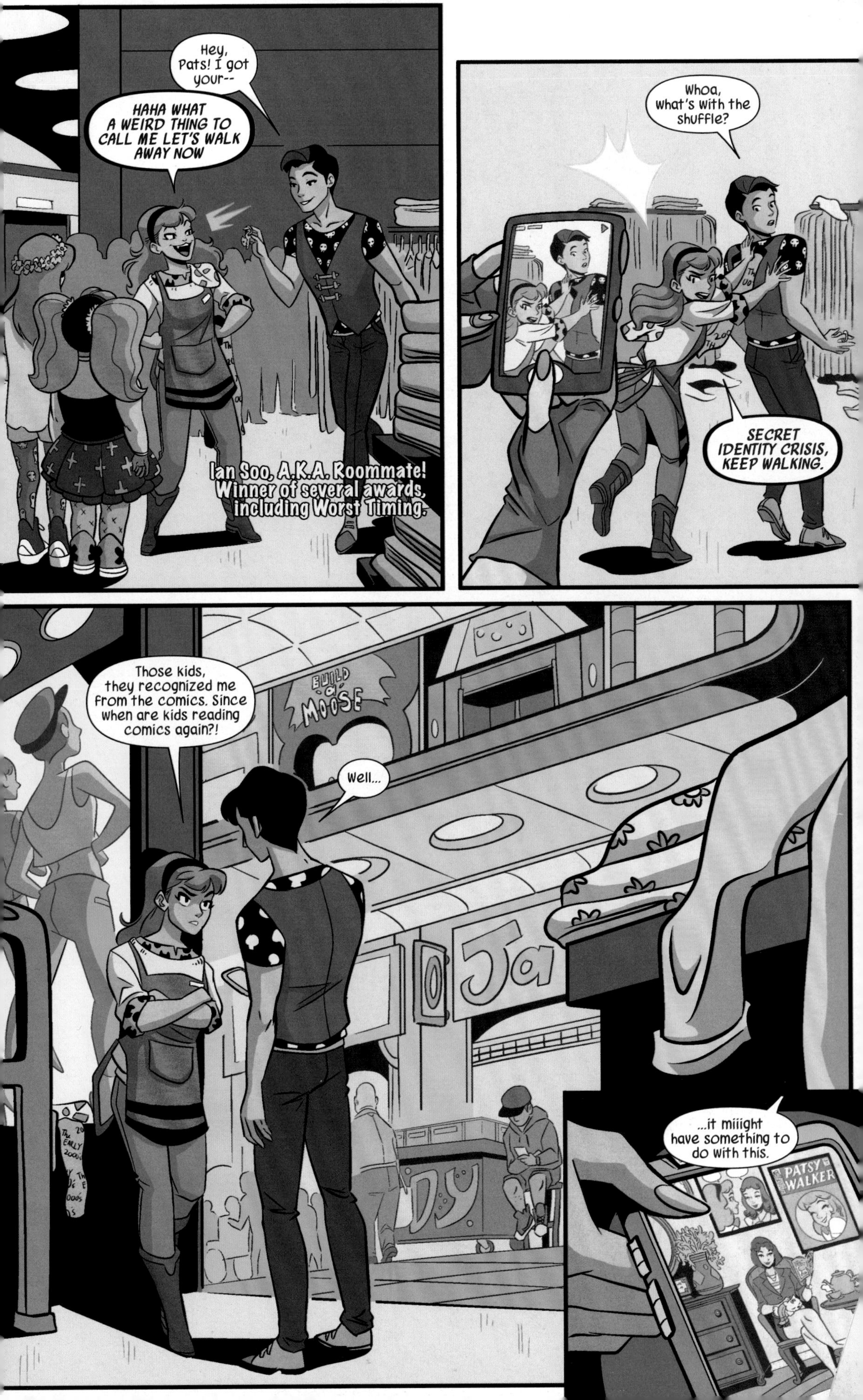
Hey, Pats! I got your--
HAHA WHAT A WEIRD THING TO CALL ME LET'S WALK AWAY NOW
Ian Soo, A.K.A. Roommate! Winner of several awards, including Worst Timing.
Whoa, what's with the shuffle?
SECRET IDENTITY CRISIS, KEEP WALKING.
Those kids, they recognized me from the comics. Since when are kids reading comics again?!
Well...
...it miiight have something to do with this.
PATSY WALKER

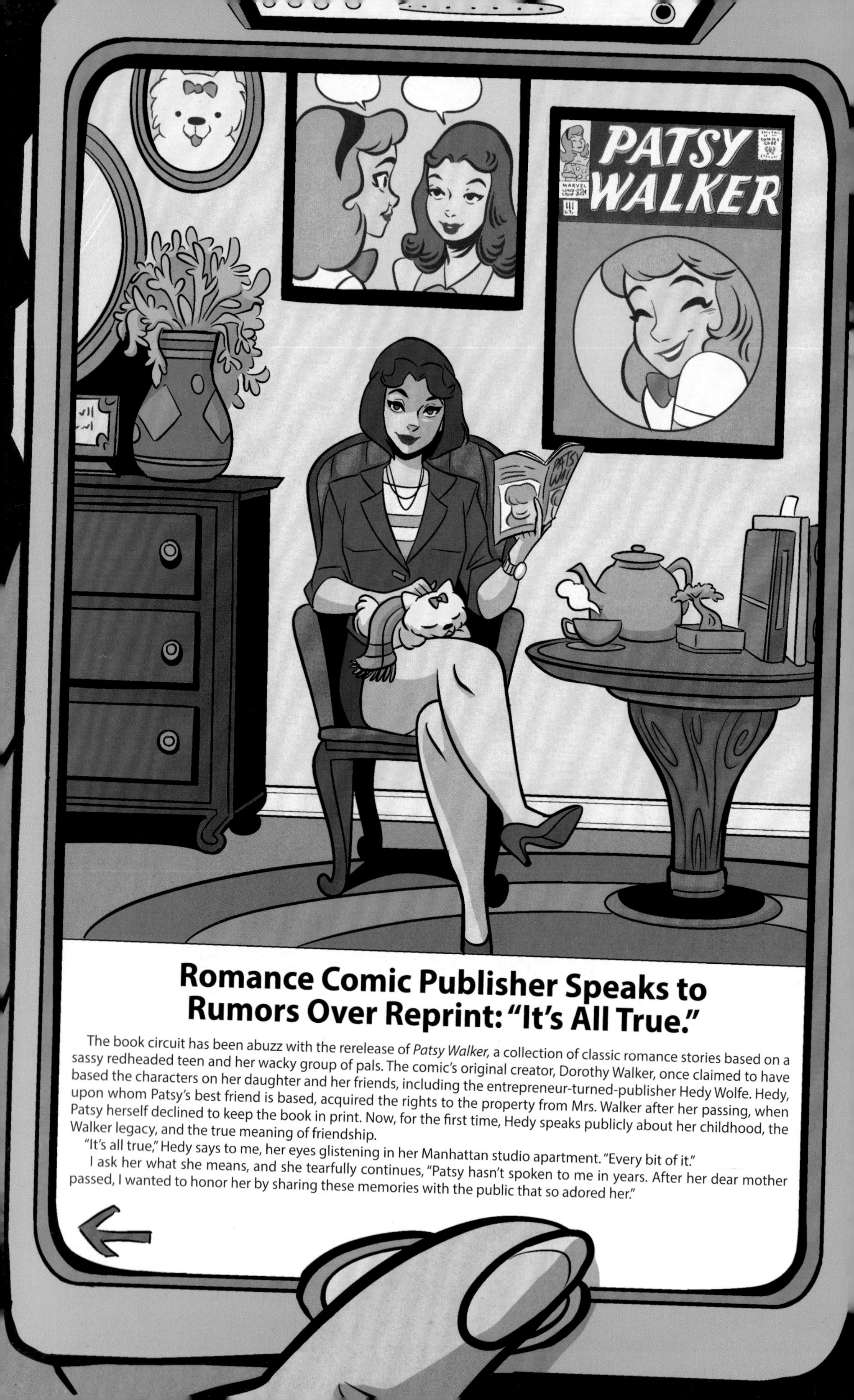
PATSY WALKER
Romance Comic Publisher Speaks to Rumors Over Reprint: "It's All True."
The book circuit has been abuzz with the rerelease of *Patsy Walker,* a collection of classic romance stories based on a sassy redheaded teen and her wacky group of pals. The comic's original creator, Dorothy Walker, once claimed to have based the characters on her daughter and her friends, including the entrepreneur-turned-publisher Hedy Wolfe. Hedy, upon whom Patsy's best friend is based, acquired the rights to the property from Mrs. Walker after her passing, when Patsy herself declined to keep the book in print. Now, for the first time, Hedy speaks publicly about her childhood, the Walker legacy, and the true meaning of friendship.
"It's all true," Hedy says to me, her eyes glistening in her Manhattan studio apartment. "Every bit of it."
I ask her what she means, and she tearfully continues, "Patsy hasn't spoken to me in years. After her dear mother passed, I wanted to honor her by sharing these memories with the public that so adored her."

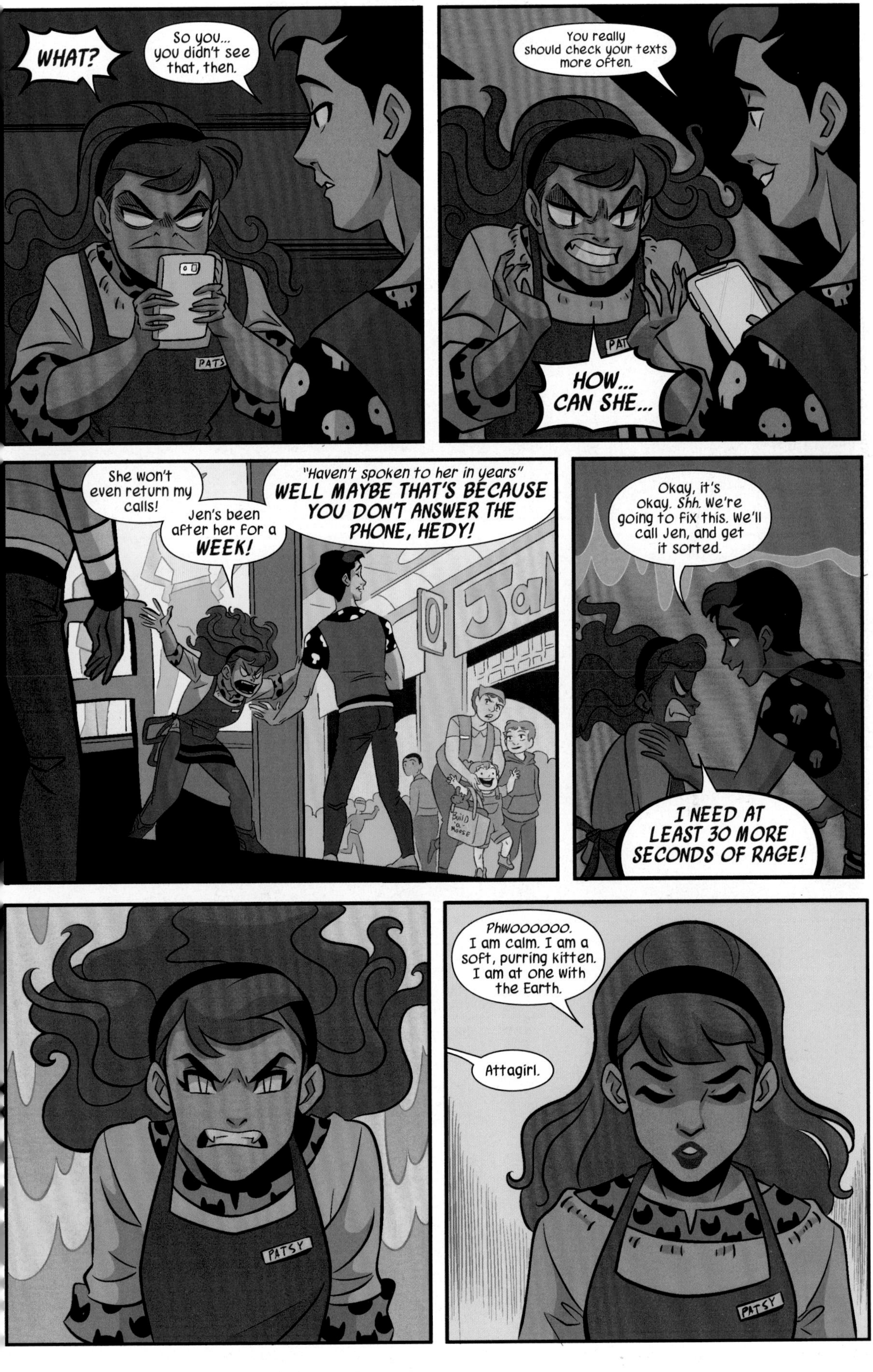
WHAT?
So you... you didn't see that, then.
You really should check your texts more often.
HOW... CAN SHE...
She won't even return my calls!
Jen's been after her for a WEEK!
"Haven't spoken to her in years"
WELL MAYBE THAT'S BECAUSE YOU DON'T ANSWER THE PHONE, HEDY!
Okay, it's okay. Shh. We're going to fix this. We'll call Jen, and get it sorted.
I NEED AT LEAST 30 MORE SECONDS OF RAGE!
Phwoooooo. I am calm. I am a soft, purring kitten. I am at one with the Earth.
Attagirl.

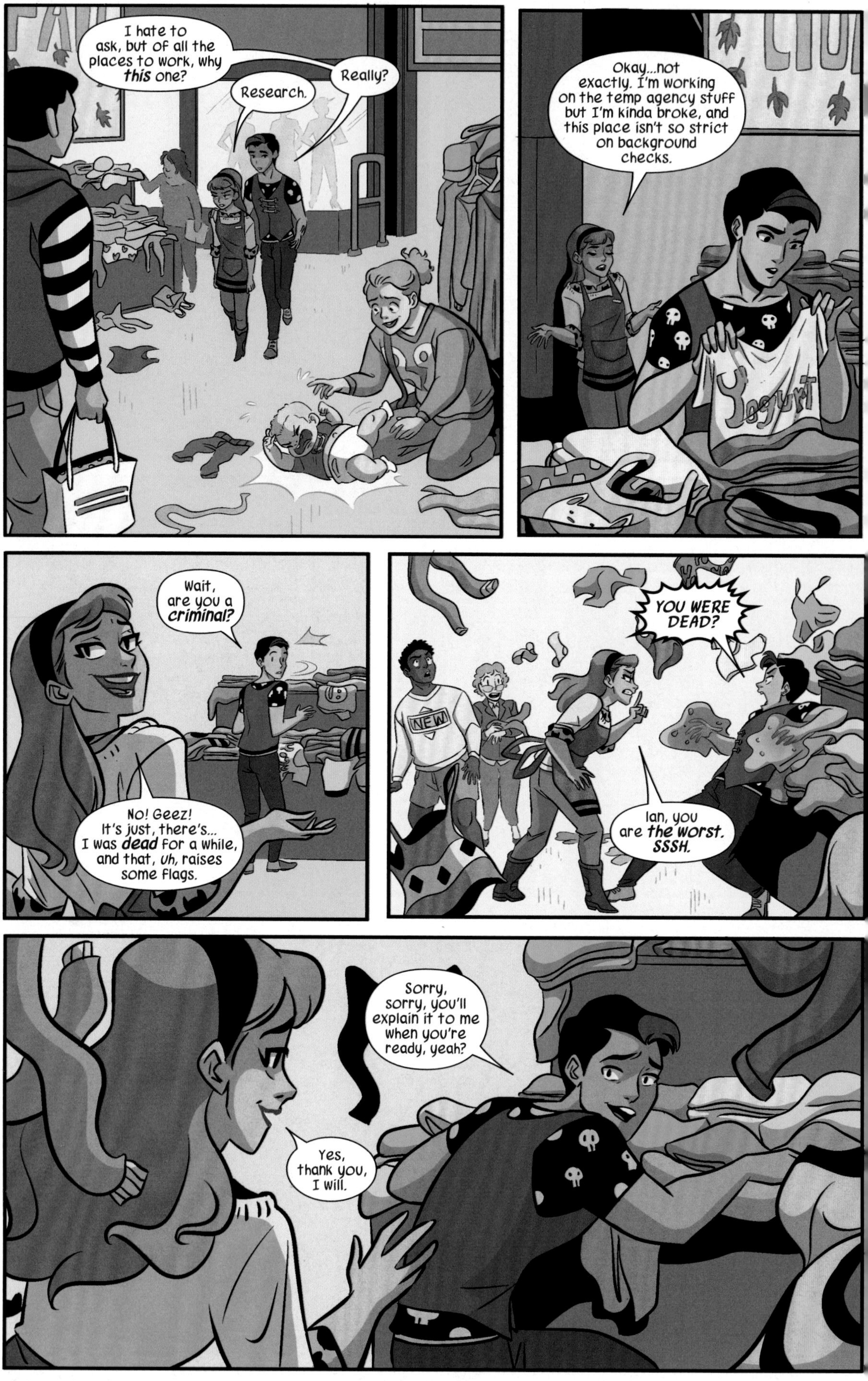
I hate to ask, but of all the places to work, why *this* one?
Research.
Really?
Okay...not exactly. I'm working on the temp agency stuff but I'm kinda broke, and this place isn't so strict on background checks.
Yogurt
Wait, are you a *criminal?*
No! Geez! It's just, there's... I was *dead* for a while, and that, *uh*, raises some flags.
YOU WERE DEAD?
NEW
Ian, you are *the worst. SSSH.*
Sorry, sorry, you'll explain it to me when you're ready, yeah?
Yes, thank you, I will.

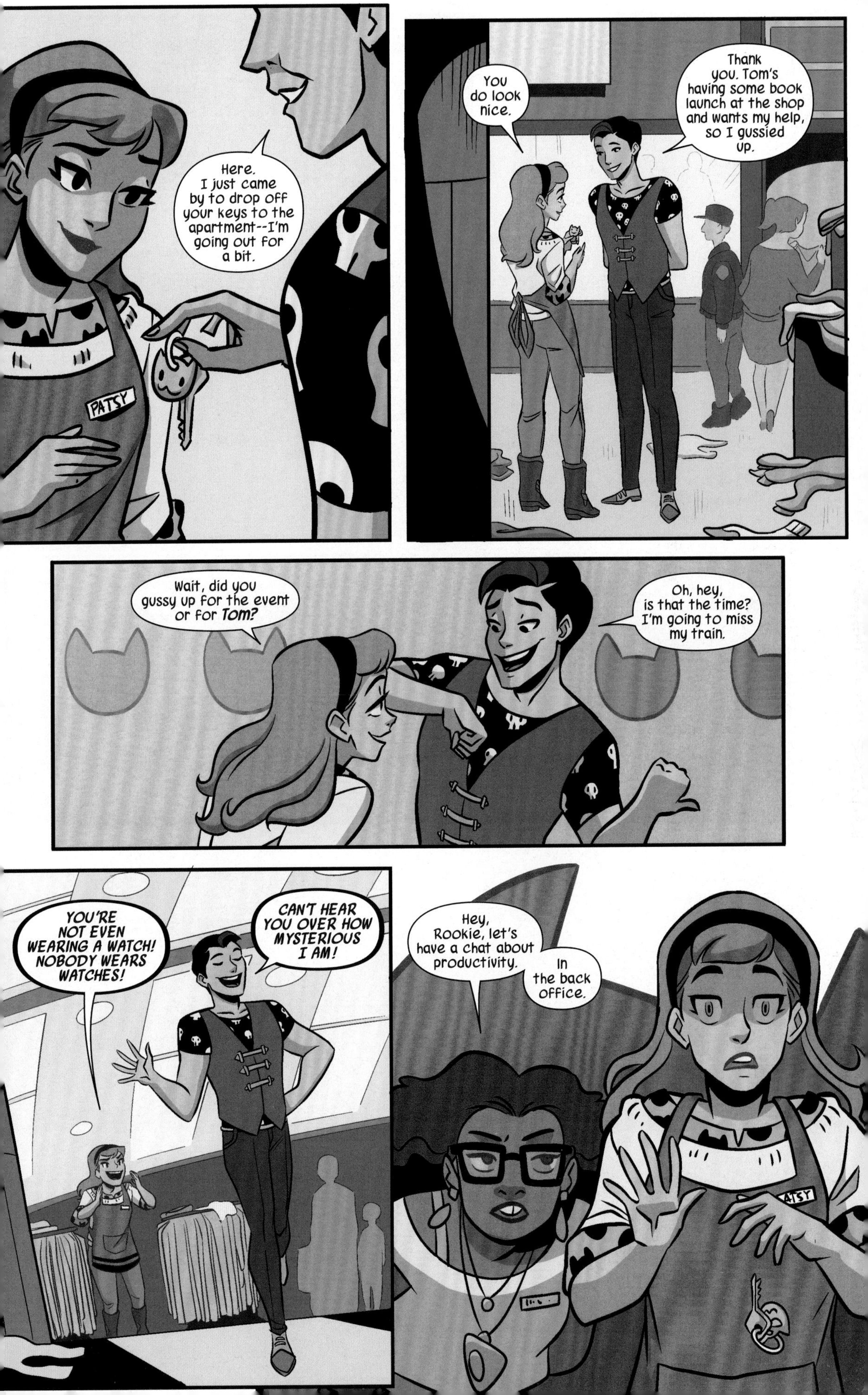

PATSY
Here. I just came by to drop off your keys to the apartment--I'm going out for a bit.
You do look nice.
Thank you. Tom's having some book launch at the shop and wants my help, so I gussied up.
Wait, did you gussy up for the event or for *Tom?*
Oh, hey, is that the time? I'm going to miss my train.
YOU'RE NOT EVEN WEARING A WATCH! NOBODY WEARS WATCHES!
CAN'T HEAR YOU OVER HOW MYSTERIOUS I AM!
Hey, Rookie, let's have a chat about productivity.
In the back office.

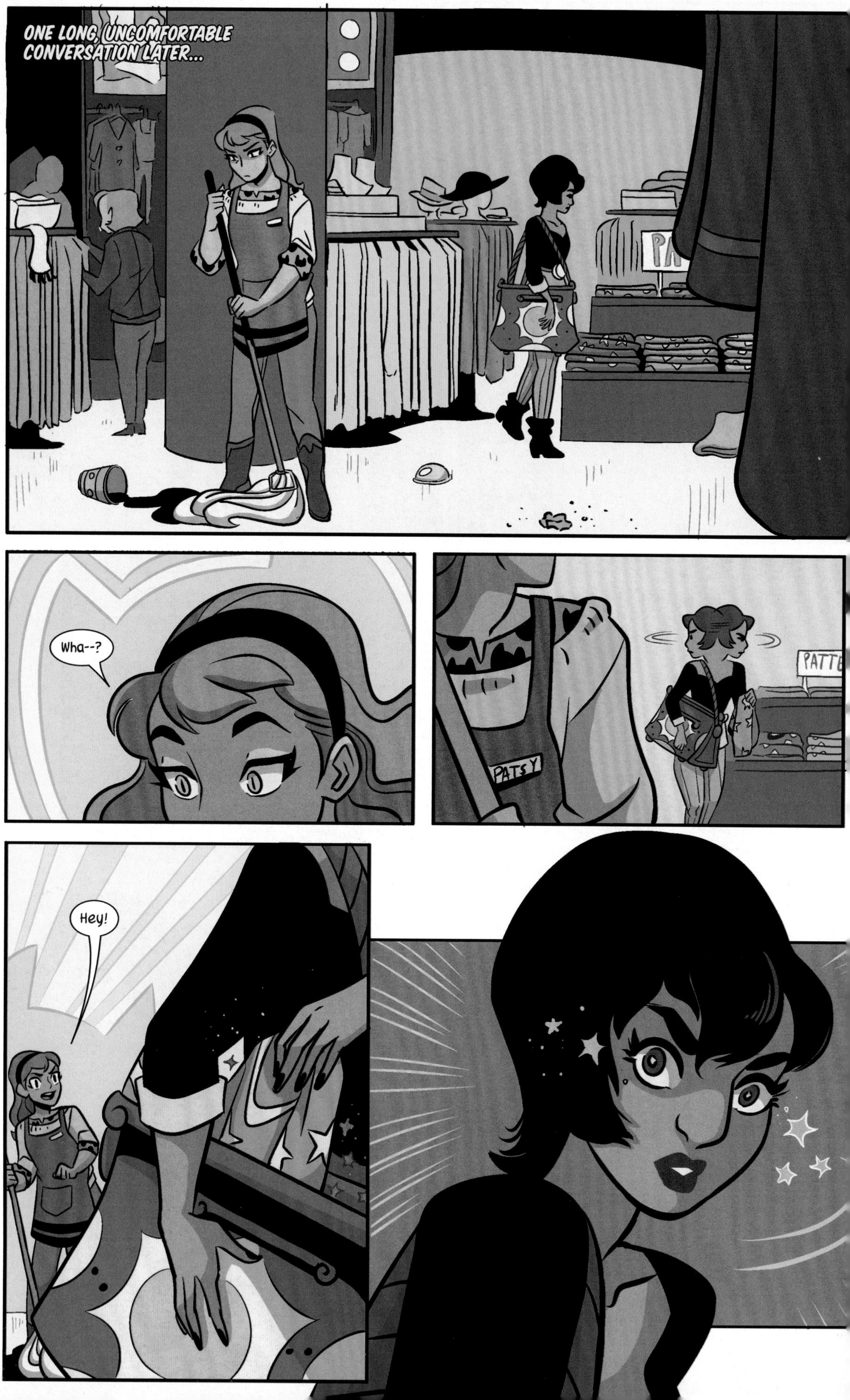
ONE LONG, UNCOMFORTABLE CONVERSATION LATER...
PA
Wha--?
PATSY
PATTE
Hey!

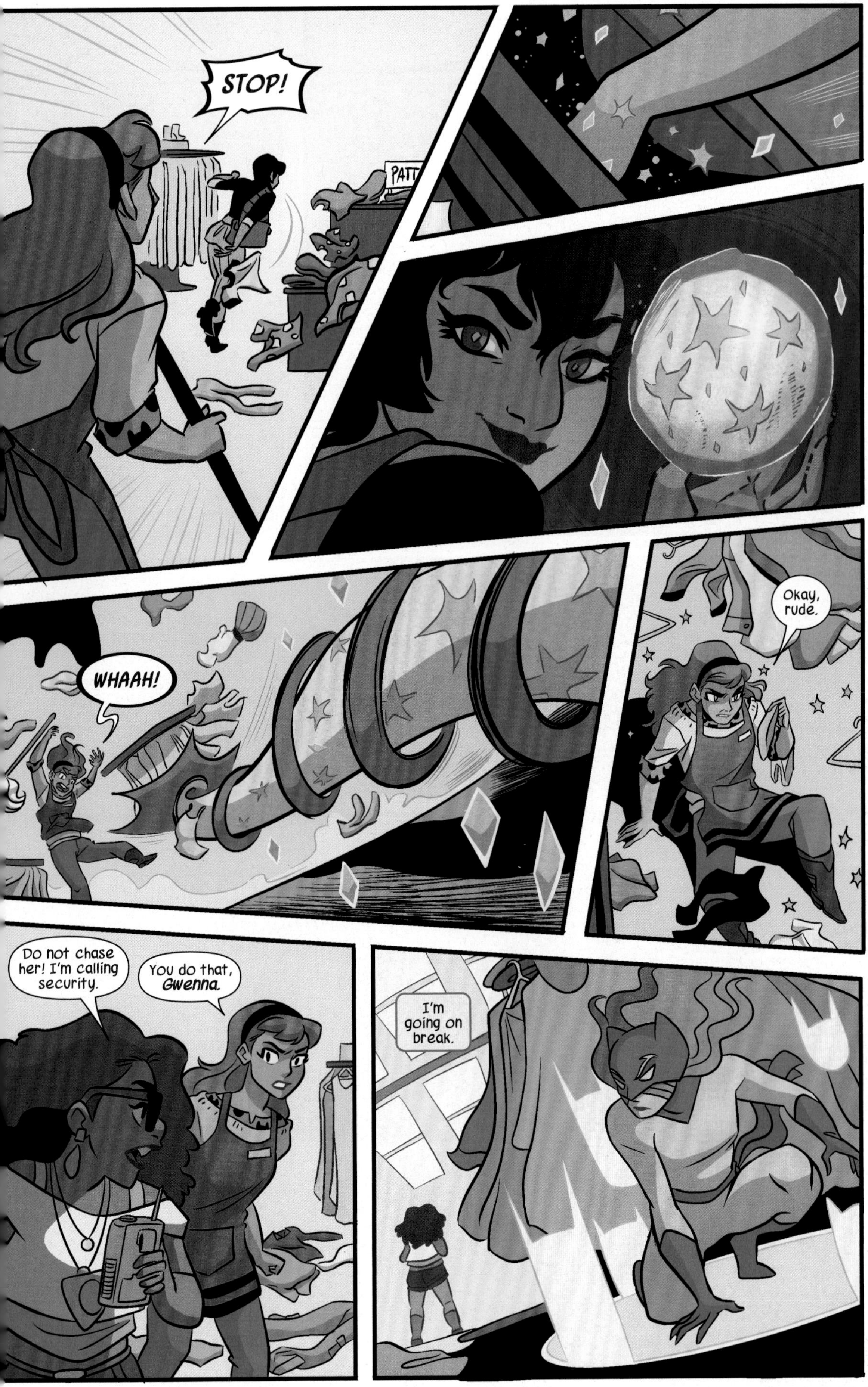
STOP!
PATT
WHAAH!
Okay, rude.
Do not chase her! I'm calling security.
You do that, *Gwenna.*
I'm going on break.

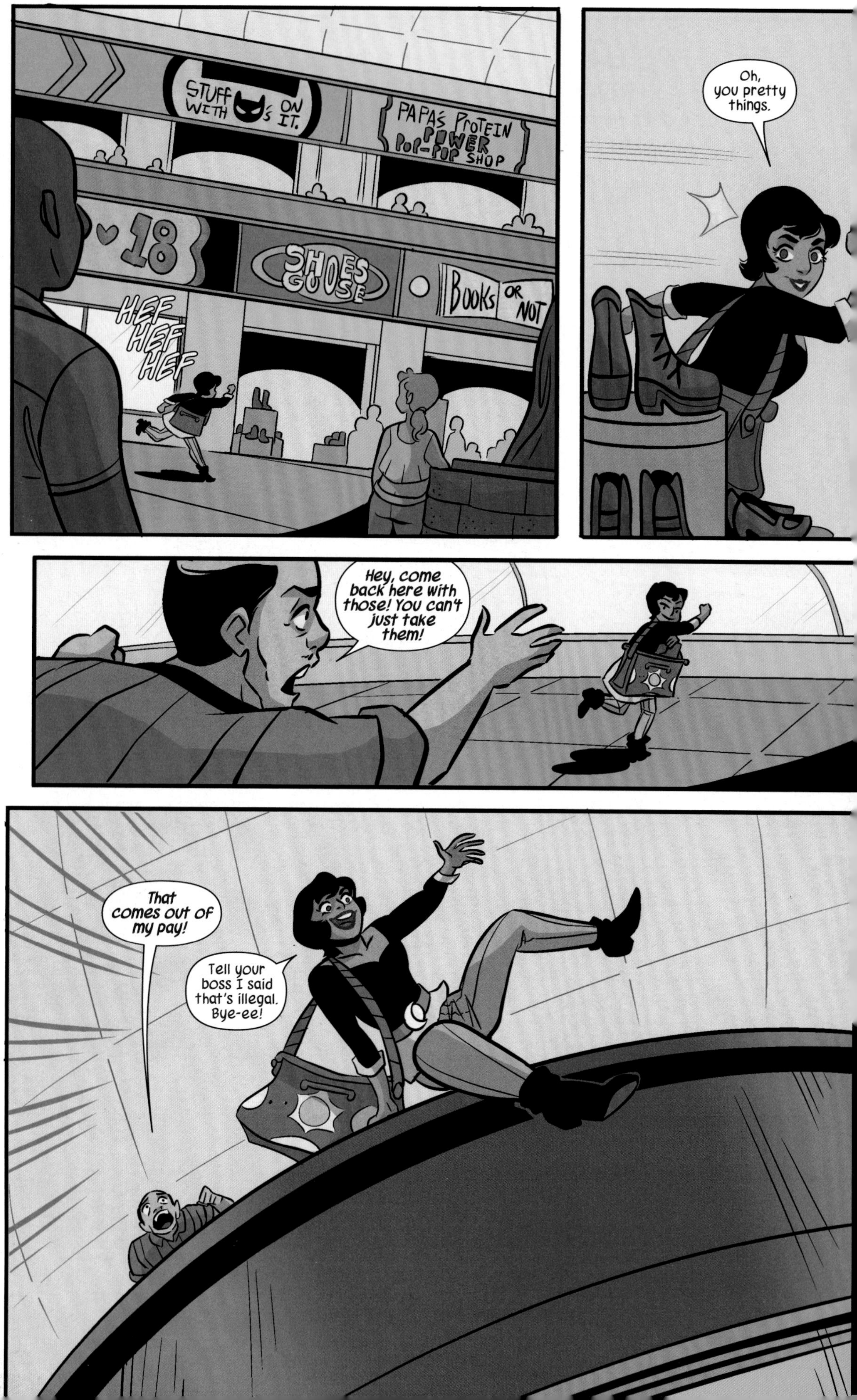
STUFF WITH 's ON IT.
PAPA'S PROTEIN POWER POP-POP SHOP
18
SHOES GOOSE
BOOKS OR NOT
HEF HEF HEF
Oh, you pretty things.
Hey, come back here with those! You can't just take them!
That comes out of my pay!
Tell your boss I said that's illegal. Bye-ee!

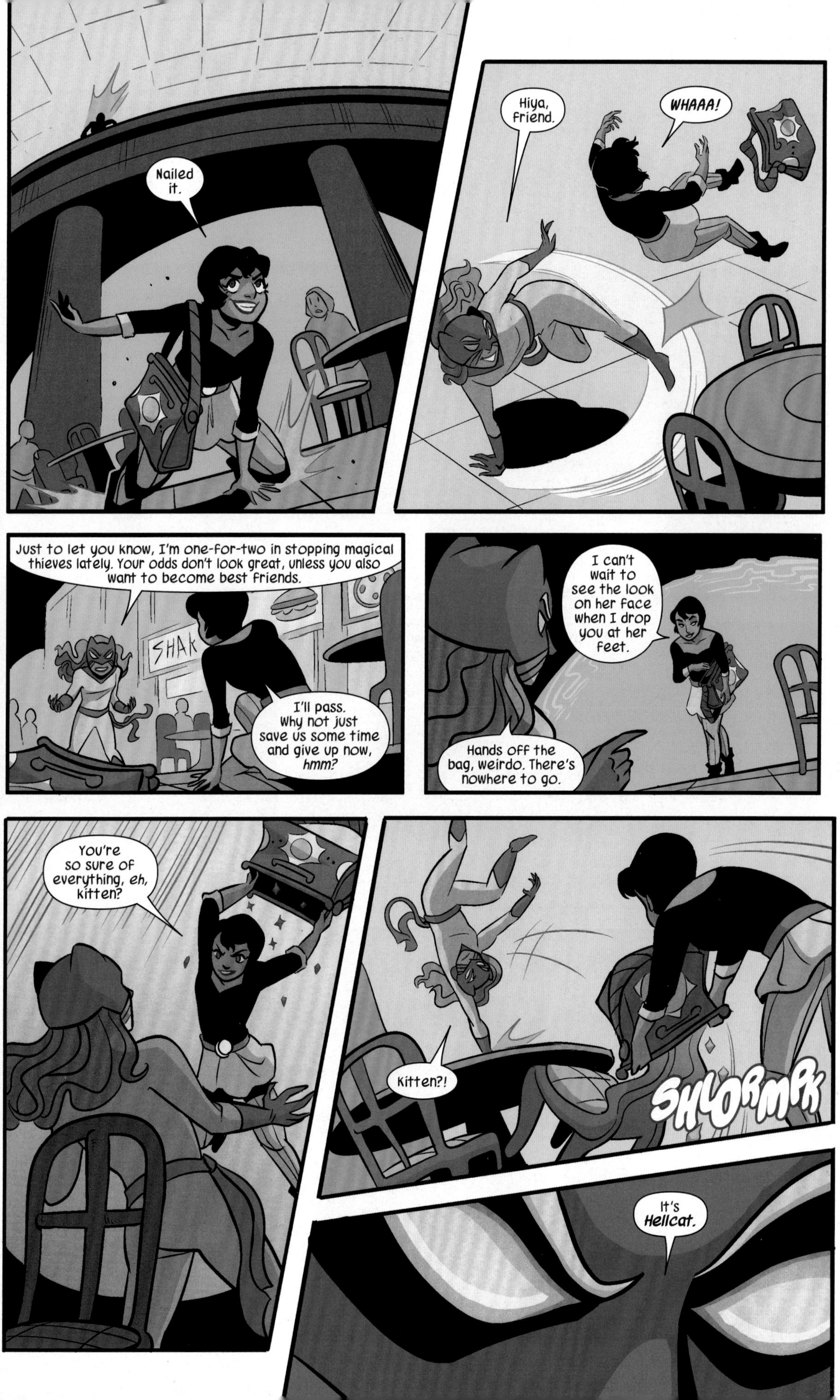
Nailed it.
Hiya, friend.
WHAAA!
Just to let you know, I'm one-for-two in stopping magical thieves lately. Your odds don't look great, unless you also want to become best friends.
SHAK
I'll pass. Why not just save us some time and give up now, *hmm?*
I can't wait to see the look on her face when I drop you at her feet.
Hands off the bag, weirdo. There's nowhere to go.
You're so sure of everything, *eh,* kitten?
Kitten?!
SHLORMPK
It's *Hellcat.*

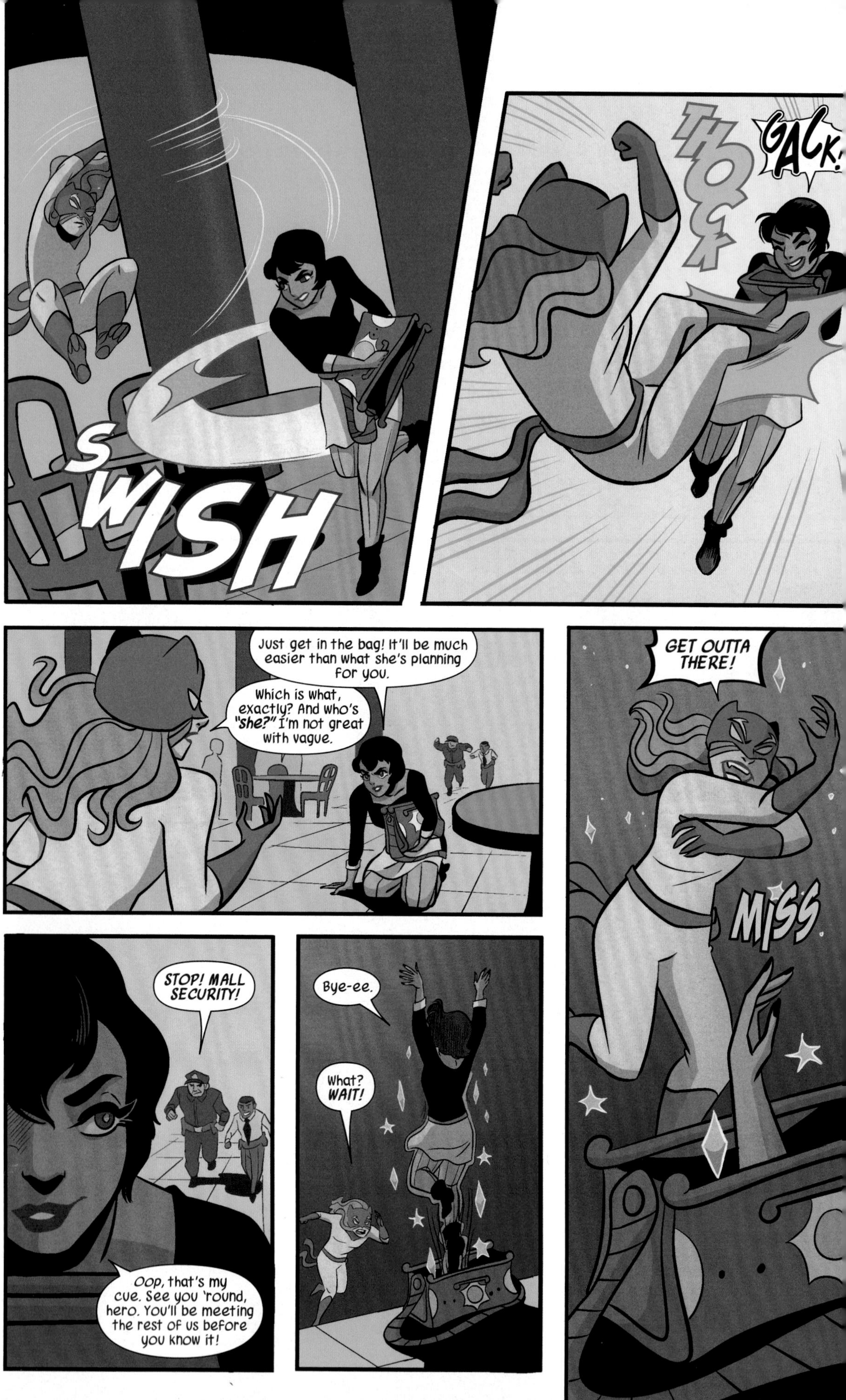
SWISH
THOCK
GACK!
Just get in the bag! It'll be much easier than what she's planning for you.
Which is what, exactly? And who's "she?" I'm not great with vague.
GET OUTTA THERE!
MISS
STOP! MALL SECURITY!
Oop, that's my cue. See you 'round, hero. You'll be meeting the rest of us before you know it!
Bye-ee.
What? WAIT!

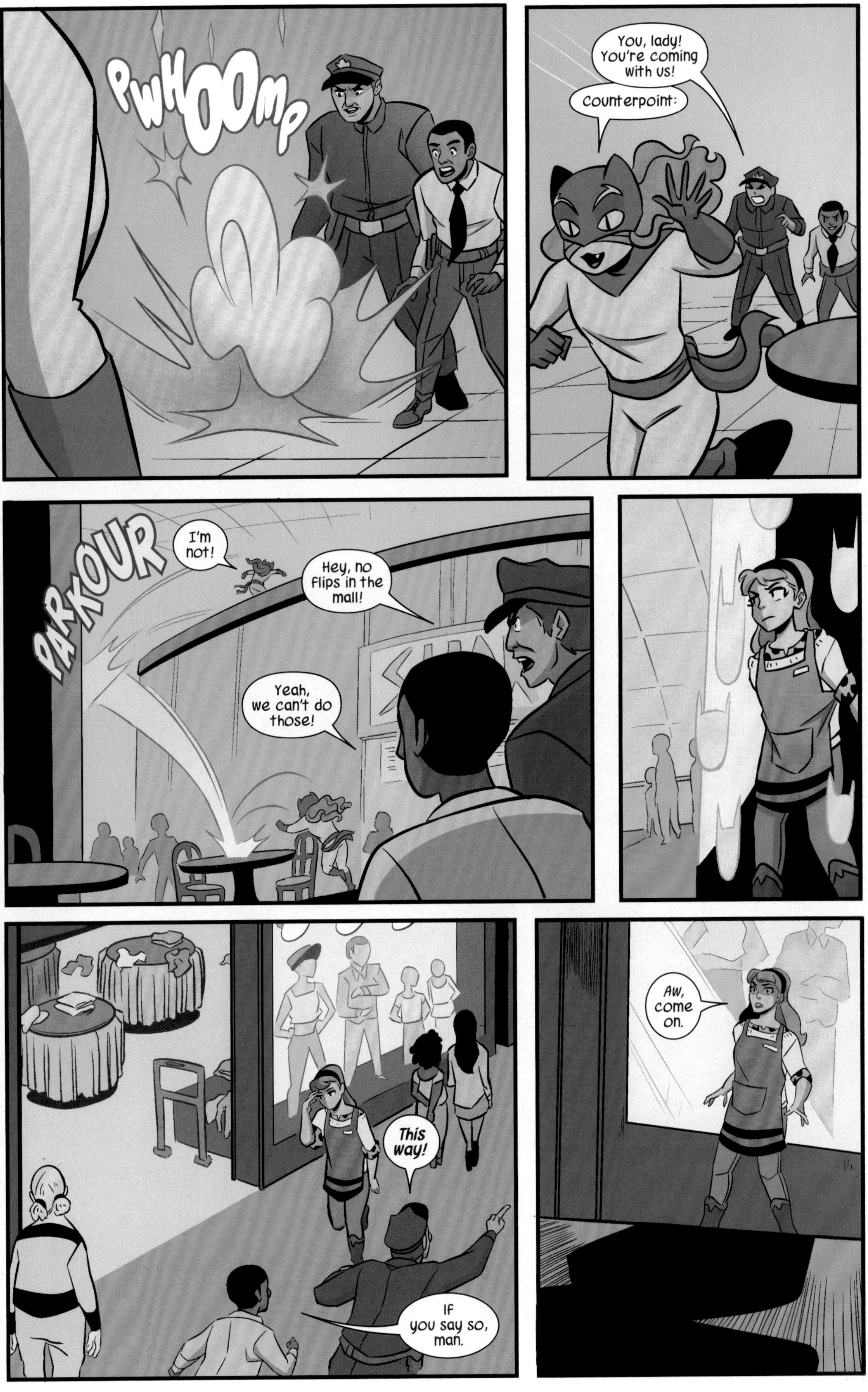
PWHOOOMP
You, lady! You're coming with us!
Counterpoint:
PARKOUR
I'm not!
Hey, no flips in the mall!
Yeah, we can't do those!
This way!
If you say so, man.
Aw, come on.

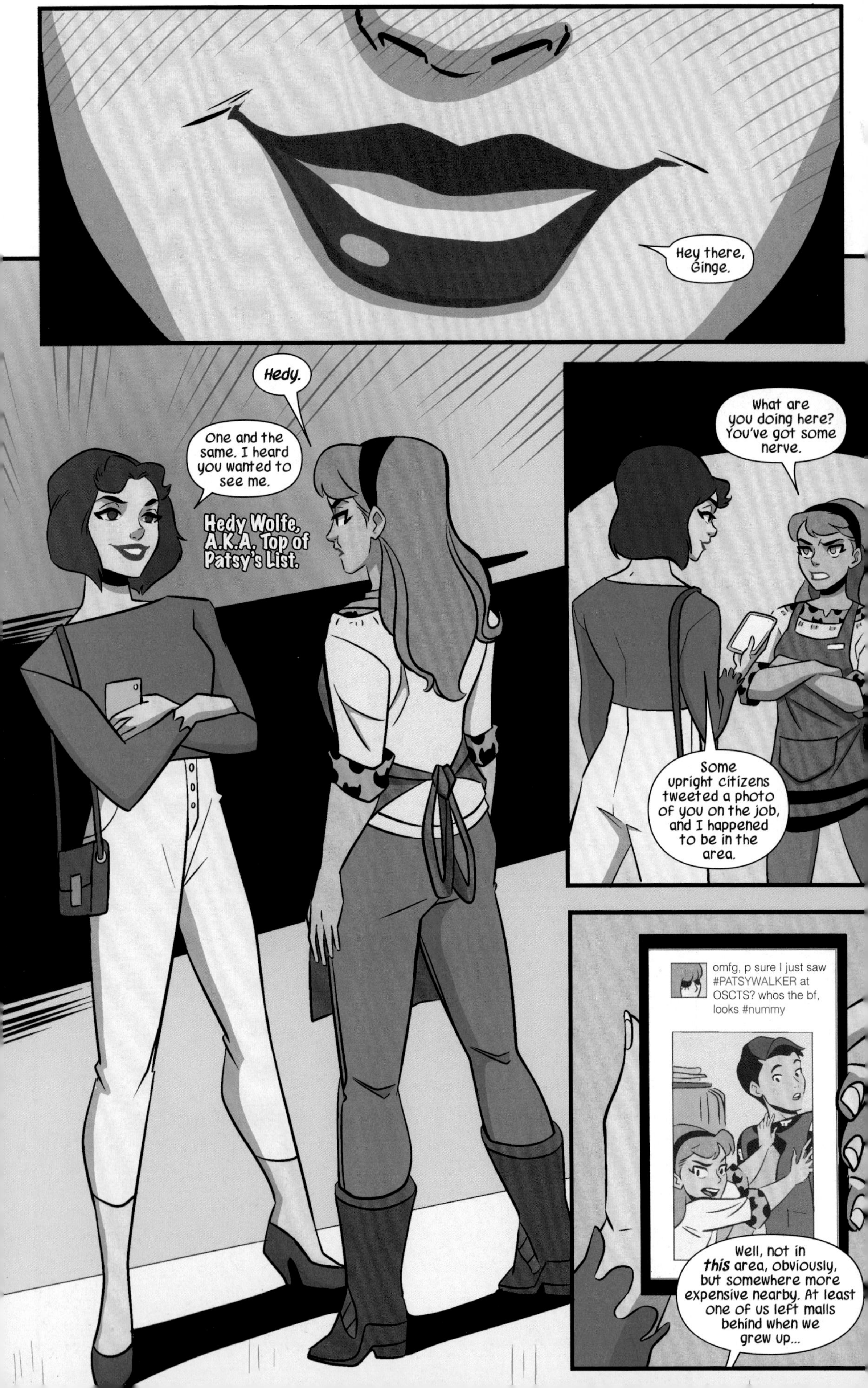
Hey there, Ginge.
Hedy.
One and the same. I heard you wanted to see me.
Hedy Wolfe, A.K.A. Top of Patsy's List.
What are you doing here? You've got some nerve.
Some upright citizens tweeted a photo of you on the job, and I happened to be in the area.
omfg, p sure I just saw #PATSYWALKER at OSCTS? whos the bf, looks #nummy
Well, not in *this* area, obviously, but somewhere more expensive nearby. At least one of us left malls behind when we grew up...

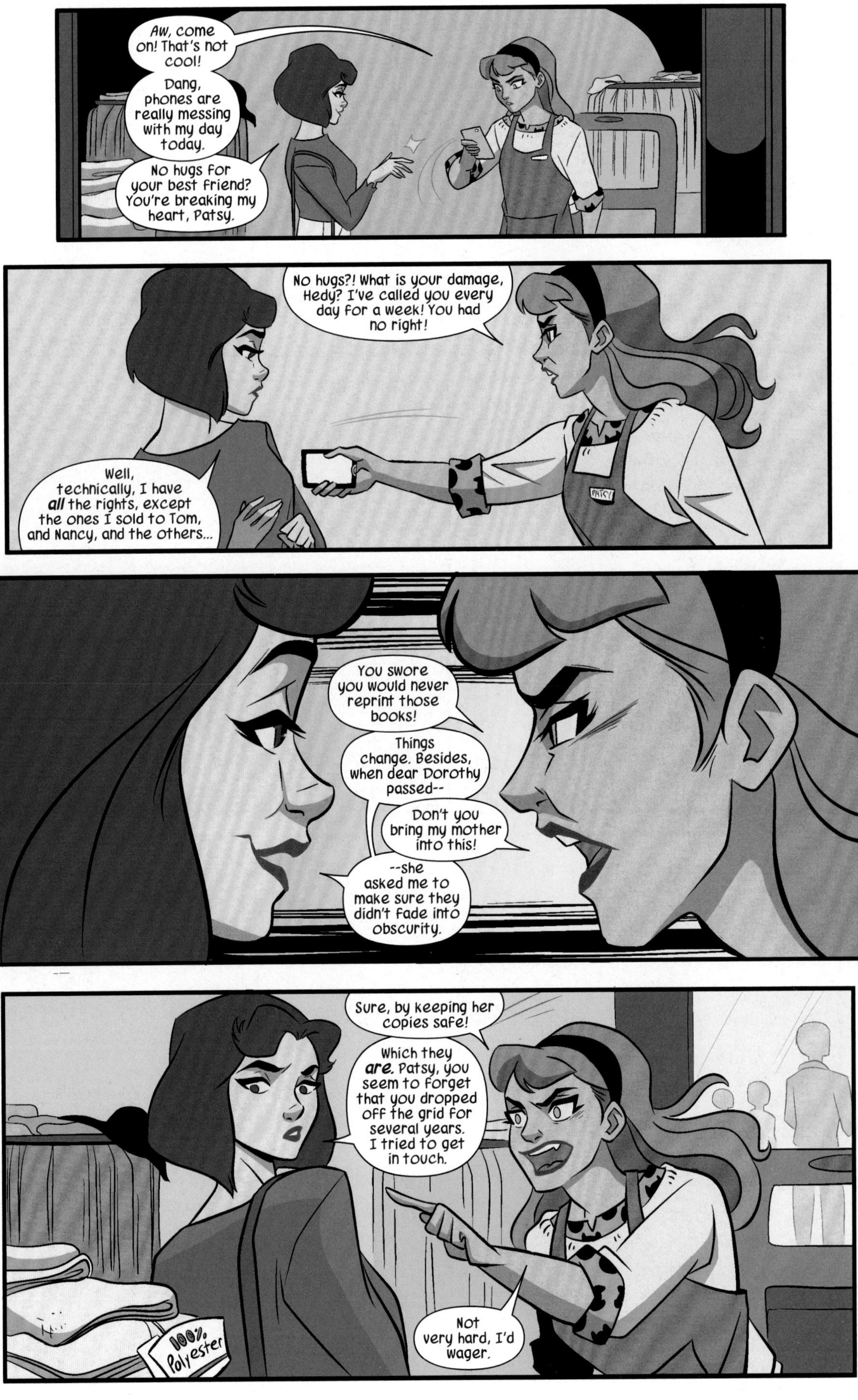
Aw, come on! That's not cool!
Dang, phones are really messing with my day today.
No hugs for your best friend? You're breaking my heart, Patsy.
No hugs?! What is your damage, Hedy? I've called you every day for a week! You had no right!
Well, technically, I have ***all*** the rights, except the ones I sold to Tom, and Nancy, and the others...
PATSY
You swore you would never reprint those books!
Things change. Besides, when dear Dorothy passed--
Don't you bring my mother into this!
--she asked me to make sure they didn't fade into obscurity.
Sure, by keeping her copies safe!
Which they ***are.*** Patsy, you seem to forget that you dropped off the grid for several years. I tried to get in touch.
Not very hard, I'd wager.
100% Polyester

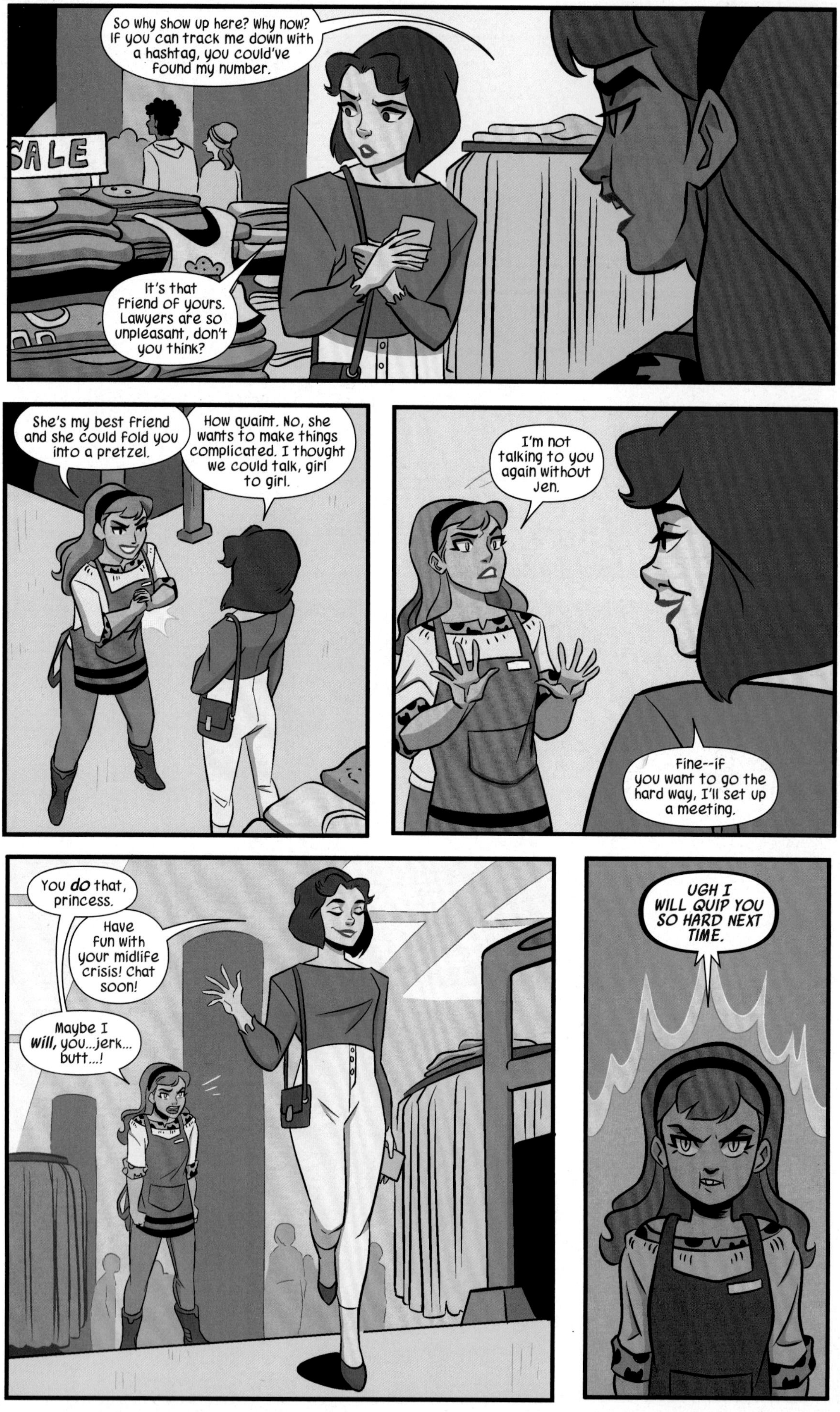
So why show up here? Why now? If you can track me down with a hashtag, you could've found my number.
SALE
It's that friend of yours. Lawyers are so unpleasant, don't you think?
She's my best friend and she could fold you into a pretzel.
How quaint. No, she wants to make things complicated. I thought we could talk, girl to girl.
I'm not talking to you again without Jen.
Fine--if you want to go the hard way, I'll set up a meeting.
You **do** that, princess.
Have fun with your midlife crisis! Chat soon!
Maybe I ***will***, you...jerk... butt...!
UGH I WILL QUIP YOU SO HARD NEXT TIME.

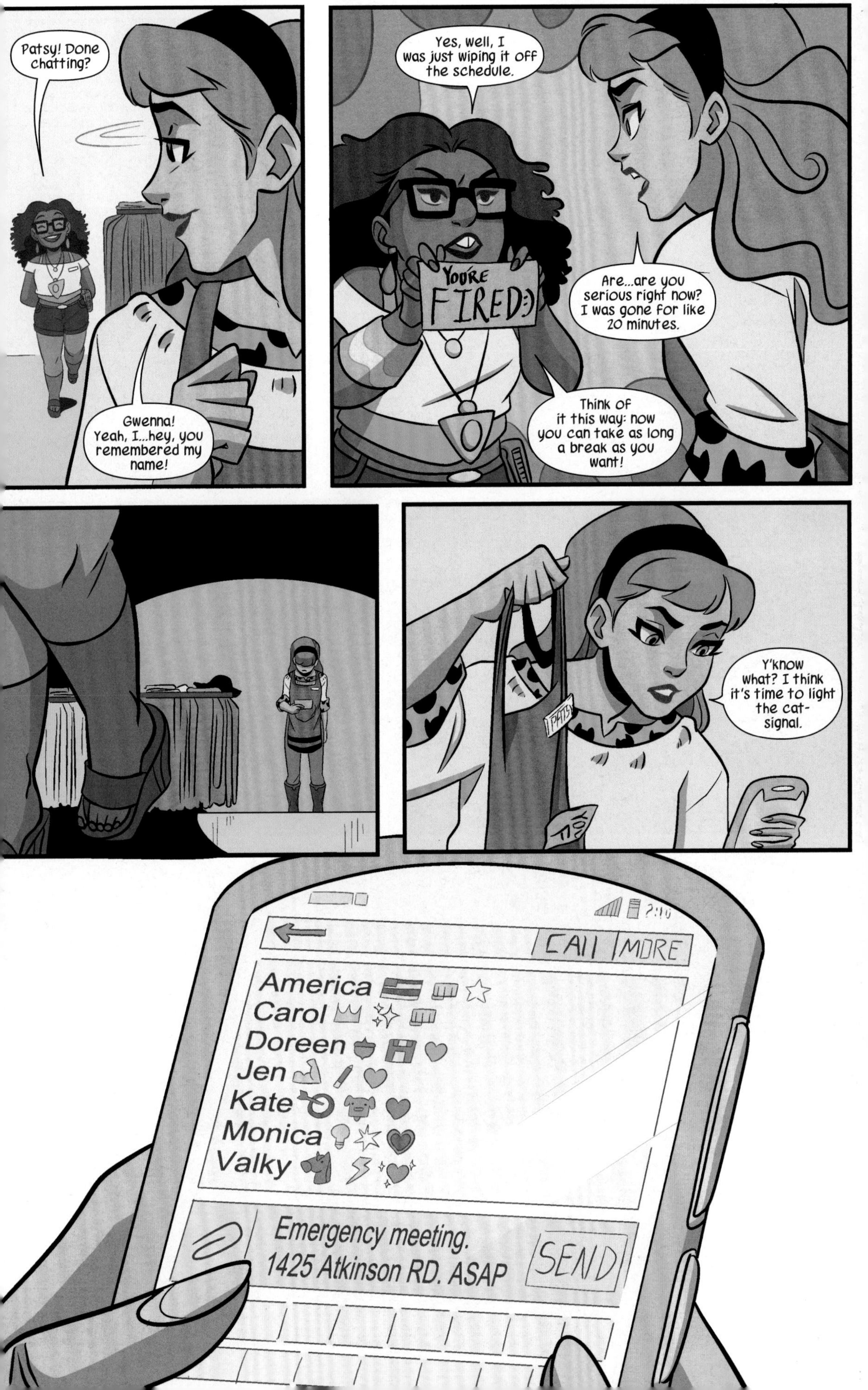
Patsy! Done chatting?
Gwenna! Yeah, I...hey, you remembered my name!
Yes, well, I was just wiping it off the schedule.
YOU'RE FIRED :)
Are...are you serious right now? I was gone for like 20 minutes.
Think of it this way: now you can take as long a break as you want!
Y'know what? I think it's time to light the cat-signal.
CALL
MORE
America
Carol
Doreen
Jen
Kate
Monica
Valky
Emergency meeting.
1425 Atkinson RD. ASAP
SEND

LINDA'S BURGERS

Patsy!

Kate Bishop, A.K.A. Hawkeye/Hawkguy/ Lady Hawkguy

America Chavez, A.K.A. Ms. America (Chavez)

Doreen Green, A.K.A. The Unbeatable Squirrel Girl

Monica Rambeau, A.K.A. Spectrum

I got here as fast as I could. Are you okay?!

Oh, yeah! Yeah. I just *really* needed to blow off some steam.

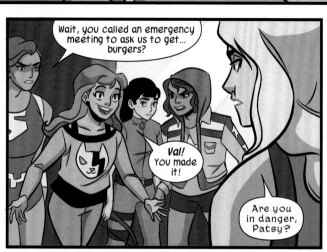

Wait, you called an emergency meeting to ask us to get... burgers?

Val! You made it!

Are you in danger, Patsy?

Only of getting more *hangry.* Naww, I just wanted to get you guys all out for a lunch. I had the worst friggin' day.

You are a terrible person and are lucky I am your friend.

Be very, very grateful I wasn't in court.

As far as I'm concerned, not eating burgers *is* an emergency.

I want your problems.

Oh, I also fight dinosaurs and stuff, and you know what? It works up an *appetite.*

That's my *girls!*

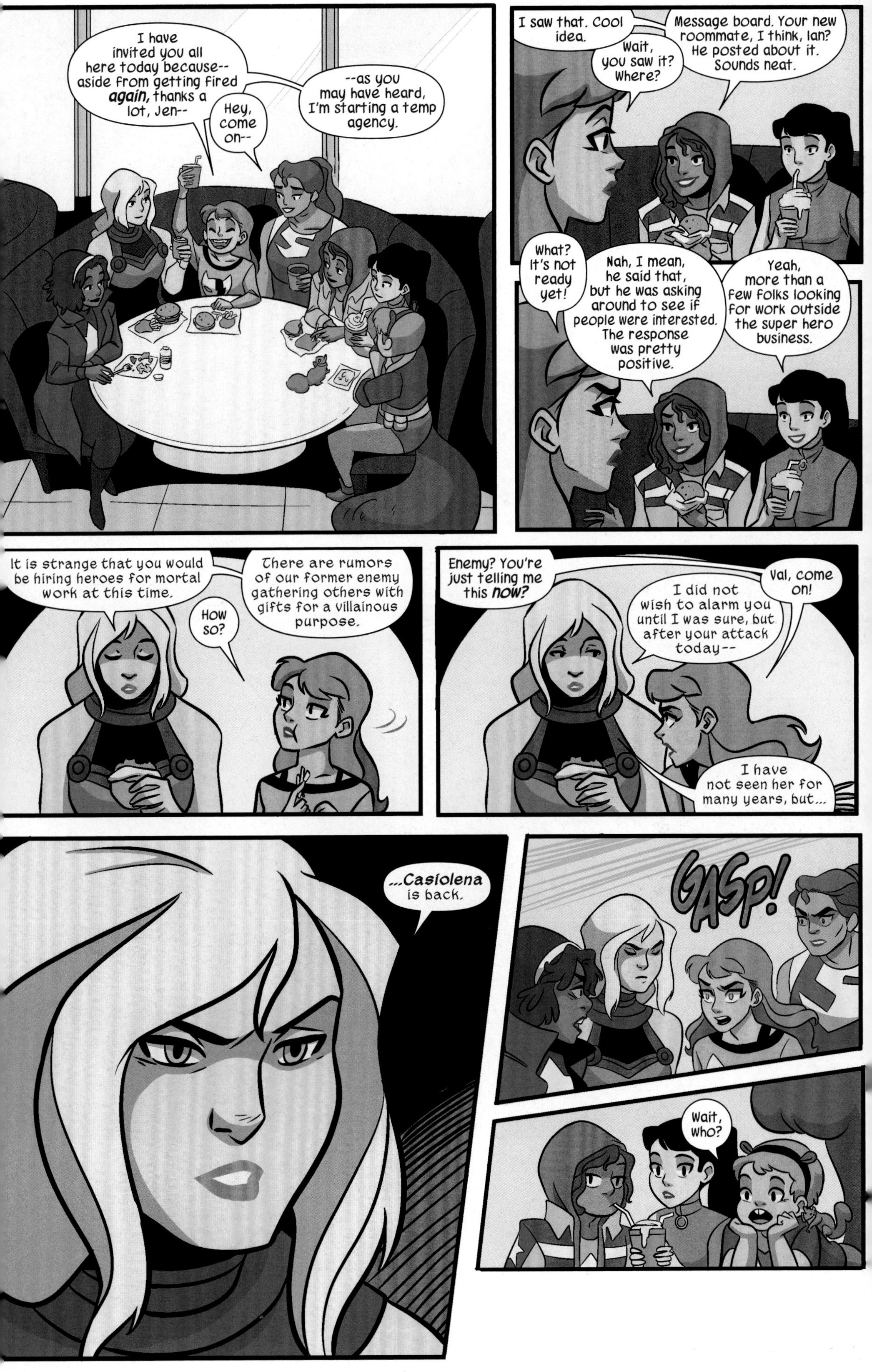
I have invited you all here today because-- aside from getting fired **again,** thanks a lot, Jen--
Hey, come on--
--as you may have heard, I'm starting a temp agency.
I saw that. Cool idea.
Wait, you saw it? Where?
Message board. Your new roommate, I think, Ian? He posted about it. Sounds neat.
What? It's not ready yet!
Nah, I mean, he said that, but he was asking around to see if people were interested. The response was pretty positive.
Yeah, more than a few folks looking for work outside the super hero business.
It is strange that you would be hiring heroes for mortal work at this time.
How so?
There are rumors of our former enemy gathering others with gifts for a villainous purpose.
Enemy? You're just telling me this **NOW?**
I did not wish to alarm you until I was sure, but after your attack today--
Val, come on!
I have not seen her for many years, but...
...Casiolena is back.
GASP!
Wait, who?

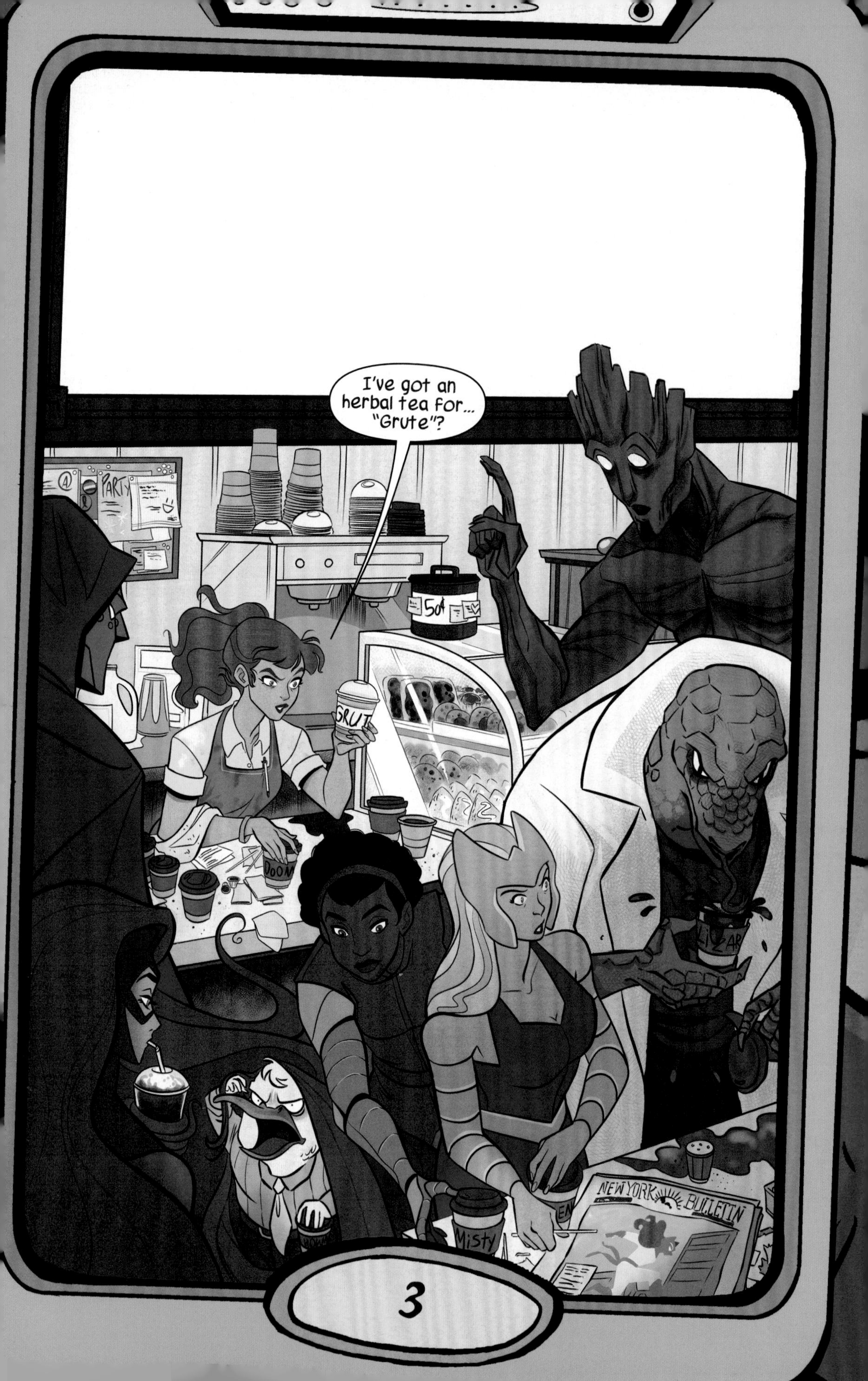
I've got an herbal tea for... "Grute"?
PARTY
50¢
GRUT
Misty
NEW YORK BULLETIN

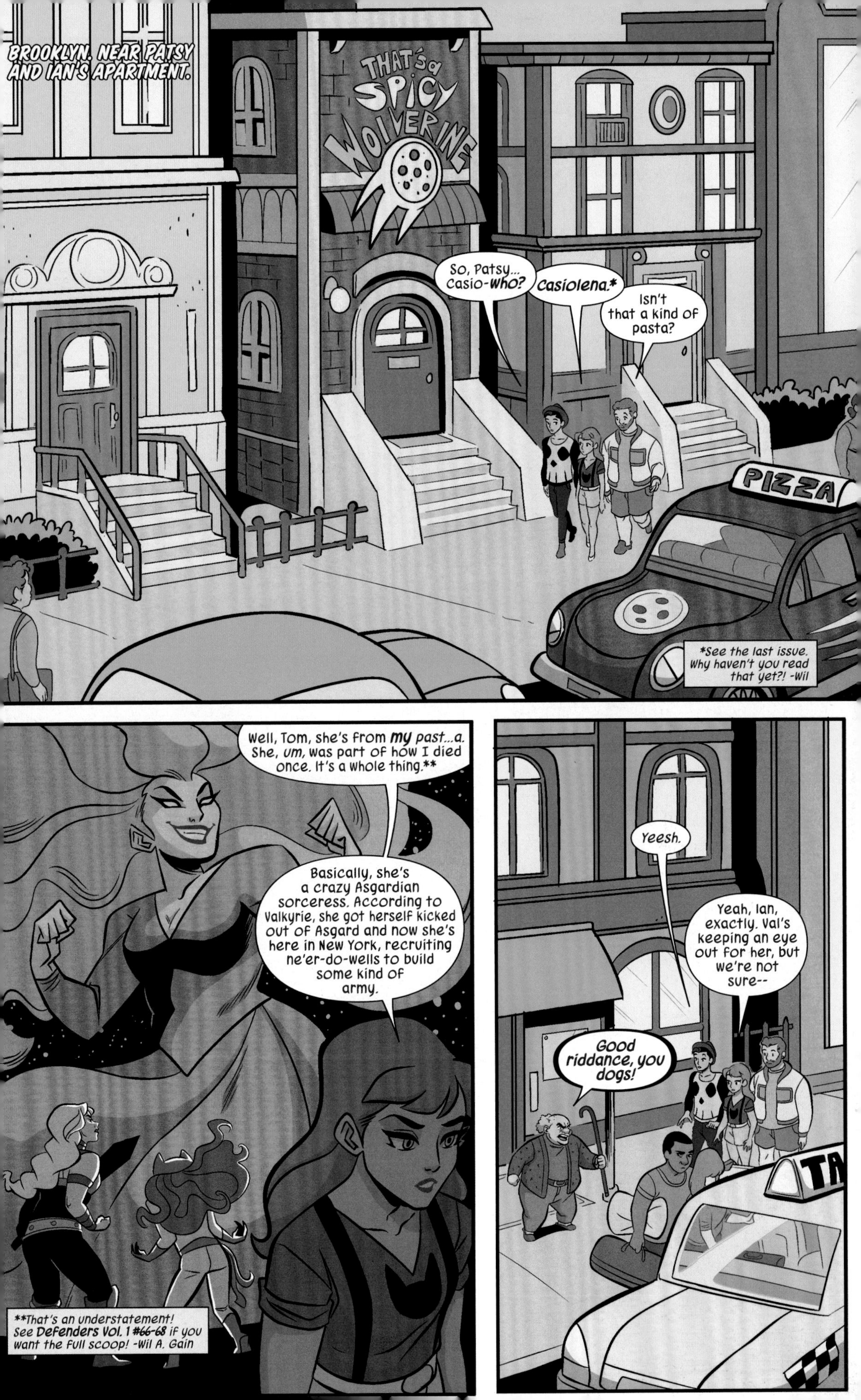
BROOKLYN. NEAR PATSY AND IAN'S APARTMENT.
THAT'S a SPICY WOLVERINE
So, Patsy... Casio-WHO?
Casiolena.*
Isn't that a kind of pasta?
PIZZA
*See the last issue. Why haven't you read that yet?! -Wil
Well, Tom, she's from my past...a. She, um, was part of how I died once. It's a whole thing.**
Basically, she's a crazy Asgardian sorceress. According to Valkyrie, she got herself kicked out of Asgard and now she's here in New York, recruiting ne'er-do-wells to build some kind of army.
**That's an understatement! See Defenders Vol. 1 #66-68 if you want the full scoop! -Wil A. Gain
Yeesh.
Yeah, Ian, exactly. Val's keeping an eye out for her, but we're not sure--
Good riddance, you dogs!
TA

Whoa, is there a problem here?

Is no problem. Who are you, lady?

Uh, Mr. Ravina, this is my new roommate, Patsy Walker. Patsy, meet your new landlord.

You still here? I thought we kicked you out!

Well, heh, you tried, but I found someone to help with rent.

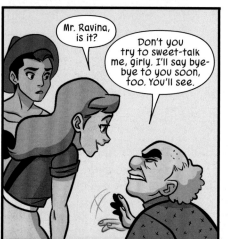

Mr. Ravina, is it?

Don't you try to sweet-talk me, girly. I'll say bye-bye to you soon, too. You'll see.

Look, did something happen to that couple? Are they all right?

Pah!

Please excuse my father, he can be a little... cantankerous. He's not a big fan of anyone under 40.

Hi there.

Uh... hello.

My name's Federigo. Are you just moving in?

I...

Come on, Patsy. We're done here.

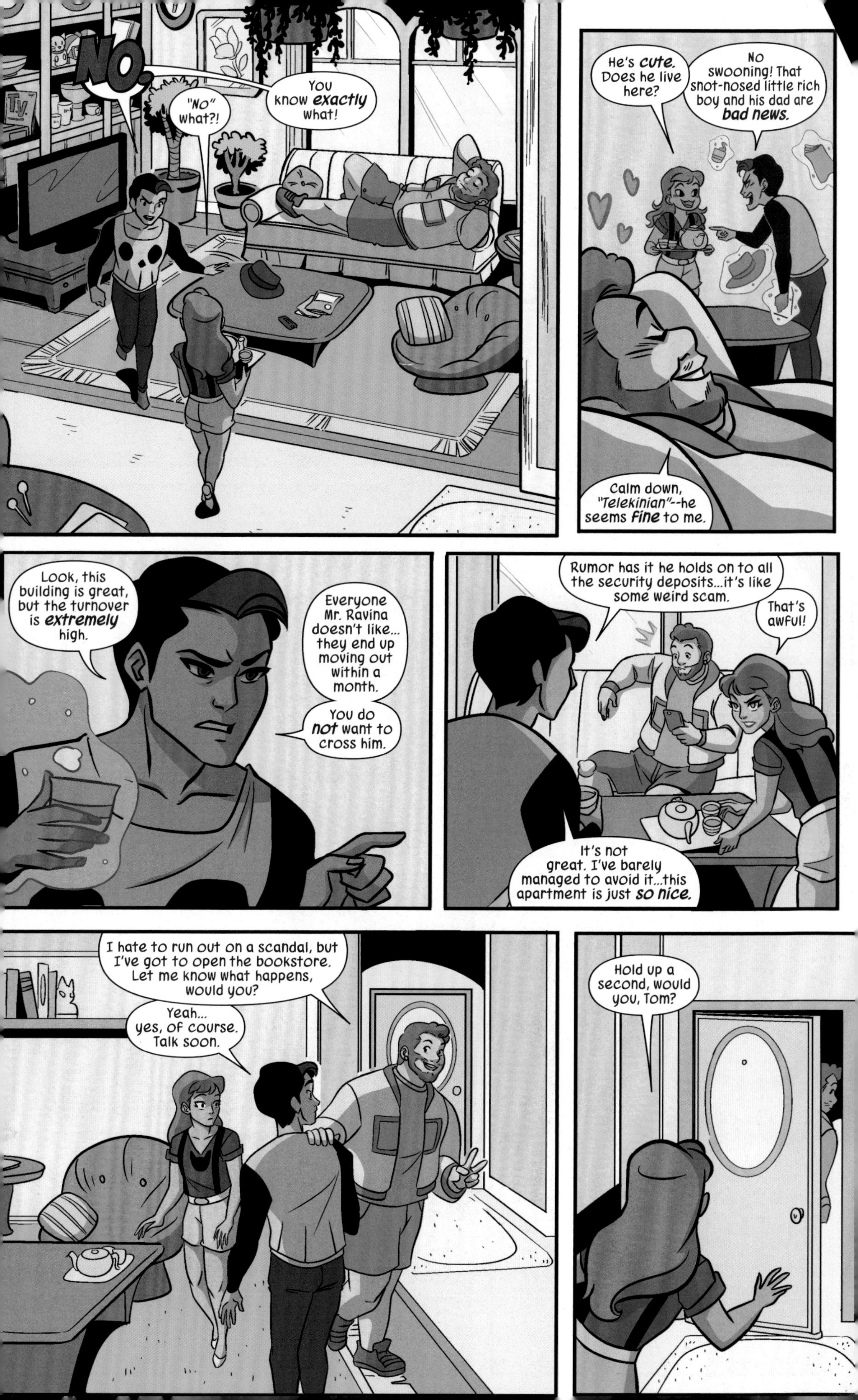
NO.
"NO" what?!
You know exactly what!
He's cute. Does he live here?
No swooning! That snot-nosed little rich boy and his dad are bad news.
Calm down, "Telekinian"--he seems fine to me.
Look, this building is great, but the turnover is extremely high.
Everyone Mr. Ravina doesn't like... they end up moving out within a month.
You do not want to cross him.
Rumor has it he holds on to all the security deposits...it's like some weird scam.
That's awful!
It's not great. I've barely managed to avoid it...this apartment is just so nice.
I hate to run out on a scandal, but I've got to open the bookstore. Let me know what happens, would you?
Yeah... yes, of course. Talk soon.
Hold up a second, would you, Tom?

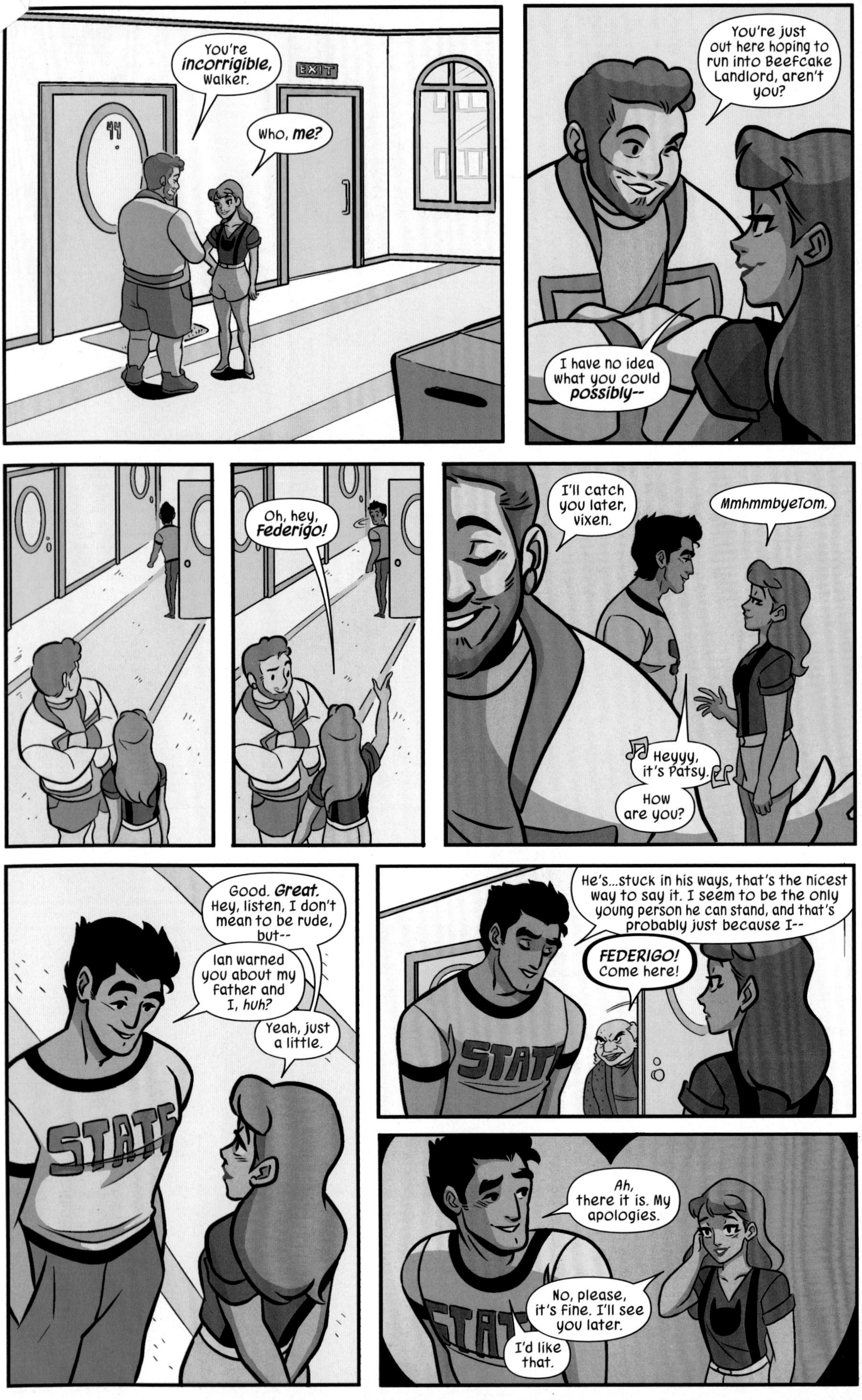
You're *incorrigible,* Walker.
EXIT
Who, *me?*
You're just out here hoping to run into Beefcake Landlord, aren't you?
I have no idea what you could *possibly--*
Oh, hey, *Federigo!*
I'll catch you later, vixen.
MmhmmbyeTom.
Heyyy, it's Patsy.
How are you?
Good. *Great.* Hey, listen, I don't mean to be rude, but--
Ian warned you about my father and I, *huh?*
Yeah, just a little.
STATE
He's...stuck in his ways, that's the nicest way to say it. I seem to be the only young person he can stand, and that's probably just because I--
FEDERIGO! Come here!
Ah, there it is. My apologies.
No, please, it's fine. I'll see you later.
I'd like that.

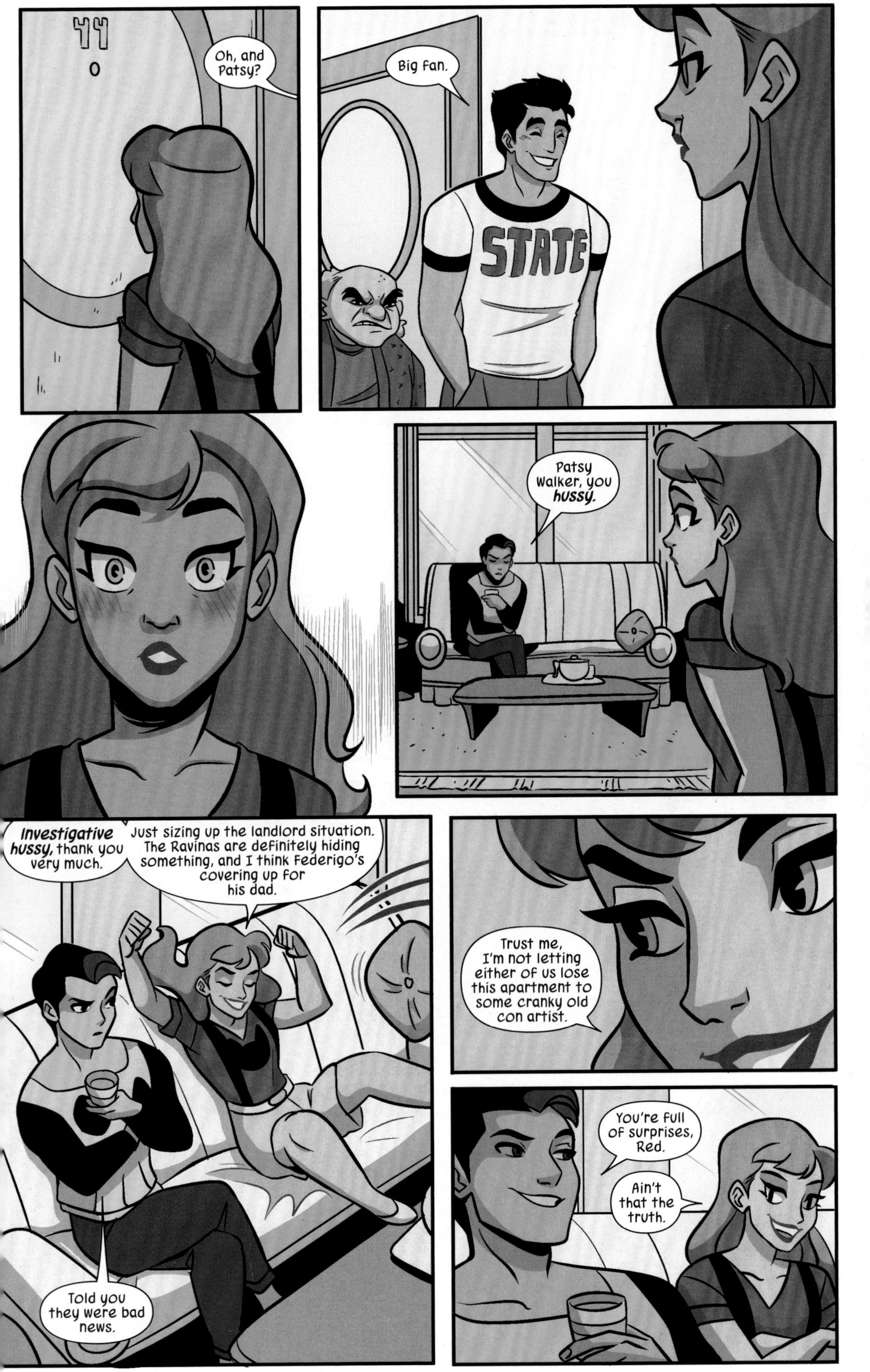

44
O
Oh, and Patsy?
Big fan.
Patsy Walker, you *hussy.*
Investigative hussy, thank you very much.
Just sizing up the landlord situation. The Ravinas are definitely hiding something, and I think Federigo's covering up for his dad.
Told you they were bad news.
Trust me, I'm not letting either of us lose this apartment to some cranky old con artist.
You're full of surprises, Red.
Ain't that the truth.

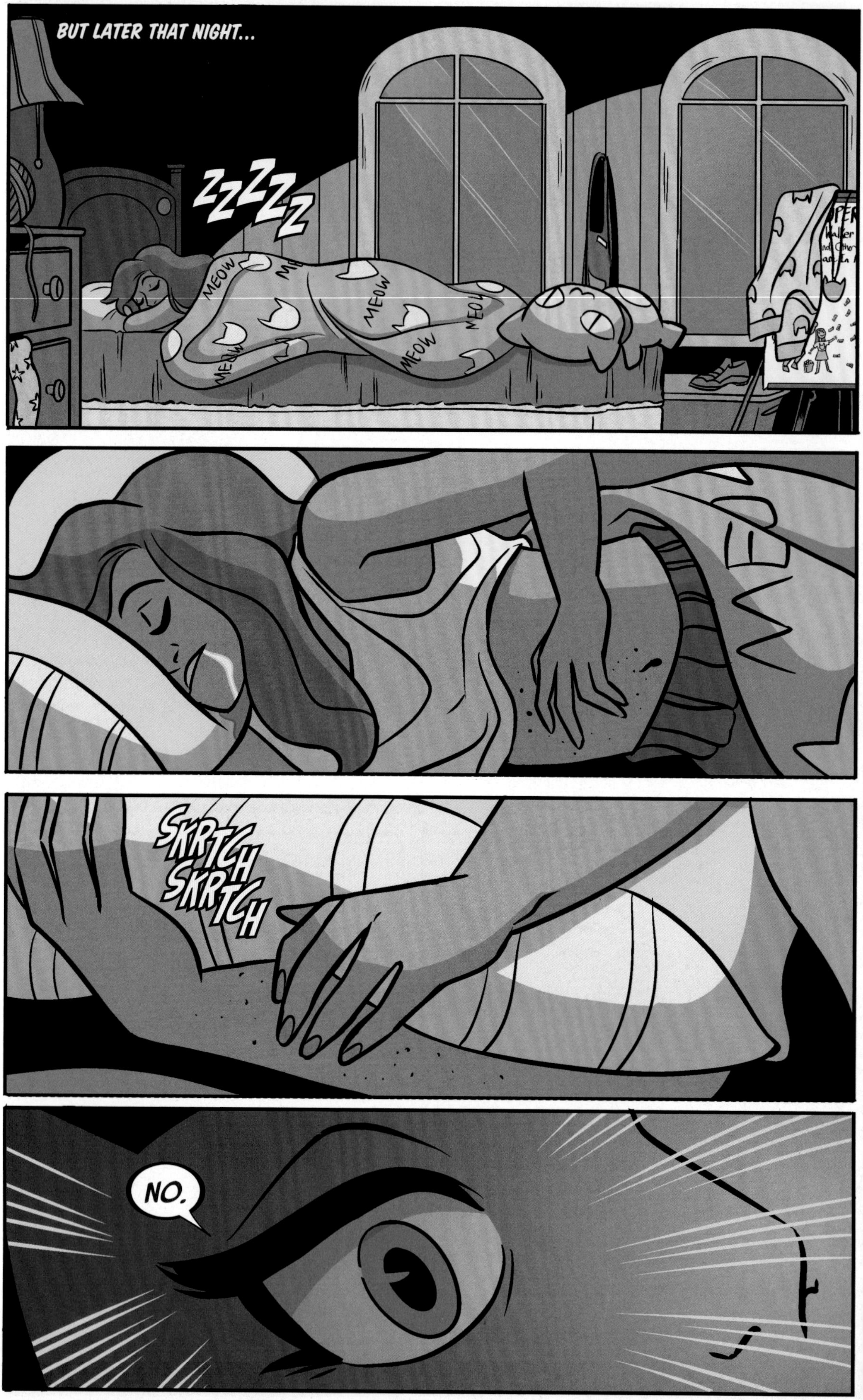
BUT LATER THAT NIGHT...
ZZZZZ
SKRTCH
SKRTCH
NO.

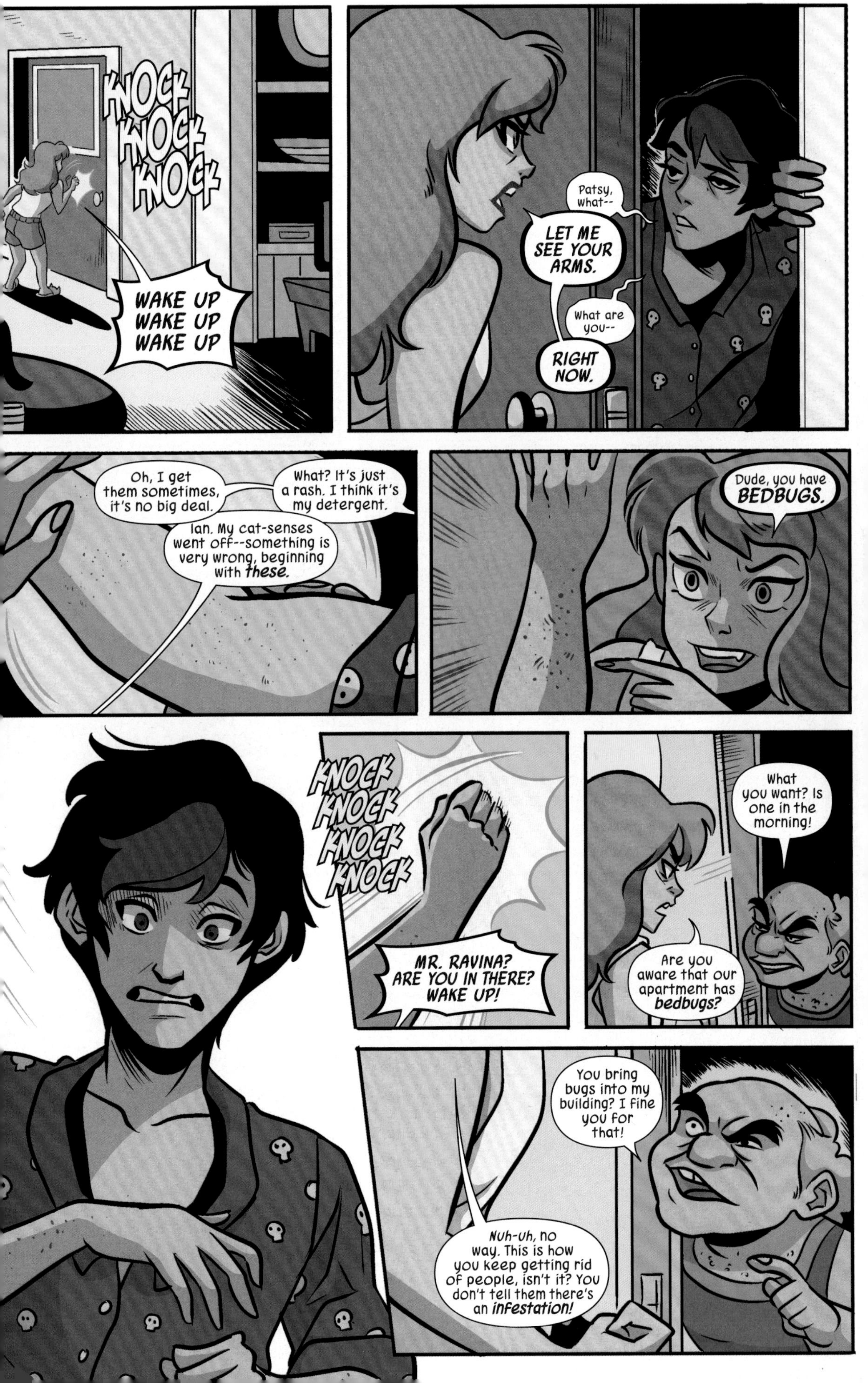
KNOCK KNOCK KNOCK
WAKE UP WAKE UP WAKE UP
Patsy, what--
LET ME SEE YOUR ARMS.
What are you--
RIGHT NOW.
What? It's just a rash. I think it's my detergent.
Oh, I get them sometimes, it's no big deal.
Ian. My cat-senses went off--something is very wrong, beginning with these.
Dude, you have BEDBUGS.
KNOCK KNOCK KNOCK KNOCK
MR. RAVINA? ARE YOU IN THERE? WAKE UP!
What you want? Is one in the morning!
Are you aware that our apartment has bedbugs?
You bring bugs into my building? I fine you for that!
Nuh-uh, no way. This is how you keep getting rid of people, isn't it? You don't tell them there's an infestation!

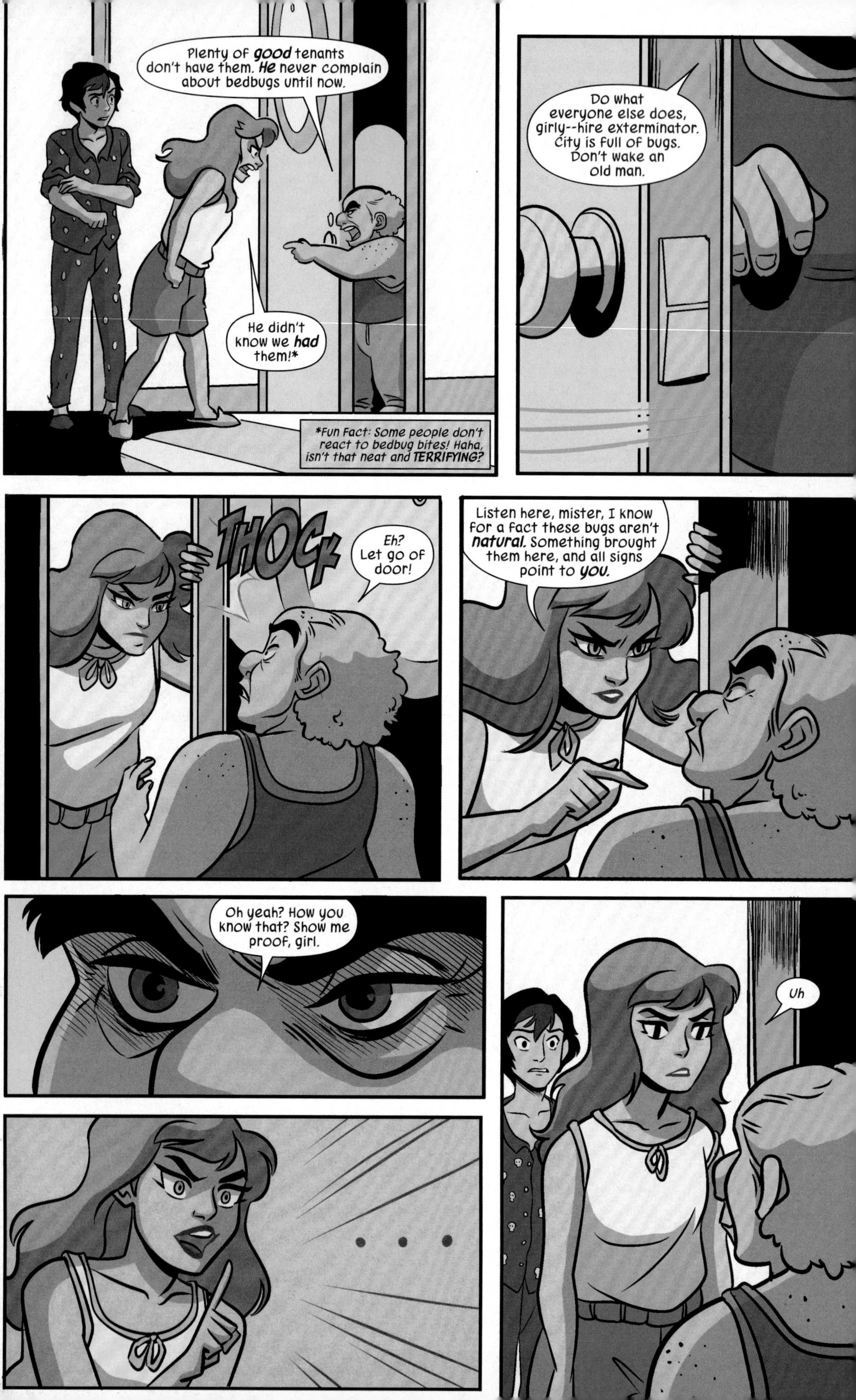
Plenty of good tenants don't have them. He never complain about bedbugs until now.
He didn't know we had them!*
*Fun Fact: Some people don't react to bedbug bites! Haha, isn't that neat and TERRIFYING?
Do what everyone else does, girly--hire exterminator. City is full of bugs. Don't wake an old man.
THOCK
Eh? Let go of door!
Listen here, mister, I know for a fact these bugs aren't natural. Something brought them here, and all signs point to you.
Oh yeah? How you know that? Show me proof, girl.
...
Uh

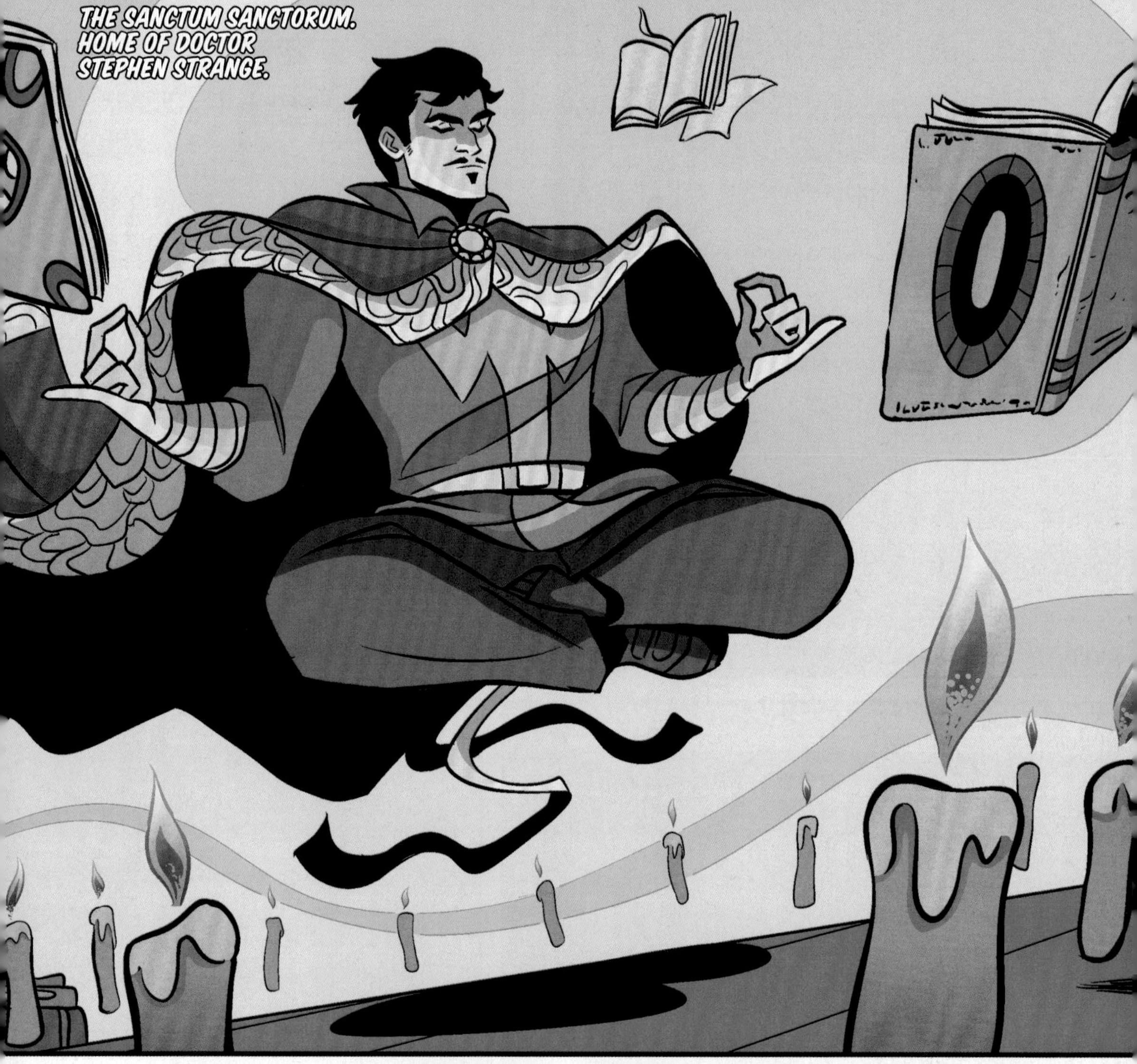
THE SANCTUM SANCTORUM. HOME OF DOCTOR STEPHEN STRANGE.

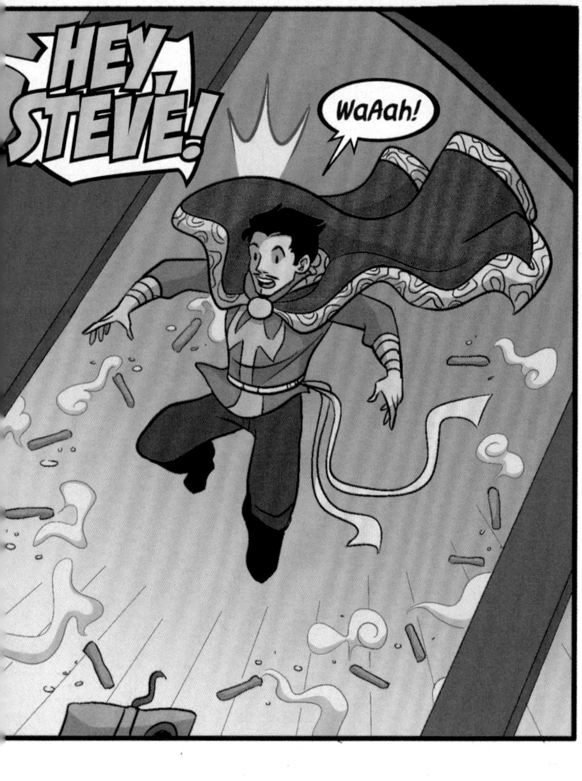
HEY, STEVE!
WaAah!

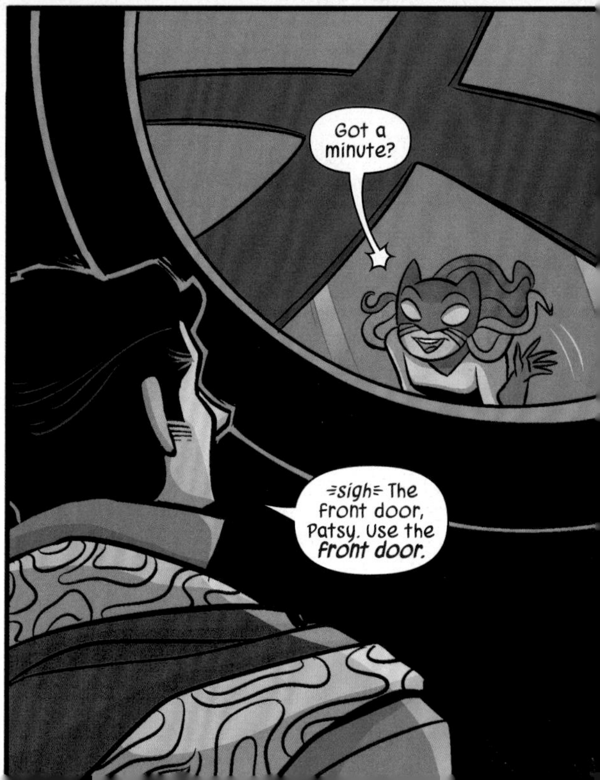
Got a minute?
=sigh= The front door, Patsy. Use the front door.

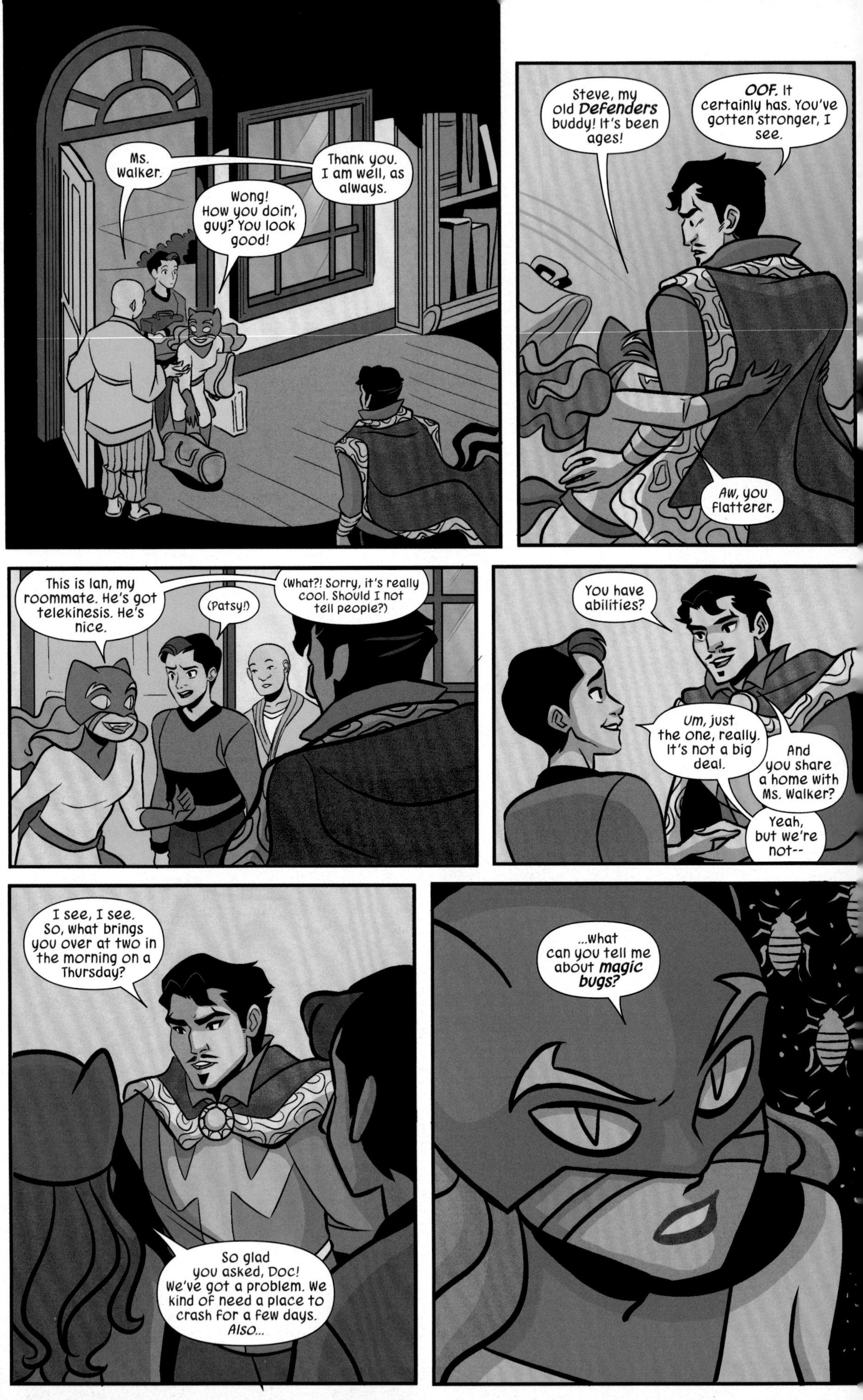
Ms. Walker.
Thank you. I am well, as always.
Wong! How you doin', guy? You look good!
Steve, my old Defenders buddy! It's been ages!
OOF. It certainly has. You've gotten stronger, I see.
Aw, you flatterer.
This is Ian, my roommate. He's got telekinesis. He's nice.
(Patsy!)
(What?! Sorry, it's really cool. Should I not tell people?)
You have abilities?
Um, just the one, really. It's not a big deal.
And you share a home with Ms. Walker?
Yeah, but we're not--
I see, I see. So, what brings you over at two in the morning on a Thursday?
So glad you asked, Doc! We've got a problem. We kind of need a place to crash for a few days. Also...
...What can you tell me about magic bugs?

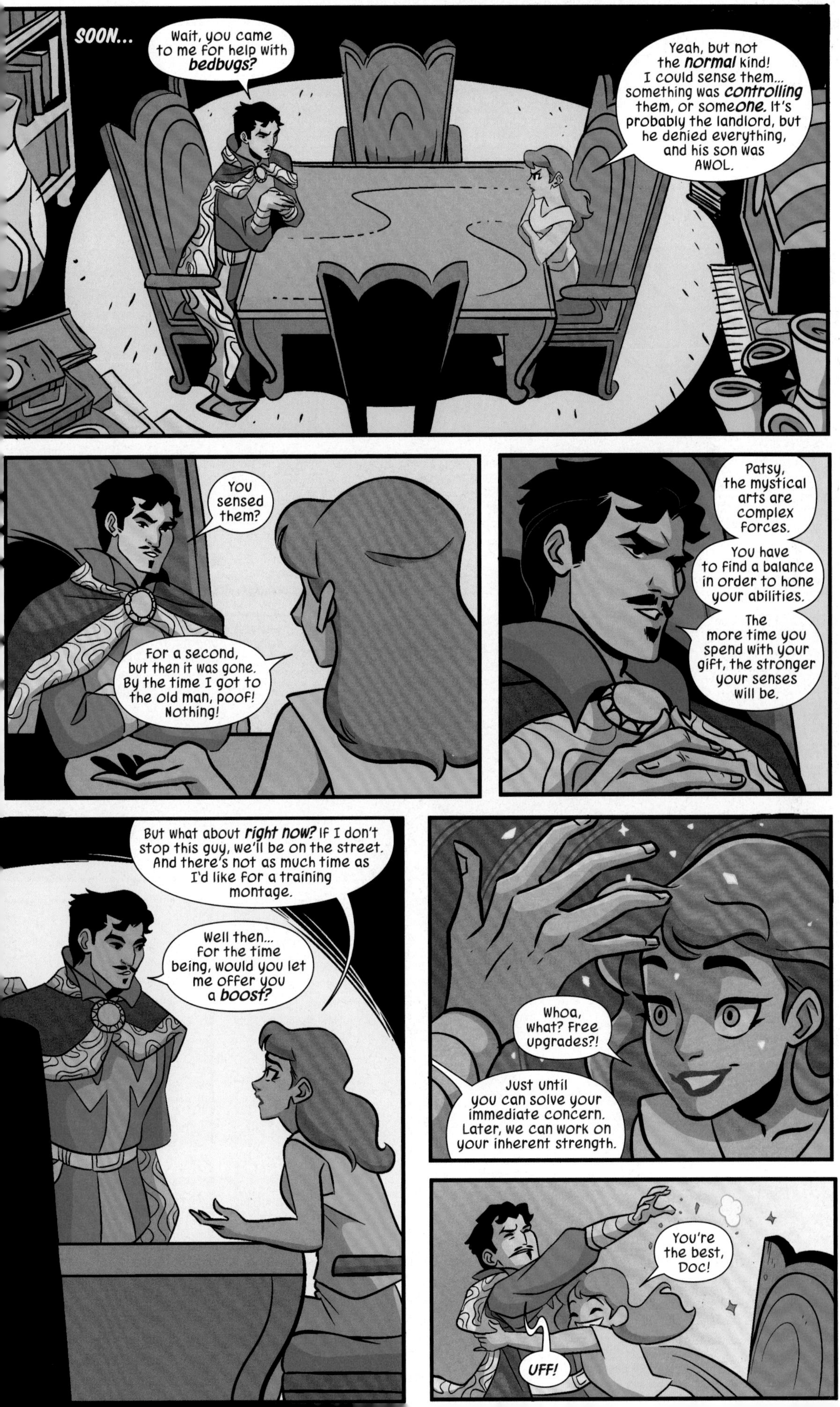
SOON...
Wait, you came to me for help with bedbugs?
Yeah, but not the normal kind! I could sense them... something was controlling them, or someone. It's probably the landlord, but he denied everything, and his son was AWOL.
You sensed them?
For a second, but then it was gone. By the time I got to the old man, poof! Nothing!
Patsy, the mystical arts are complex forces.
You have to find a balance in order to hone your abilities.
The more time you spend with your gift, the stronger your senses will be.
But what about right now? If I don't stop this guy, we'll be on the street. And there's not as much time as I'd like for a training montage.
Well then... for the time being, would you let me offer you a boost?
Whoa, what? Free upgrades?!
Just until you can solve your immediate concern. Later, we can work on your inherent strength.
You're the best, Doc!
UFF!

IAN! Can you hold the fort for a bit?

Whoa, Patsy! What got into you?

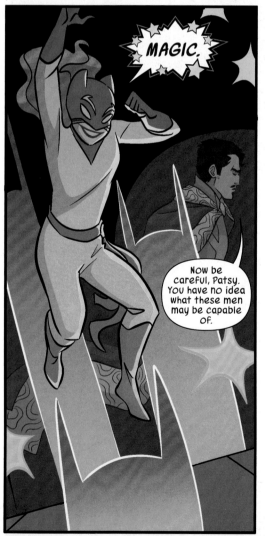

MAGIC.

Now be careful, Patsy. You have no idea what these men may be capable of.

I know they have *gross bug powers* and I *want my apartment back* and I am feeling *REALLY GOOD* right now.

Text you when I'm done, dudes! Don't have too much fun without me!

Check.

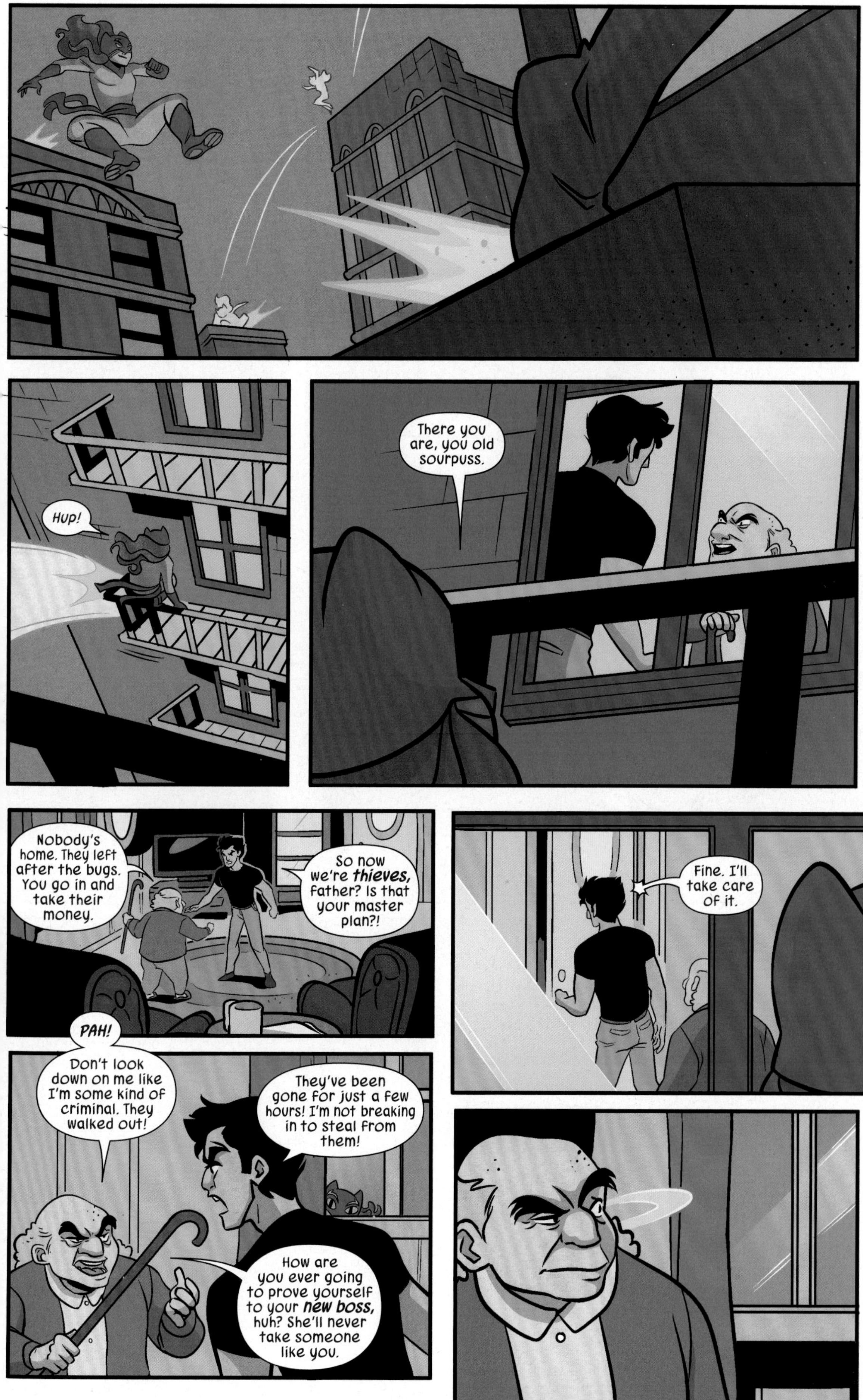
Hup!
There you are, you old sourpuss.
Nobody's home. They left after the bugs. You go in and take their money.
So now we're *thieves*, father? Is that your master plan?!
Fine. I'll take care of it.
PAH!
Don't look down on me like I'm some kind of criminal. They walked out!
They've been gone for just a few hours! I'm not breaking in to steal from them!
How are you ever going to prove yourself to your *new boss*, huh? She'll never take someone like you.

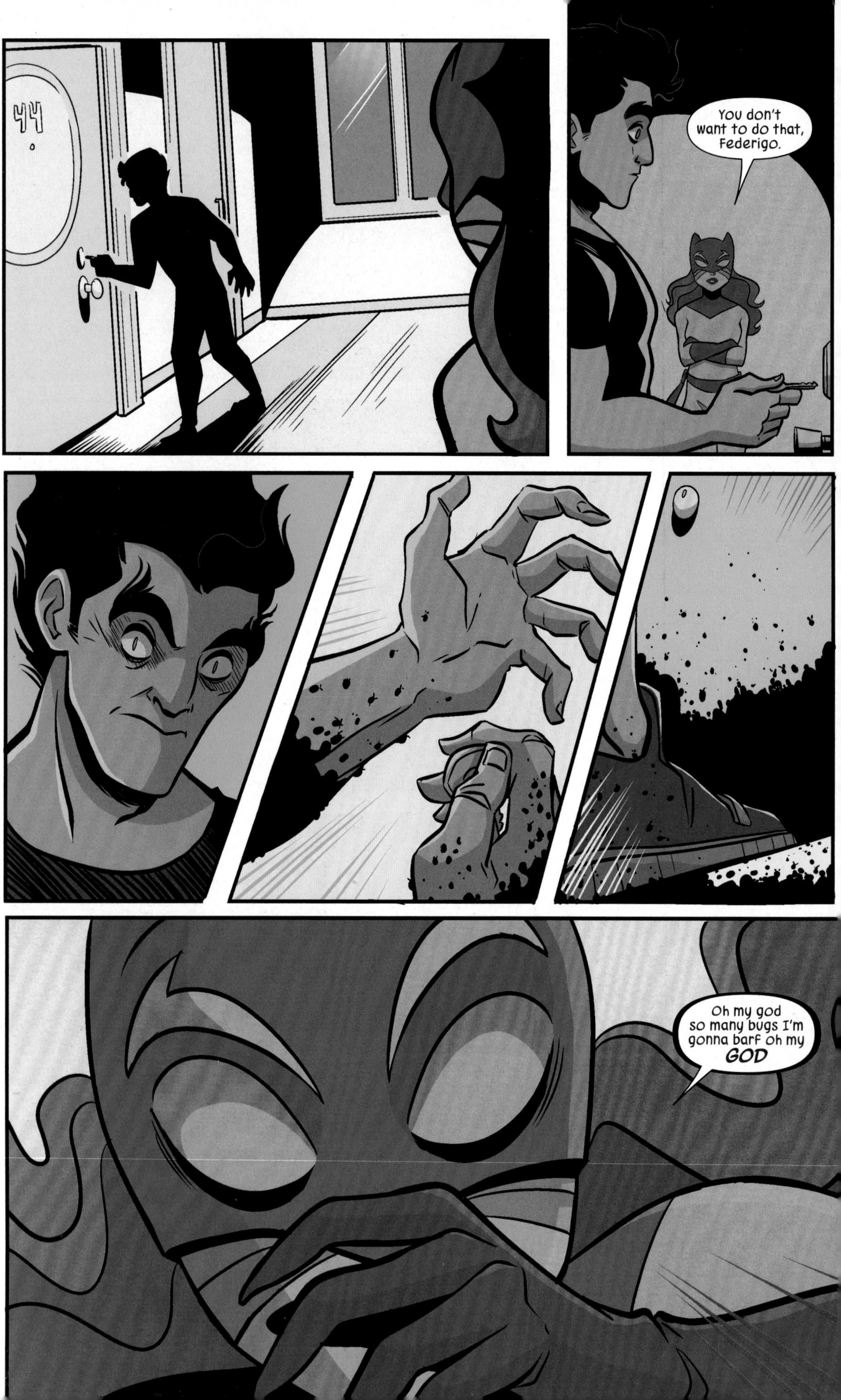
44
You don't want to do that, Federigo.
Oh my god so many bugs I'm gonna barf oh my GOD

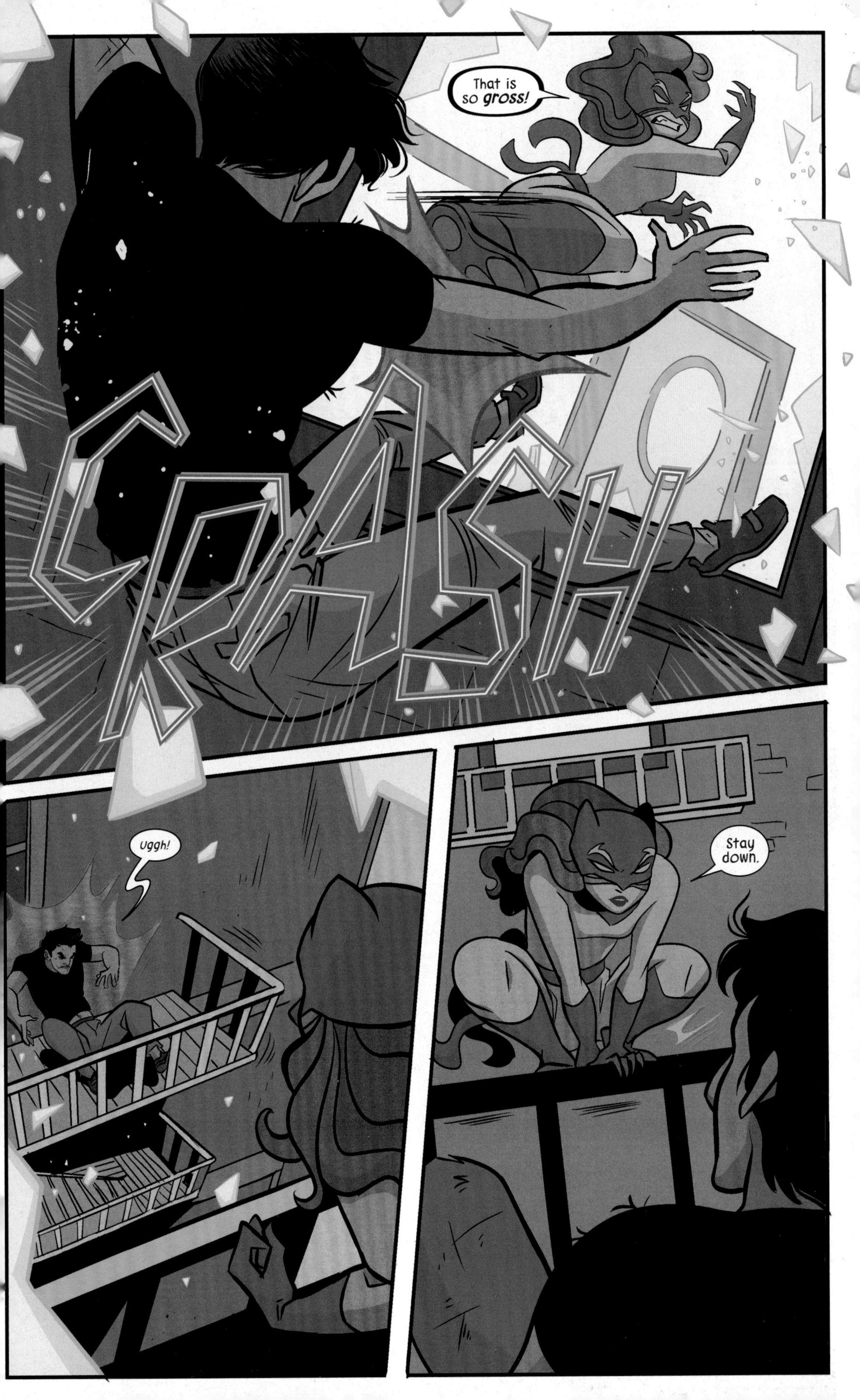
That is so *gross!*
CRASH
Uggh!
Stay down.

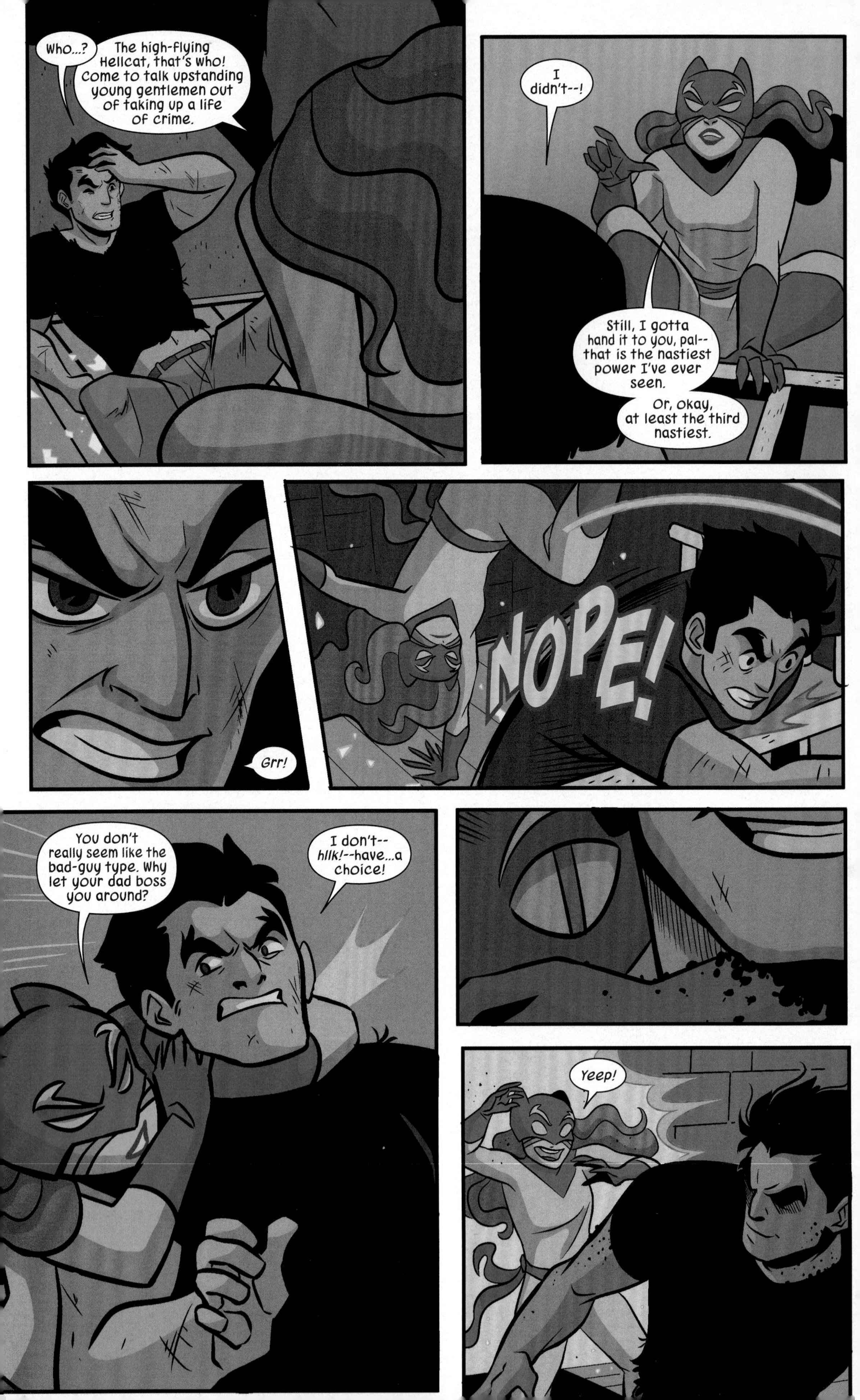
Who...?
The high-flying Hellcat, that's who! Come to talk upstanding young gentlemen out of taking up a life of crime.
I didn't--!
Still, I gotta hand it to you, pal-- that is the nastiest power I've ever seen.
Or, okay, at least the third nastiest.
Grr!
NOPE!
You don't really seem like the bad-guy type. Why let your dad boss you around?
I don't-- hllk!--have...a choice!
Yeep!

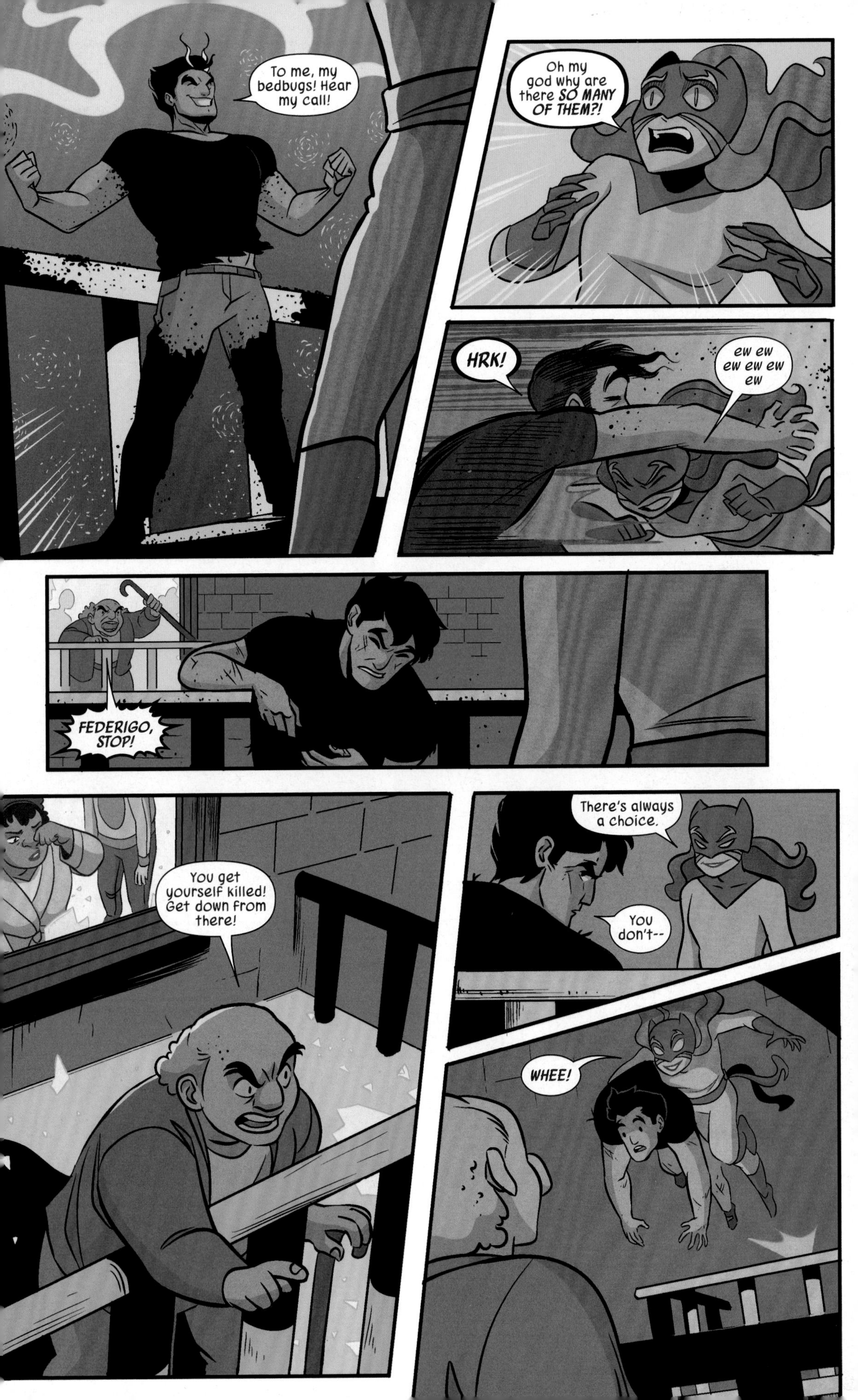
To me, my bedbugs! Hear my call!
Oh my god why are there SO MANY OF THEM?!
HRK!
ew ew ew ew ew ew
FEDERIGO, STOP!
You get yourself killed! Get down from there!
There's always a choice.
You don't--
WHEE!

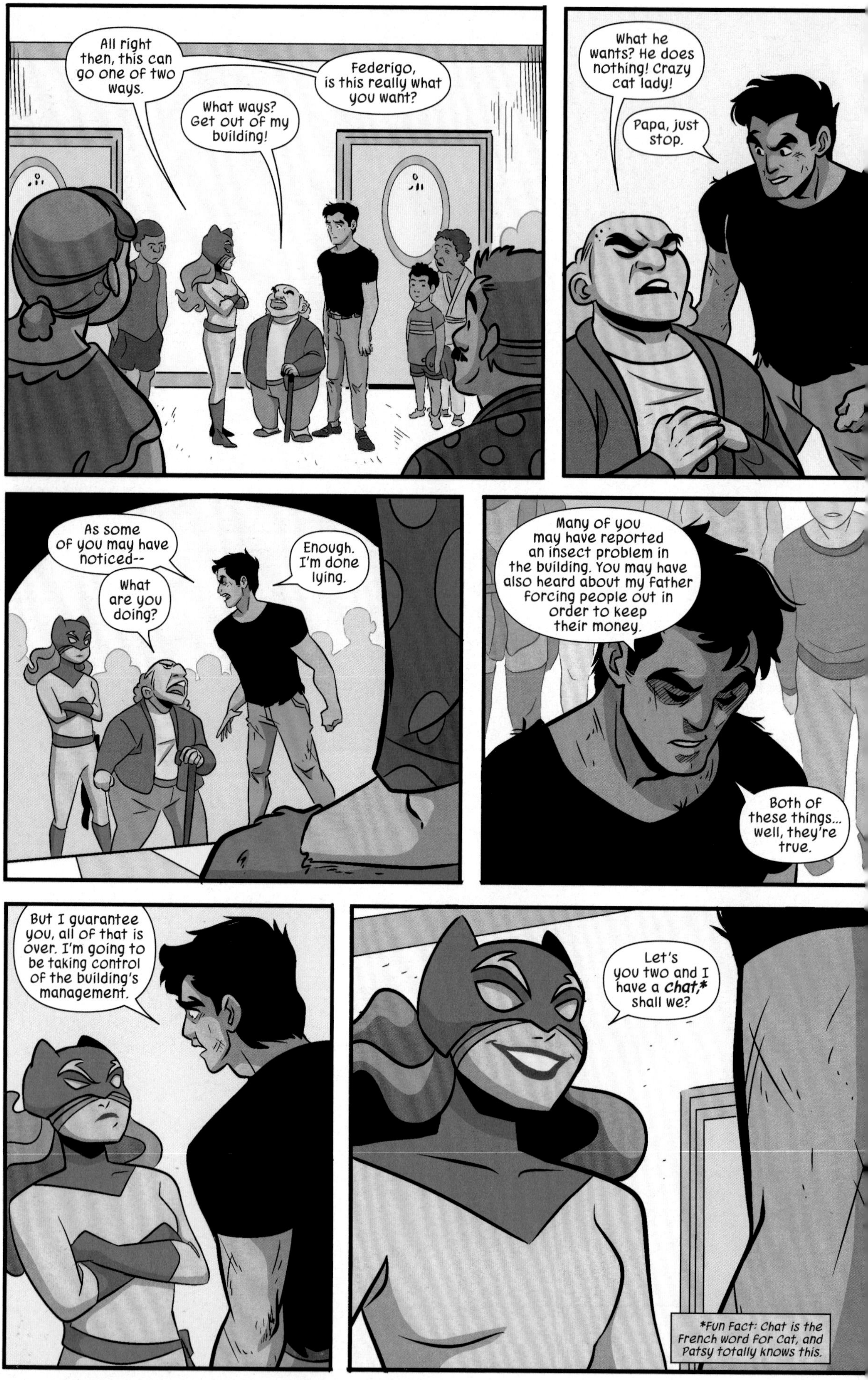
All right then, this can go one of two ways.
Federigo, is this really what you want?
What ways? Get out of my building!
What he wants? He does nothing! Crazy cat lady!
Papa, just stop.
As some of you may have noticed--
What are you doing?
Enough. I'm done lying.
Many of you may have reported an insect problem in the building. You may have also heard about my father forcing people out in order to keep their money.
Both of these things... well, they're true.
But I guarantee you, all of that is over. I'm going to be taking control of the building's management.
Let's you two and I have a ***chat,**** shall we?
*Fun Fact: Chat is the French word for cat, and Patsy totally knows this.

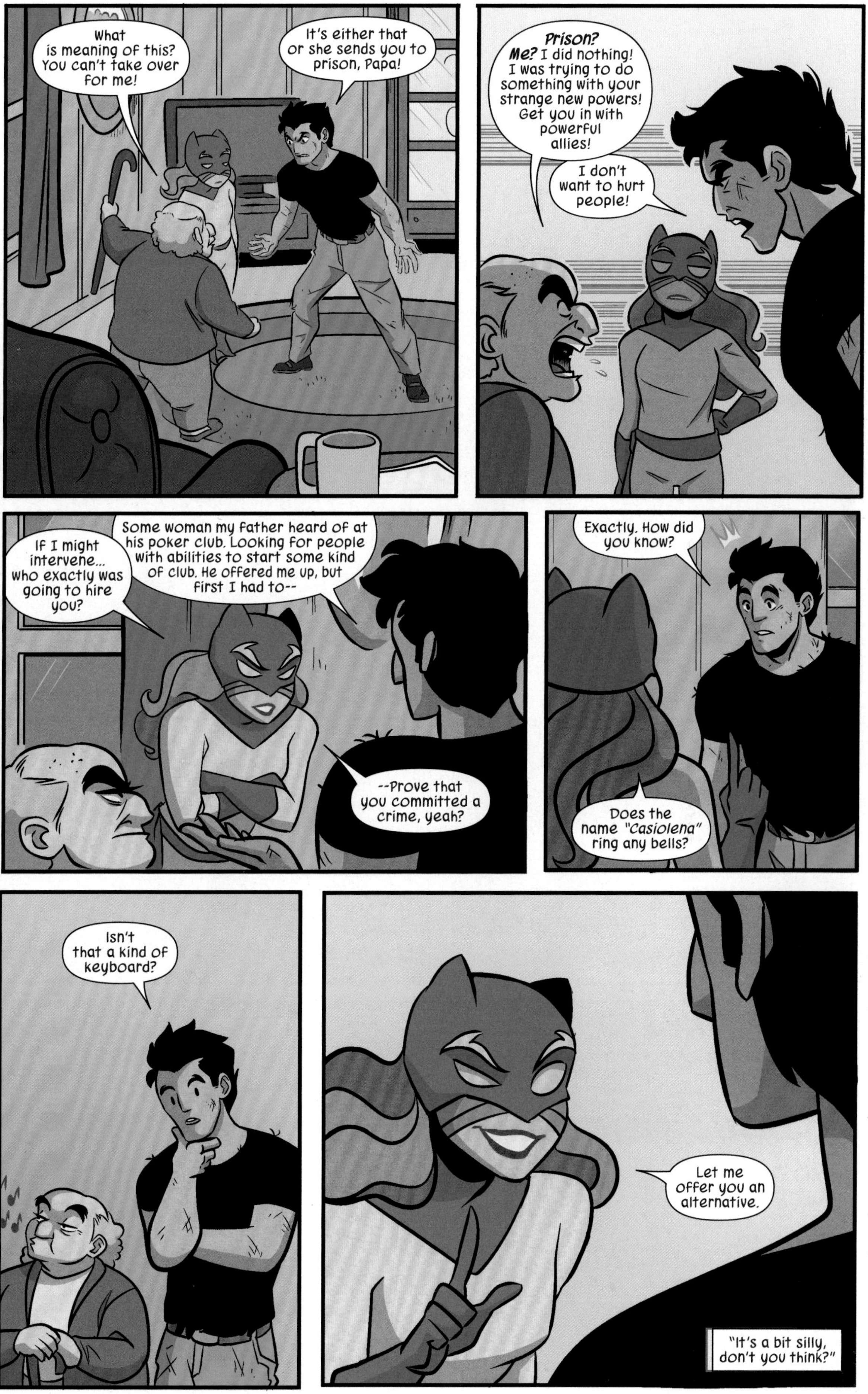
What is meaning of this? You can't take over for me!
It's either that or she sends you to prison, Papa!
Prison? Me? I did nothing! I was trying to do something with your strange new powers! Get you in with powerful allies!
I don't want to hurt people!
If I might intervene... who exactly was going to hire you?
Some woman my father heard of at his poker club. Looking for people with abilities to start some kind of club. He offered me up, but first I had to--
--Prove that you committed a crime, yeah?
Exactly. How did you know?
Does the name "Casiolena" ring any bells?
Isn't that a kind of keyboard?
Let me offer you an alternative.
"It's a bit silly, don't you think?"

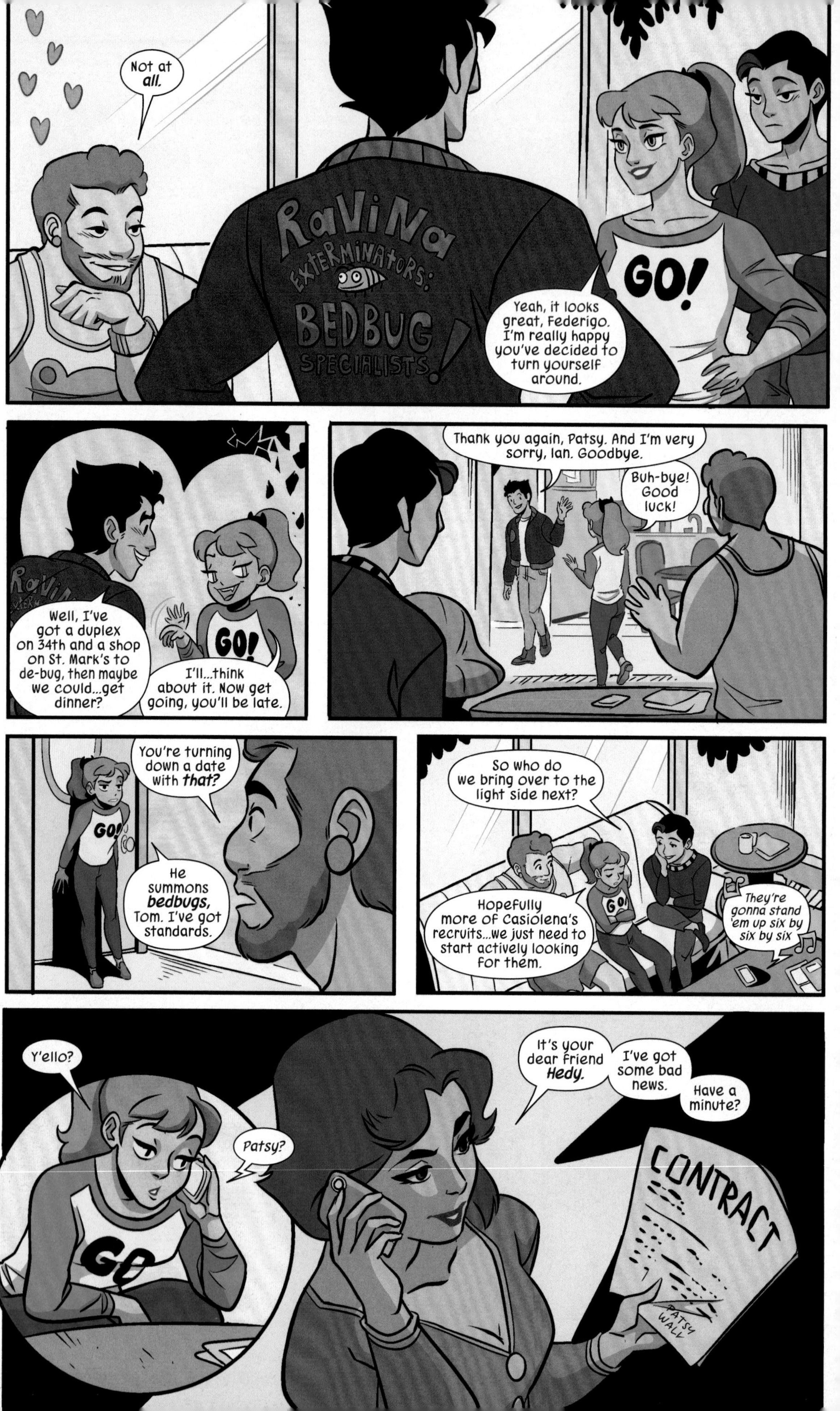

Not at all.
RaViNa EXTERMINATORS: BEDBUG SPECIALISTS!
GO!
Yeah, it looks great, Federigo. I'm really happy you've decided to turn yourself around.
Well, I've got a duplex on 34th and a shop on St. Mark's to de-bug, then maybe we could...get dinner?
I'll...think about it. Now get going, you'll be late.
Thank you again, Patsy. And I'm very sorry, Ian. Goodbye.
Buh-bye! Good luck!
You're turning down a date with that?
He summons bedbugs, Tom. I've got standards.
So who do we bring over to the light side next?
Hopefully more of Casiolena's recruits...we just need to start actively looking for them.
They're gonna stand 'em up six by six by six
Y'ello?
Patsy?
It's your dear friend Hedy.
I've got some bad news.
Have a minute?
CONTRACT
PATSY WALL

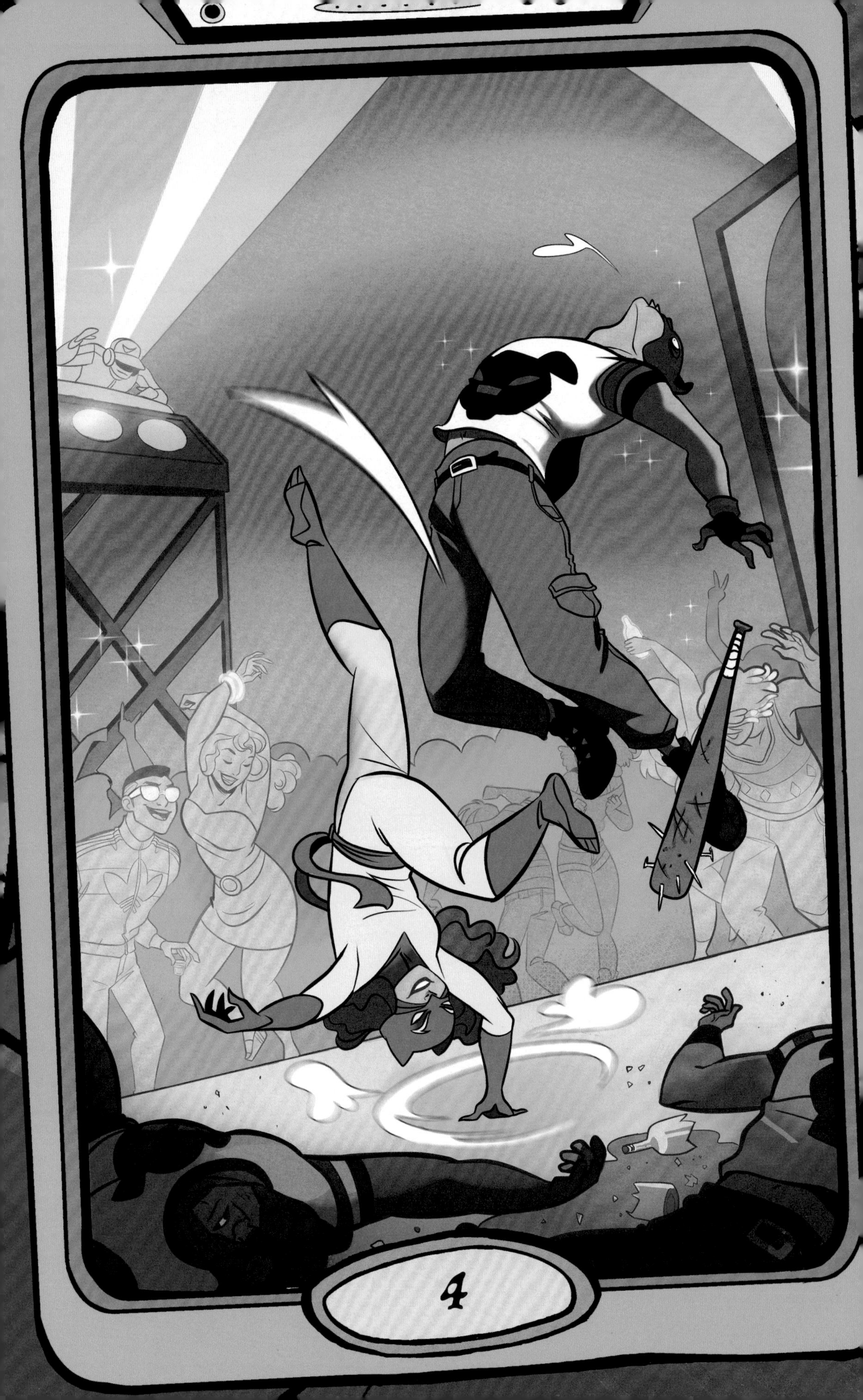
4

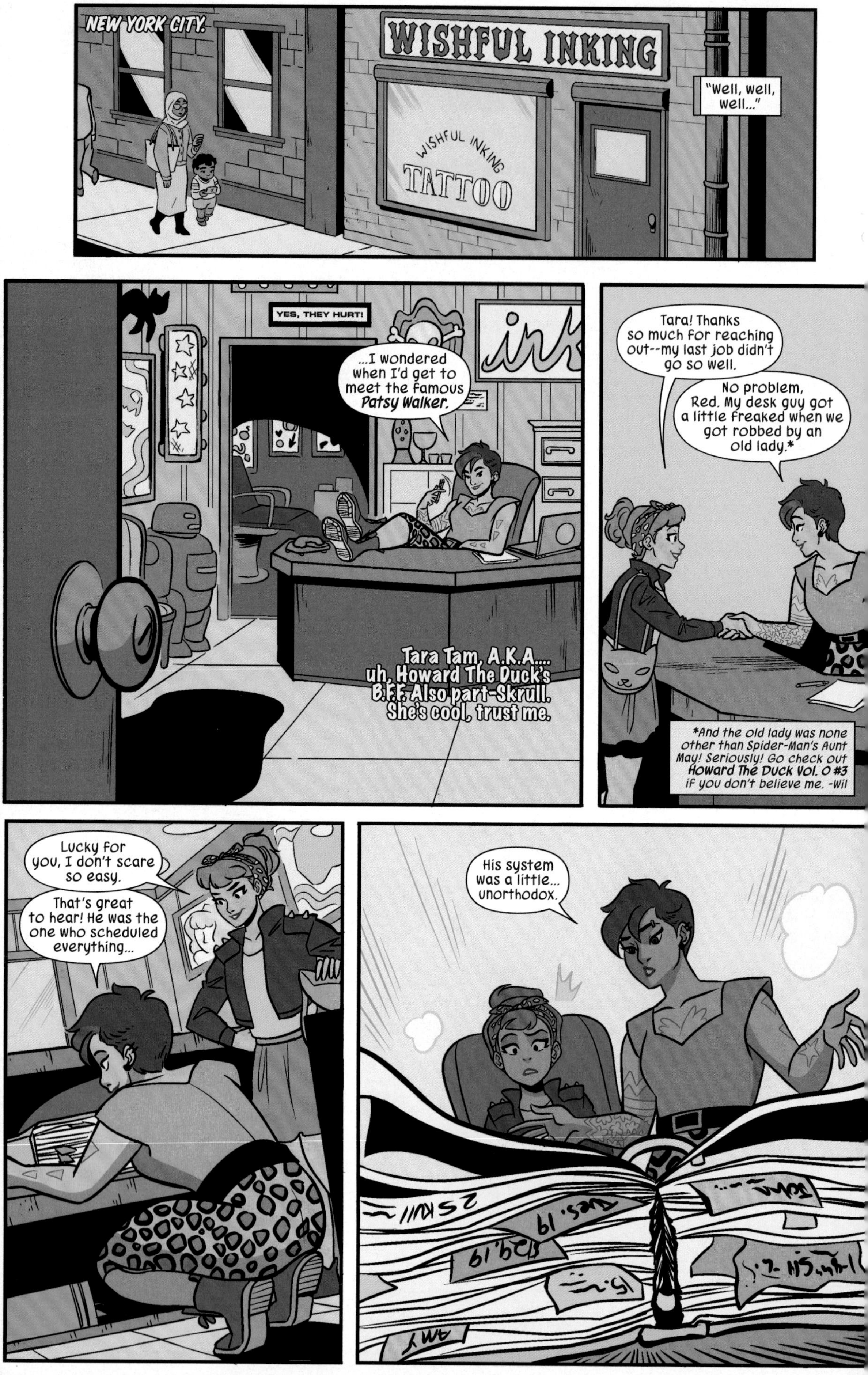
NEW YORK CITY.
WISHFUL INKING
WISHFUL INKING TATTOO
"Well, well, well..."
YES, THEY HURT!
ink
...I wondered when I'd get to meet the famous *Patsy Walker.*
Tara Tam, A.K.A.... uh, Howard The Duck's B.F.F. Also part-Skrull. She's cool, trust me.
Tara! Thanks so much for reaching out--my last job didn't go so well.
No problem, Red. My desk guy got a little freaked when we got robbed by an old lady.*
*And the old lady was none other than Spider-Man's Aunt May! Seriously! Go check out **Howard The Duck Vol. 0 #3** if you don't believe me. -Wil
Lucky for you, I don't scare so easy.
That's great to hear! He was the one who scheduled everything...
His system was a little... unorthodox.

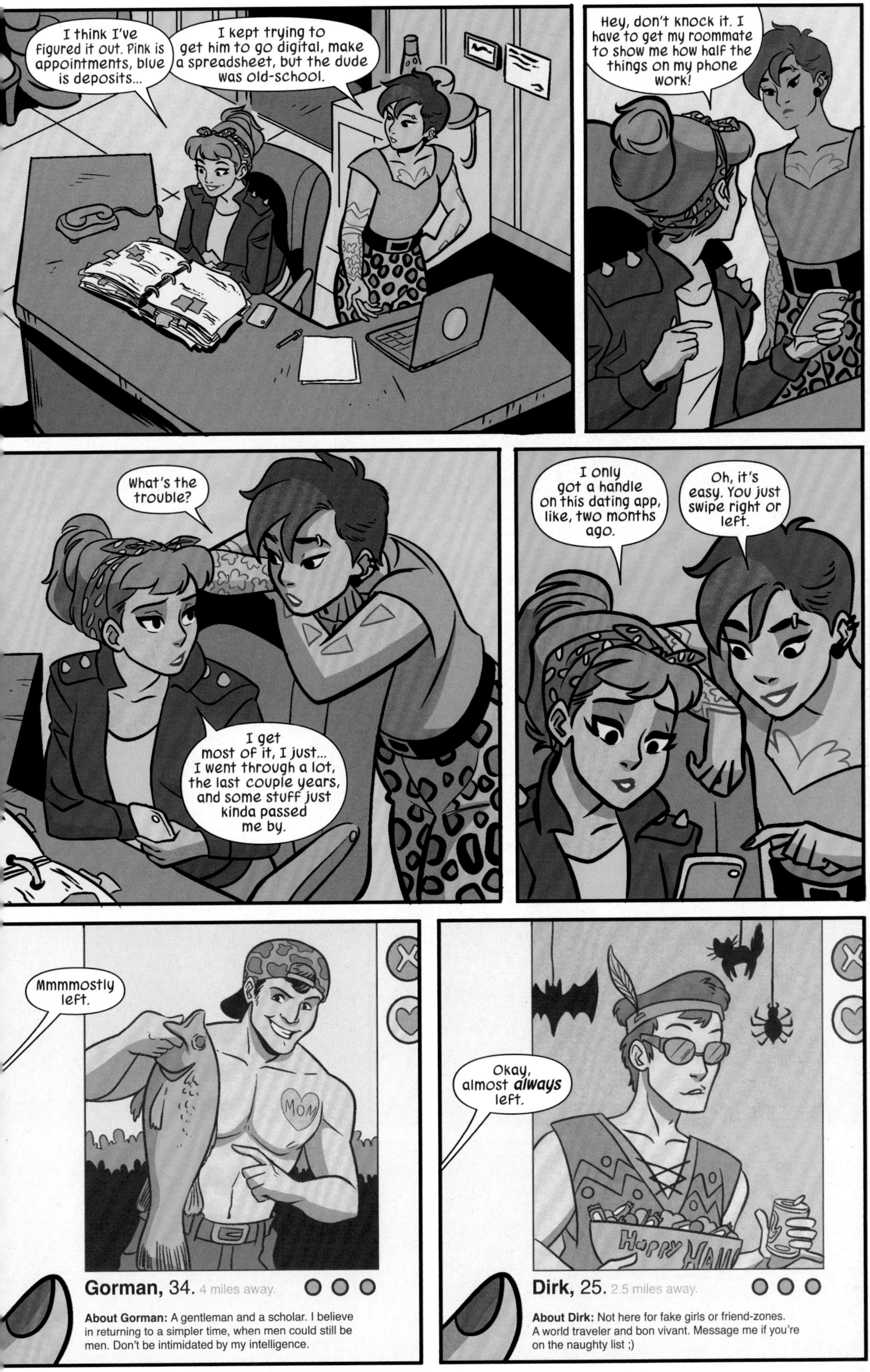

I think I've figured it out. Pink is appointments, blue is deposits...
I kept trying to get him to go digital, make a spreadsheet, but the dude was old-school.
Hey, don't knock it. I have to get my roommate to show me how half the things on my phone work!
What's the trouble?
I get most of it, I just... I went through a lot, the last couple years, and some stuff just kinda passed me by.
I only got a handle on this dating app, like, two months ago.
Oh, it's easy. You just swipe right or left.
Mmmmostly left.
MOM
Gorman, 34. 4 miles away.
About Gorman: A gentleman and a scholar. I believe in returning to a simpler time, when men could still be men. Don't be intimidated by my intelligence.
Okay, almost *always* left.
Dirk, 25. 2.5 miles away.
About Dirk: Not here for fake girls or friend-zones. A world traveler and bon vivant. Message me if you're on the naughty list ;)

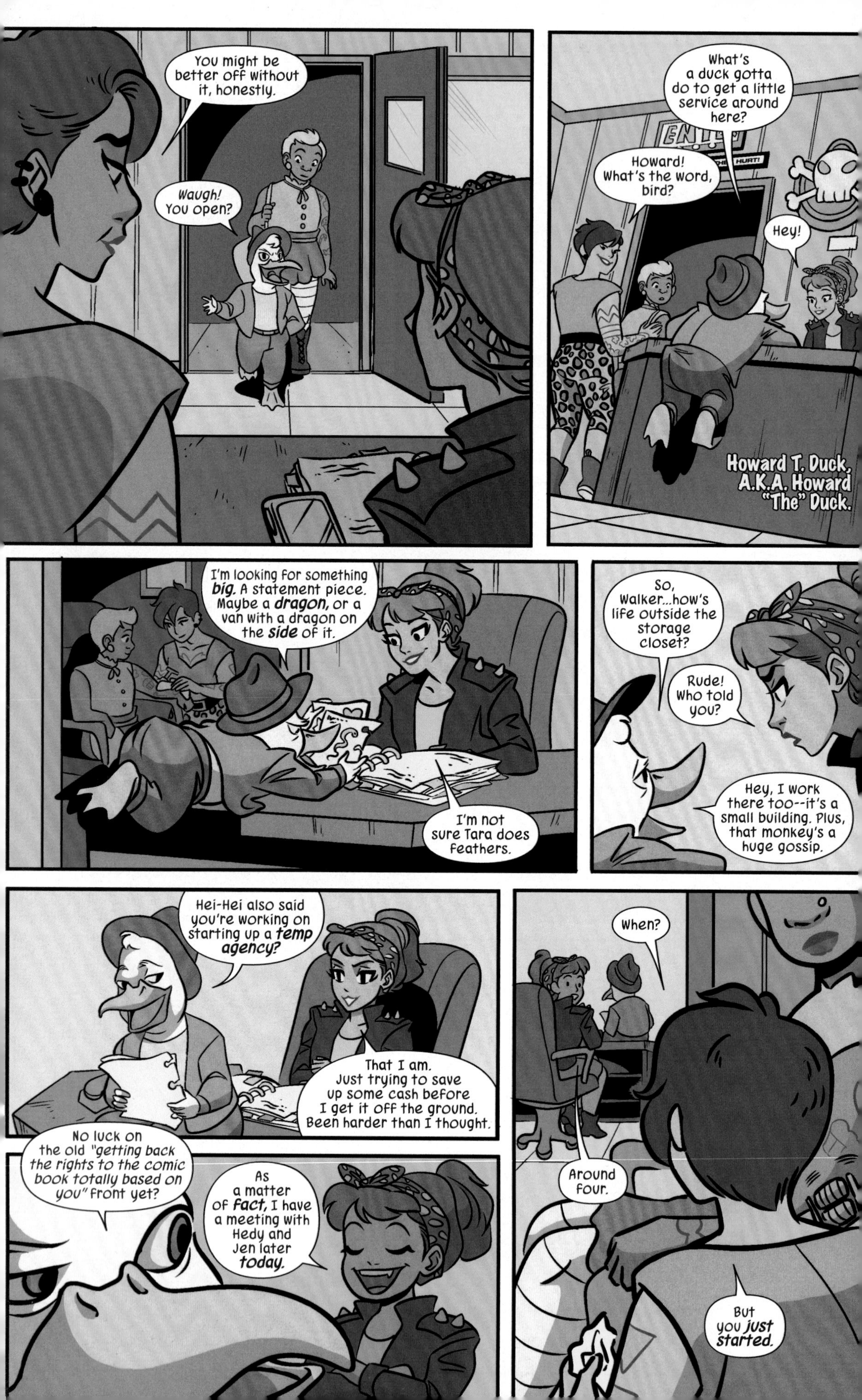
You might be better off without it, honestly.
Waugh! You open?
What's a duck gotta do to get a little service around here?
Howard! What's the word, bird?
Hey!
Howard T. Duck, A.K.A. Howard "The" Duck.
I'm looking for something *big.* A statement piece. Maybe a *dragon,* or a van with a dragon on the *side* of it.
I'm not sure Tara does feathers.
So, Walker...how's life outside the storage closet?
Rude! Who told you?
Hey, I work there too--it's a small building. Plus, that monkey's a huge gossip.
Hei-Hei also said you're working on starting up a *temp agency?*
That I am. Just trying to save up some cash before I get it off the ground. Been harder than I thought.
No luck on the old "getting back the rights to the comic book totally based on you" front yet?
As a matter of *fact,* I have a meeting with Hedy and Jen later *today.*
When?
Around four.
But you *just started.*

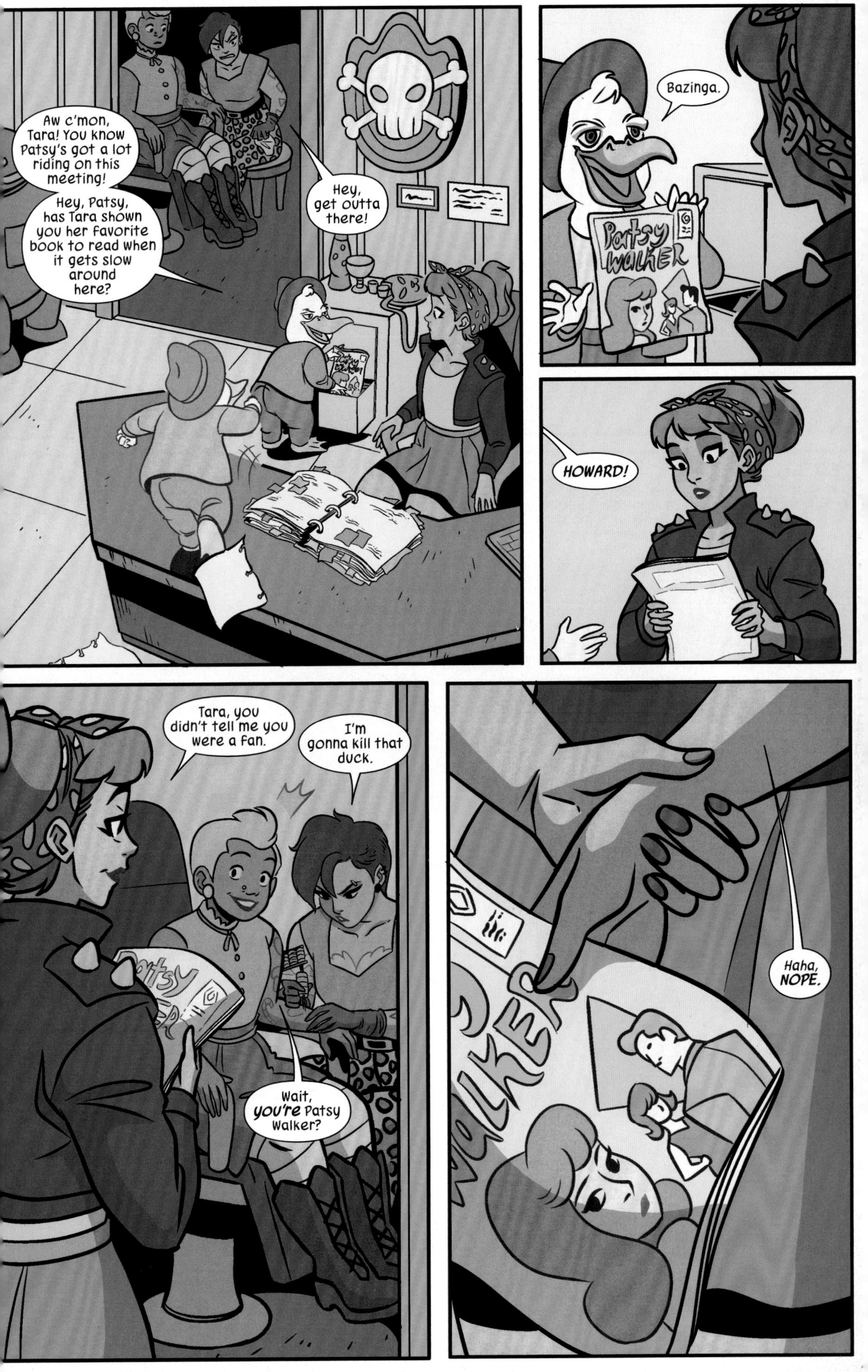

Aw c'mon, Tara! You know Patsy's got a lot riding on this meeting!
Hey, Patsy, has Tara shown you her favorite book to read when it gets slow around here?
Hey, get outta there!
Patsy Walker
Bazinga.
Patsy Walker
HOWARD!
Tara, you didn't tell me you were a fan.
I'm gonna kill that duck.
Patsy
Wait, *you're* Patsy Walker?
Walker
Haha, **NOPE.**

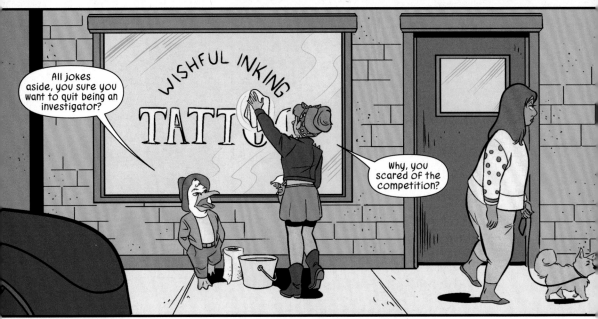

All jokes aside, you sure you want to quit being an investigator?

WISHFUL INKING TATTOO

Why, you scared of the competition?

Nah, I'd just hate to think of you wasting your talents. Jen said you were pretty good.

I was. I'm not saying I'll never go back, but I want to do something for myself. Prove that I can, y'know?

That is, if I can keep *Casiolena* from building an *army* out of all the people I'm trying to help...

Heard about that. Lot of buzz on the street, newbie super-specials joining up with some Asgardian magical baddie.

That's the one.

Is it weird to say she kinda sounds *exactly* like Enchantress?

Nah, you're not wrong. Aside from her beef with me, there's really not much difference.

Woof. That's gotta be rough for her.

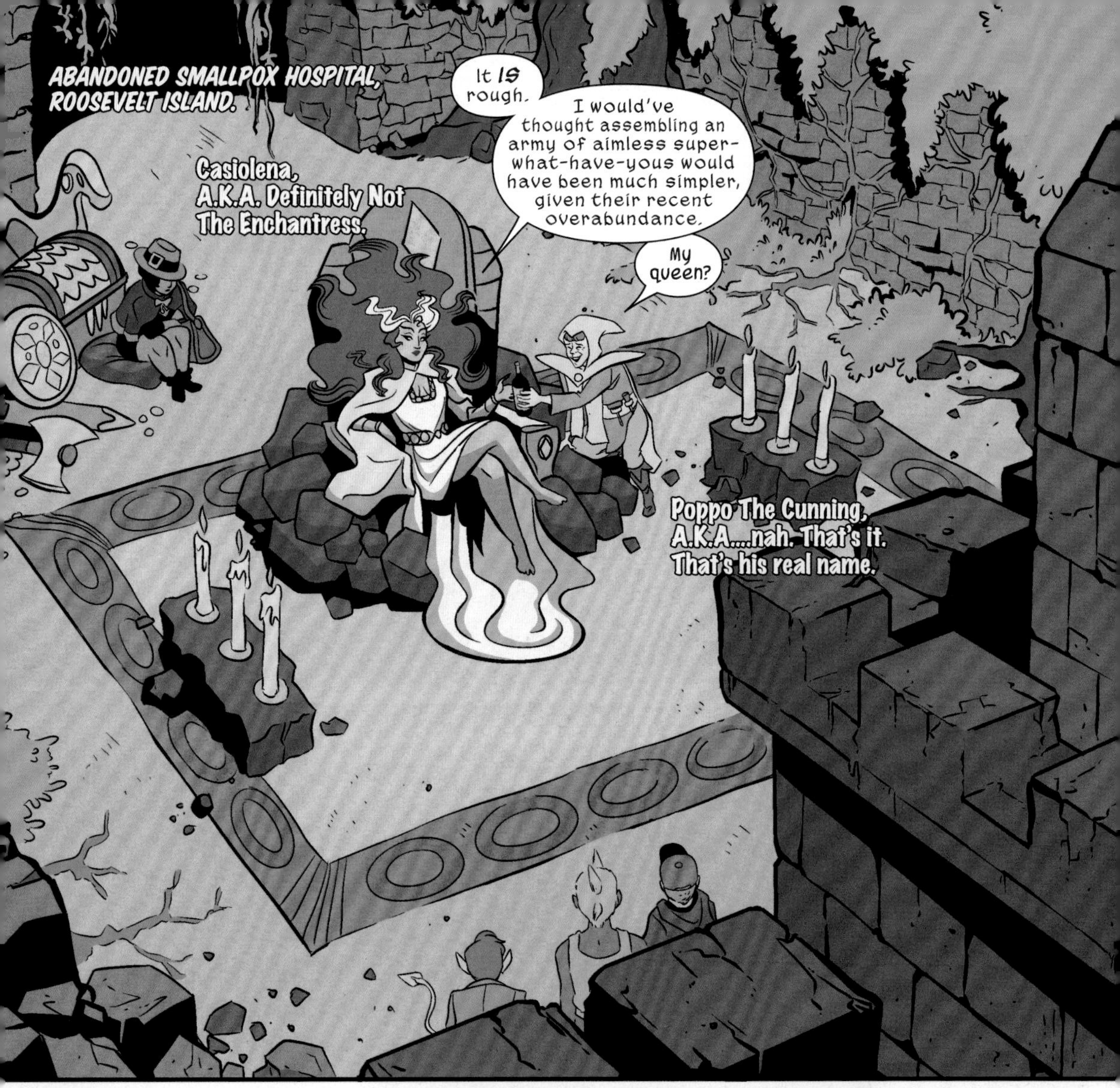
ABANDONED SMALLPOX HOSPITAL, ROOSEVELT ISLAND.
Casiolena, A.K.A. Definitely Not The Enchantress.
It IS rough.
I would've thought assembling an army of aimless super-what-have-yous would have been much simpler, given their recent overabundance.
My queen?
Poppo The Cunning, A.K.A....nah. That's it. That's his real name.

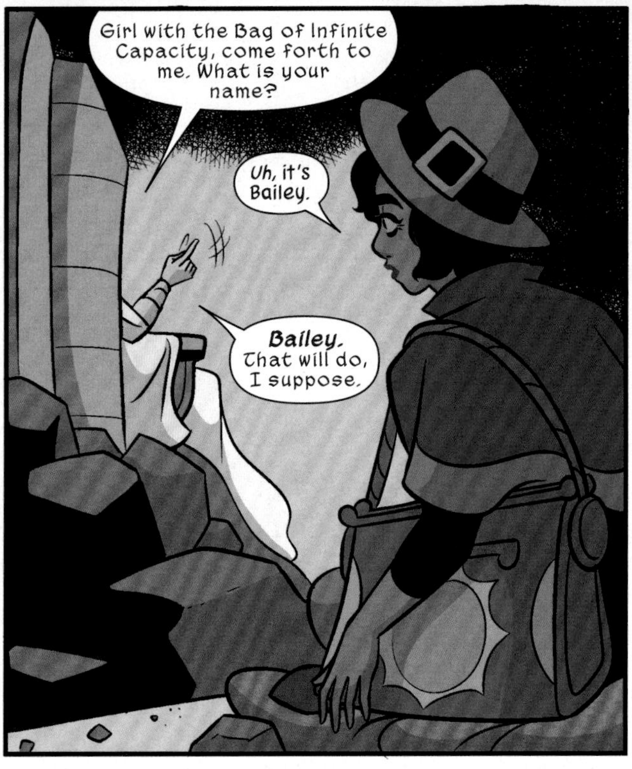
Girl with the Bag of Infinite Capacity, come forth to me. What is your name?
Uh, it's Bailey.
Bailey. That will do, I suppose.

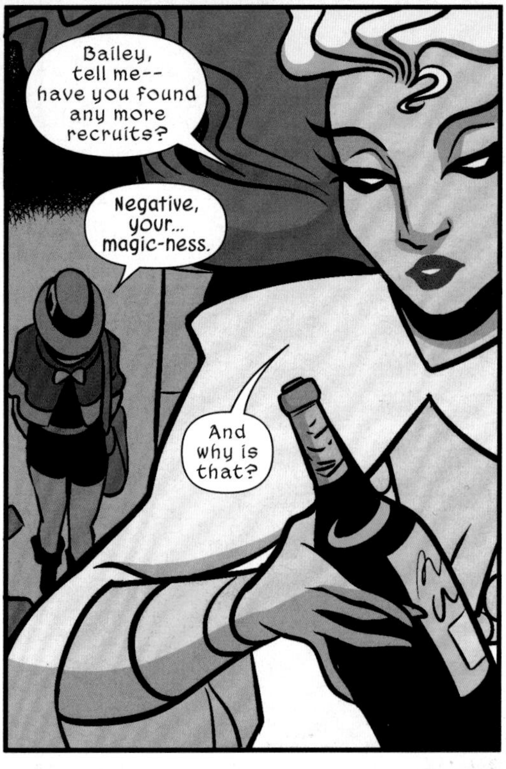
Bailey, tell me-- have you found any more recruits?
Negative, your... magic-ness.
And why is that?

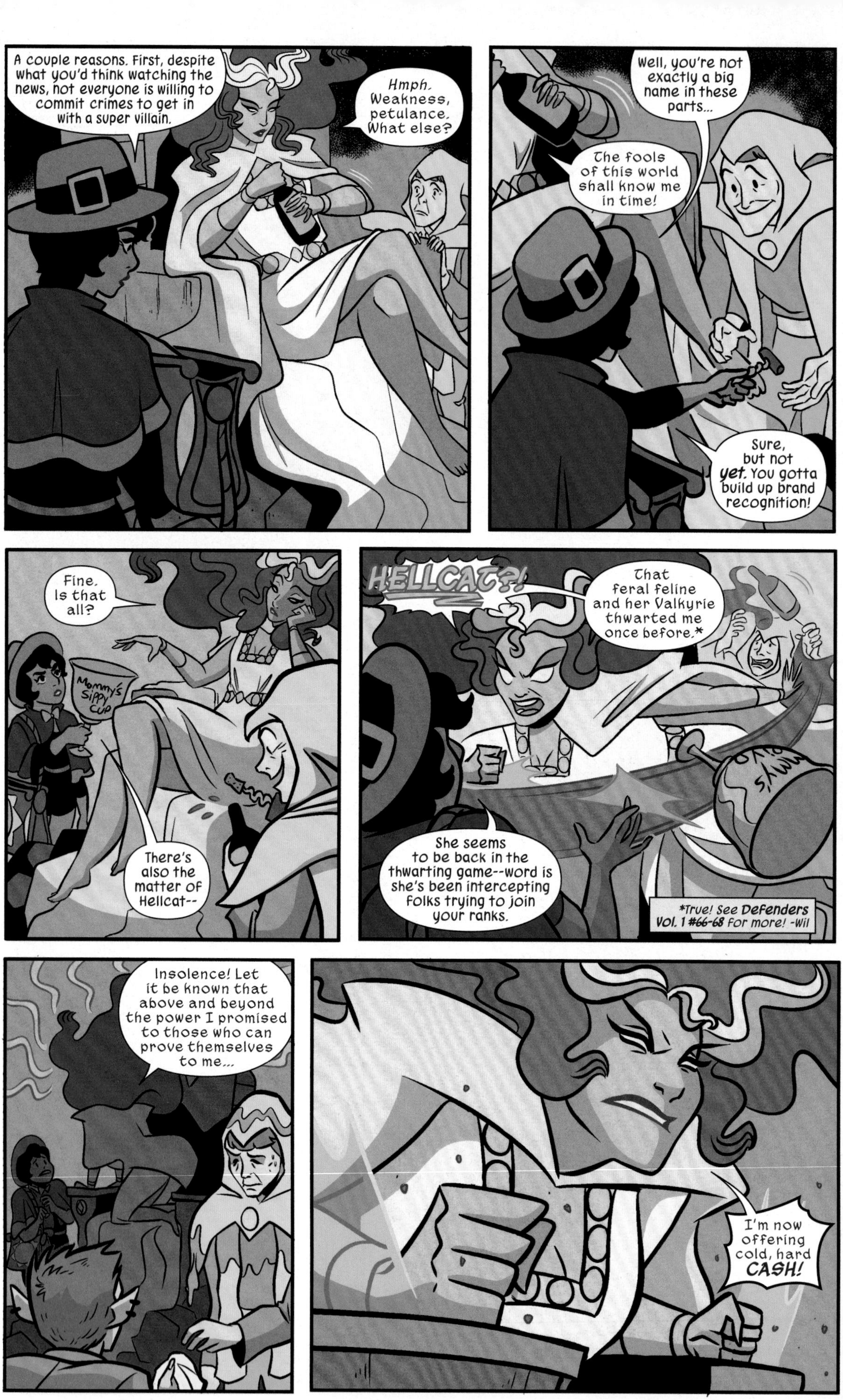
A couple reasons. First, despite what you'd think watching the news, not everyone is willing to commit crimes to get in with a super villain.
Hmph. Weakness, petulance. What else?
Well, you're not exactly a big name in these parts...
The fools of this world shall know me in time!
Sure, but not *yet.* You gotta build up brand recognition!
Fine. Is that all?
Mommy's Sippy Cup
There's also the matter of Hellcat--
HELLCAT?!
That feral feline and her Valkyrie thwarted me once before.*
She seems to be back in the thwarting game--word is she's been intercepting folks trying to join your ranks.
*True! See **Defenders** Vol. 1 #66-68 for more! -Wil
Insolence! Let it be known that above and beyond the power I promised to those who can prove themselves to me...
I'm now offering cold, hard ***CASH!***

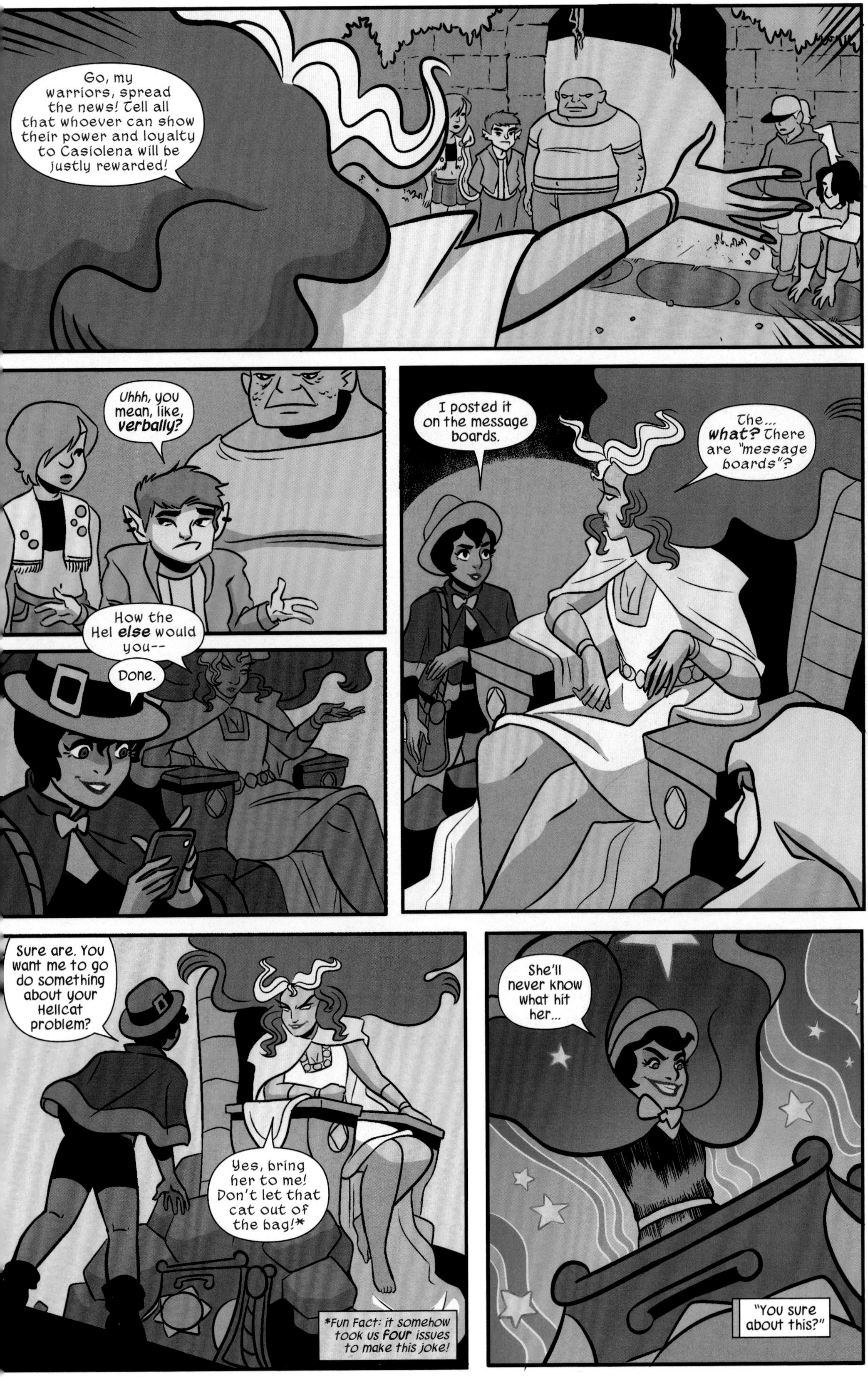
Go, my warriors, spread the news! Tell all that whoever can show their power and loyalty to Casiolena will be justly rewarded!
Uhhh, you mean, like, verbally?
I posted it on the message boards.
The... what? There are "message boards"?
How the Hel else would you--
Done.
Sure are. You want me to go do something about your Hellcat problem?
Yes, bring her to me! Don't let that cat out of the bag!*
*Fun Fact: it somehow took us FOUR issues to make this joke!
She'll never know what hit her...
"You sure about this?"

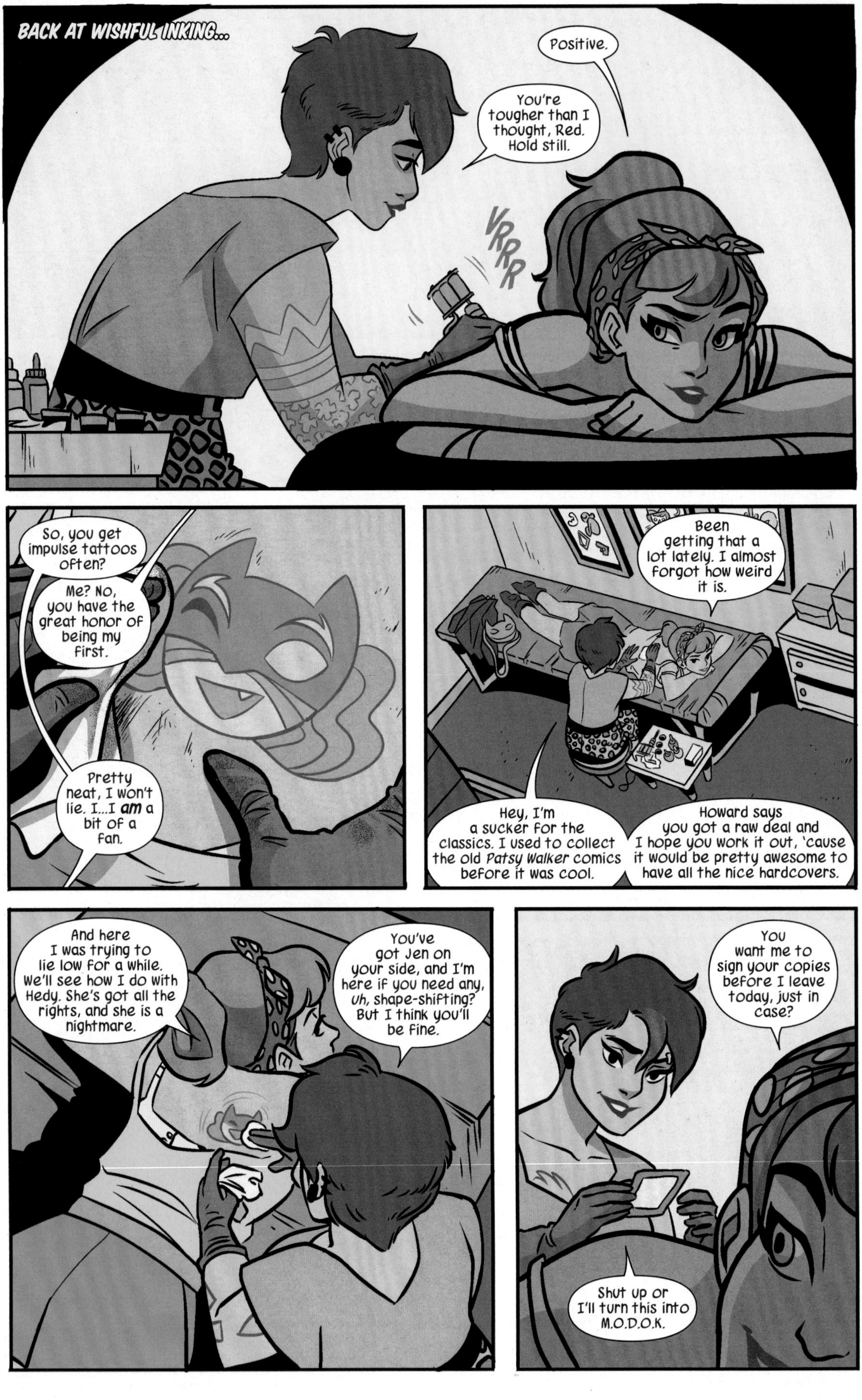
BACK AT WISHFUL INKING...
You're tougher than I thought, Red. Hold still.
Positive.
VRRR
So, you get impulse tattoos often?
Me? No, you have the great honor of being my first.
Pretty neat, I won't lie. I...I *am* a bit of a fan.
Been getting that a lot lately. I almost forgot how weird it is.
Hey, I'm a sucker for the classics. I used to collect the old *Patsy Walker* comics before it was cool.
Howard says you got a raw deal and I hope you work it out, 'cause it would be pretty awesome to have all the nice hardcovers.
And here I was trying to lie low for a while. We'll see how I do with Hedy. She's got all the rights, and she is a nightmare.
You've got Jen on your side, and I'm here if you need any, *uh*, shape-shifting? But I think you'll be fine.
You want me to sign your copies before I leave today, just in case?
Shut up or I'll turn this into M.O.D.O.K.

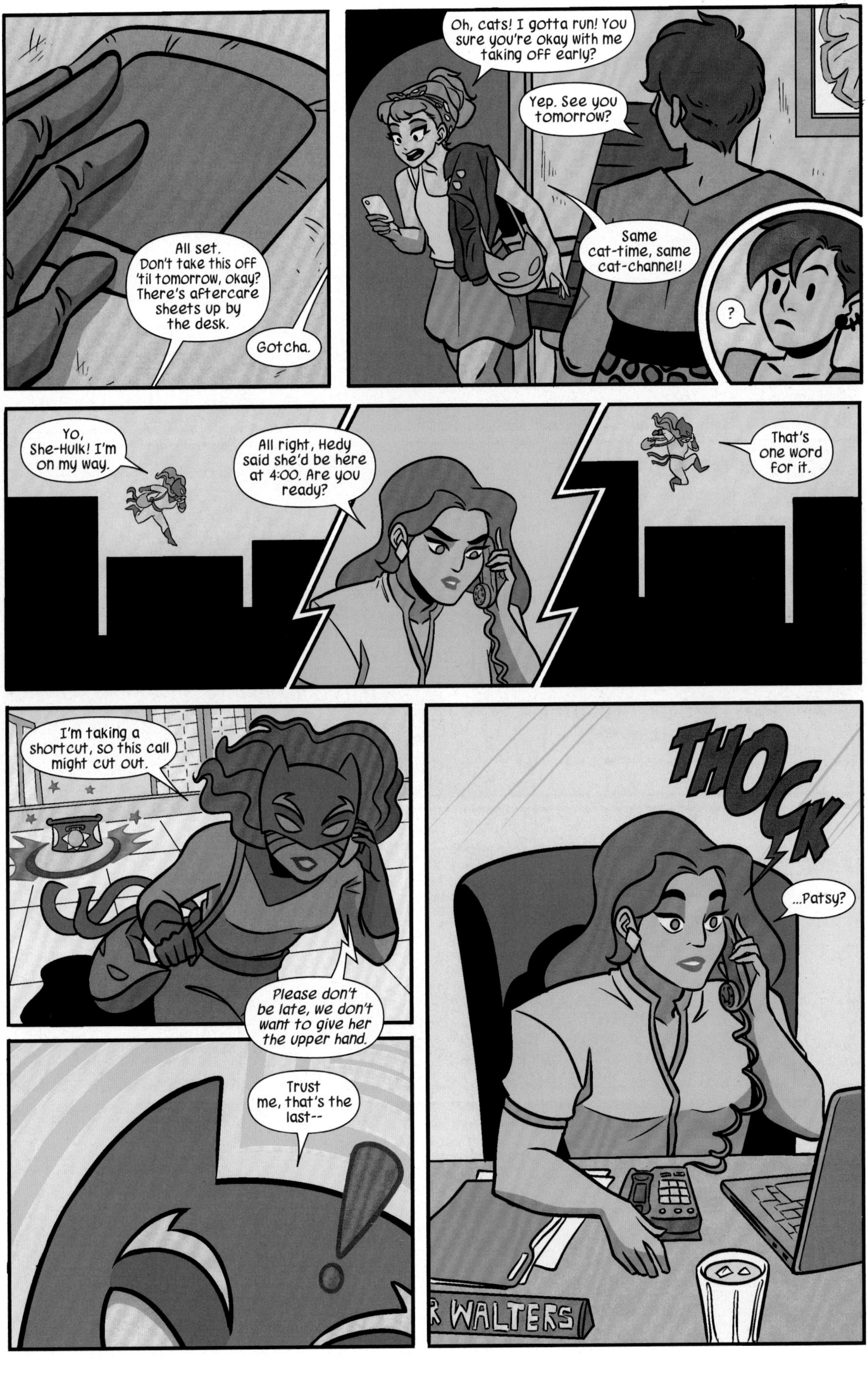
All set. Don't take this off 'til tomorrow, okay? There's aftercare sheets up by the desk.
Gotcha.
Oh, cats! I gotta run! You sure you're okay with me taking off early?
Yep. See you tomorrow?
Same cat-time, same cat-channel!
?
Yo, She-Hulk! I'm on my way.
All right, Hedy said she'd be here at 4:00. Are you ready?
That's one word for it.
I'm taking a shortcut, so this call might cut out.
Please don't be late, we don't want to give her the upper hand.
Trust me, that's the last--
THOCK
...Patsy?
R WALTERS

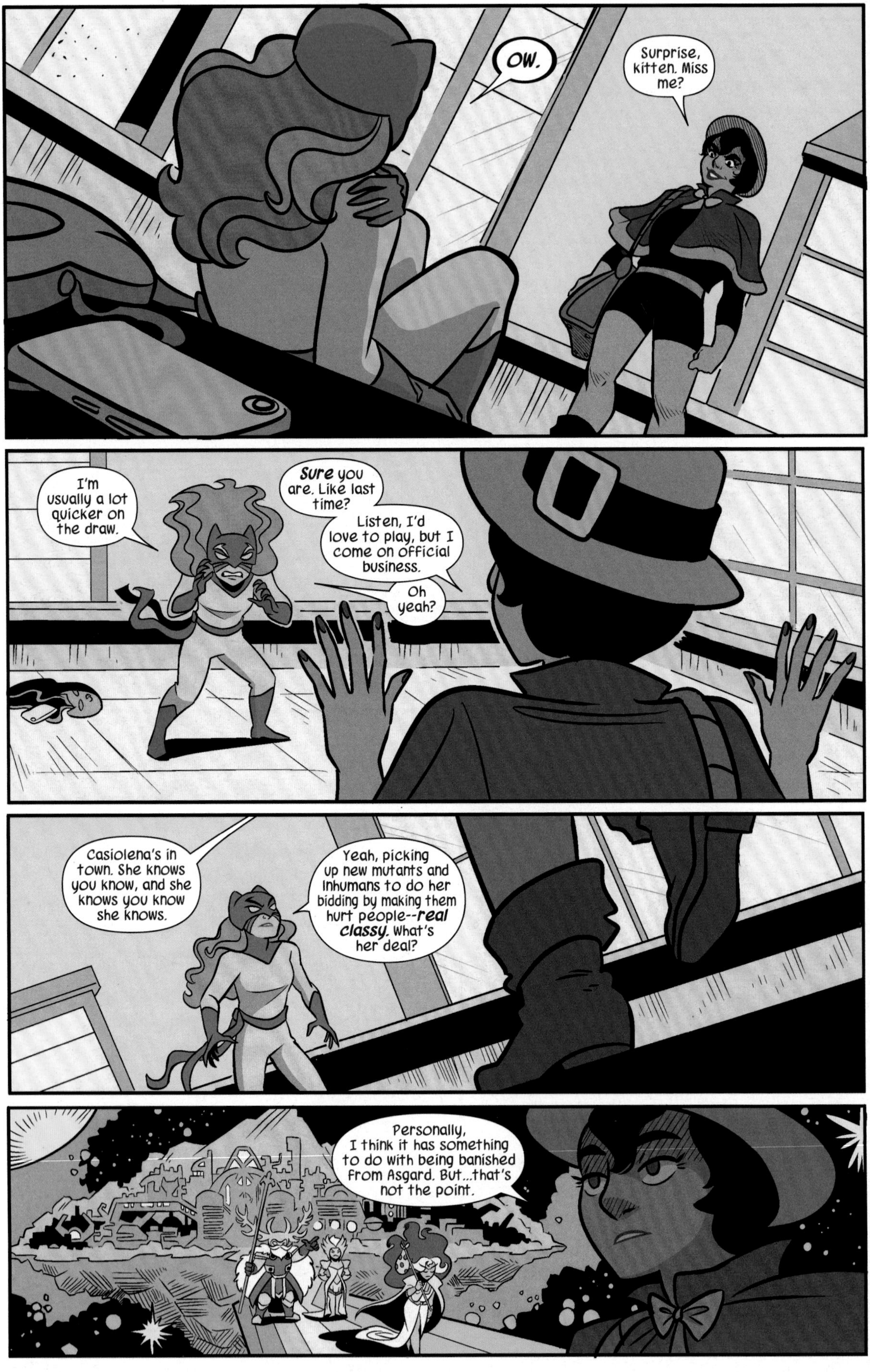
OW.
Surprise, kitten. Miss me?
I'm usually a lot quicker on the draw.
Sure you are. Like last time?
Listen, I'd love to play, but I come on official business.
Oh yeah?
Casiolena's in town. She knows you know, and she knows you know she knows.
Yeah, picking up new mutants and Inhumans to do her bidding by making them hurt people--real classy. What's her deal?
Personally, I think it has something to do with being banished from Asgard. But...that's not the point.

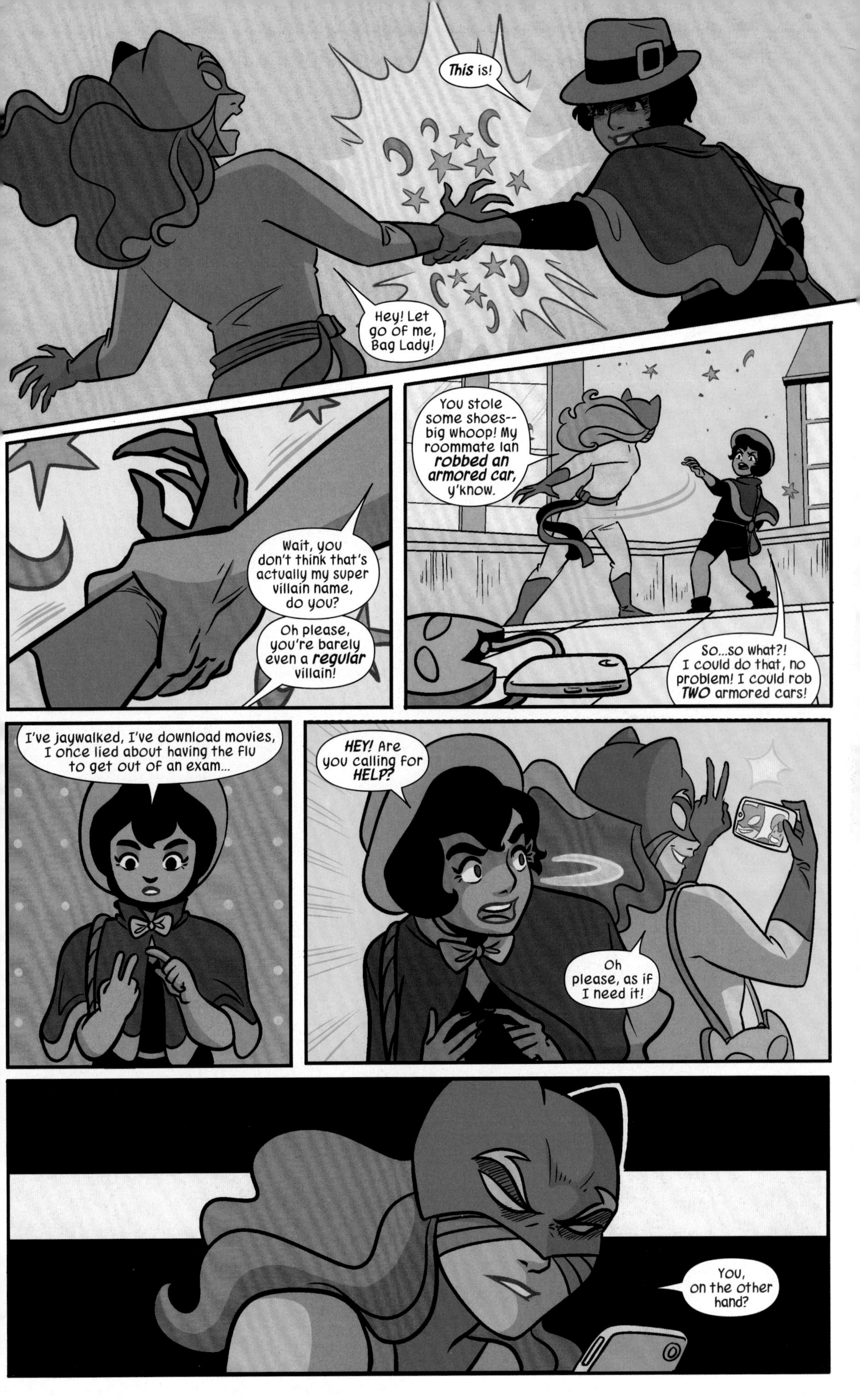
This is!
Hey! Let go of me, Bag Lady!
Wait, you don't think that's actually my super villain name, do you?
Oh please, you're barely even a regular villain!
You stole some shoes--big whoop! My roommate Ian robbed an armored car, y'know.
So...so what?! I could do that, no problem! I could rob TWO armored cars!
I've jaywalked, I've download movies, I once lied about having the flu to get out of an exam...
HEY! Are you calling for HELP?
Oh please, as if I need it!
You, on the other hand?

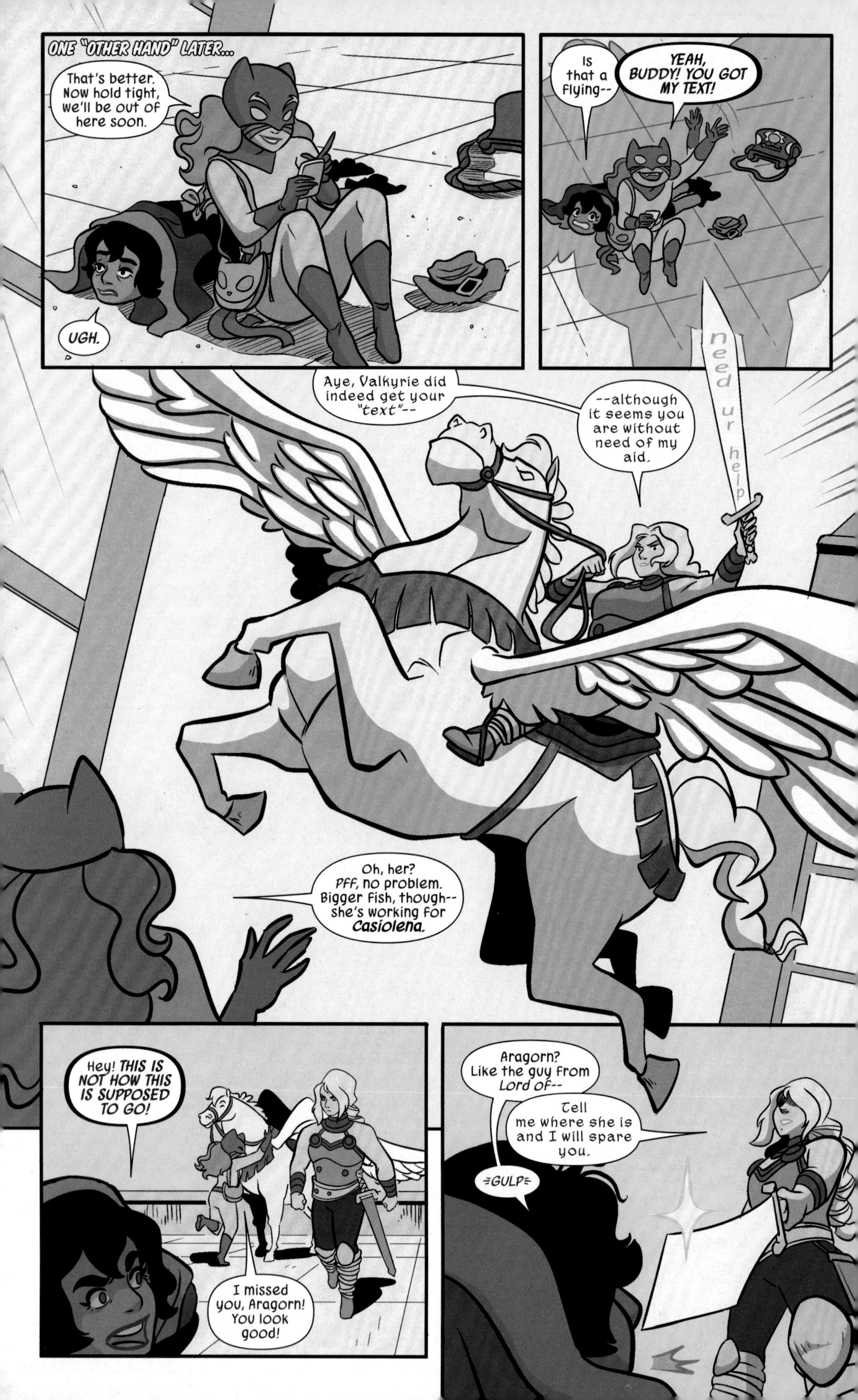

ONE "OTHER HAND" LATER...
That's better. Now hold tight, we'll be out of here soon.
UGH.
Is that a flying--
YEAH, BUDDY! YOU GOT MY TEXT!
need ur help
Aye, Valkyrie did indeed get your "text"--
--although it seems you are without need of my aid.
Oh, her? Pff, no problem. Bigger fish, though--she's working for Casiolena.
Hey! THIS IS NOT HOW THIS IS SUPPOSED TO GO!
I missed you, Aragorn! You look good!
Aragorn? Like the guy from Lord of--
Tell me where she is and I will spare you.
GULP

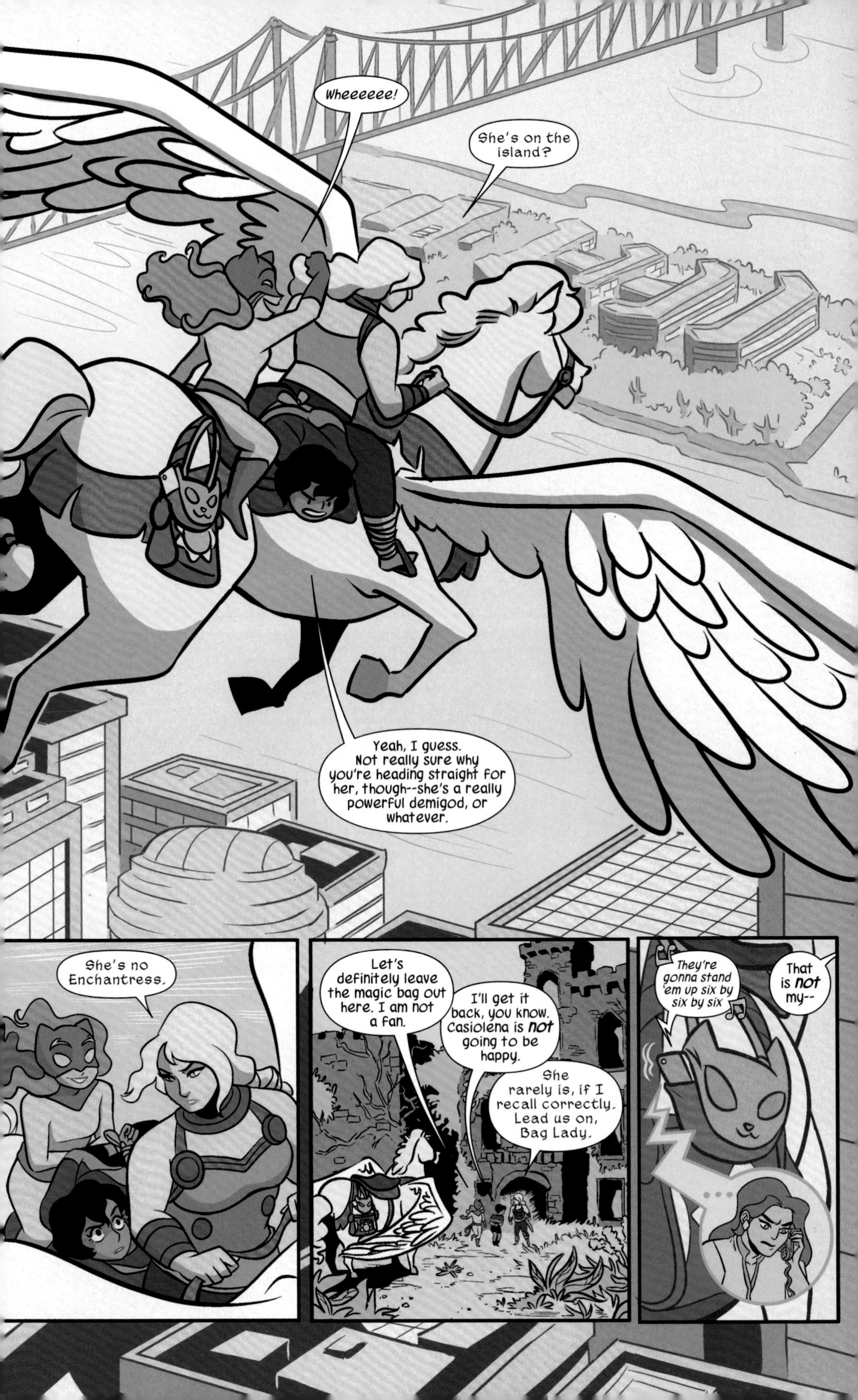
Wheeeeee!
She's on the island?
Yeah, I guess. Not really sure why you're heading straight for her, though--she's a really powerful demigod, or whatever.
She's no Enchantress.
Let's definitely leave the magic bag out here. I am not a fan.
I'll get it back, you know. Casiolena is *not* going to be happy.
She rarely is, if I recall correctly. Lead us on, Bag Lady.
They're gonna stand 'em up six by six by six
That is *not* my--

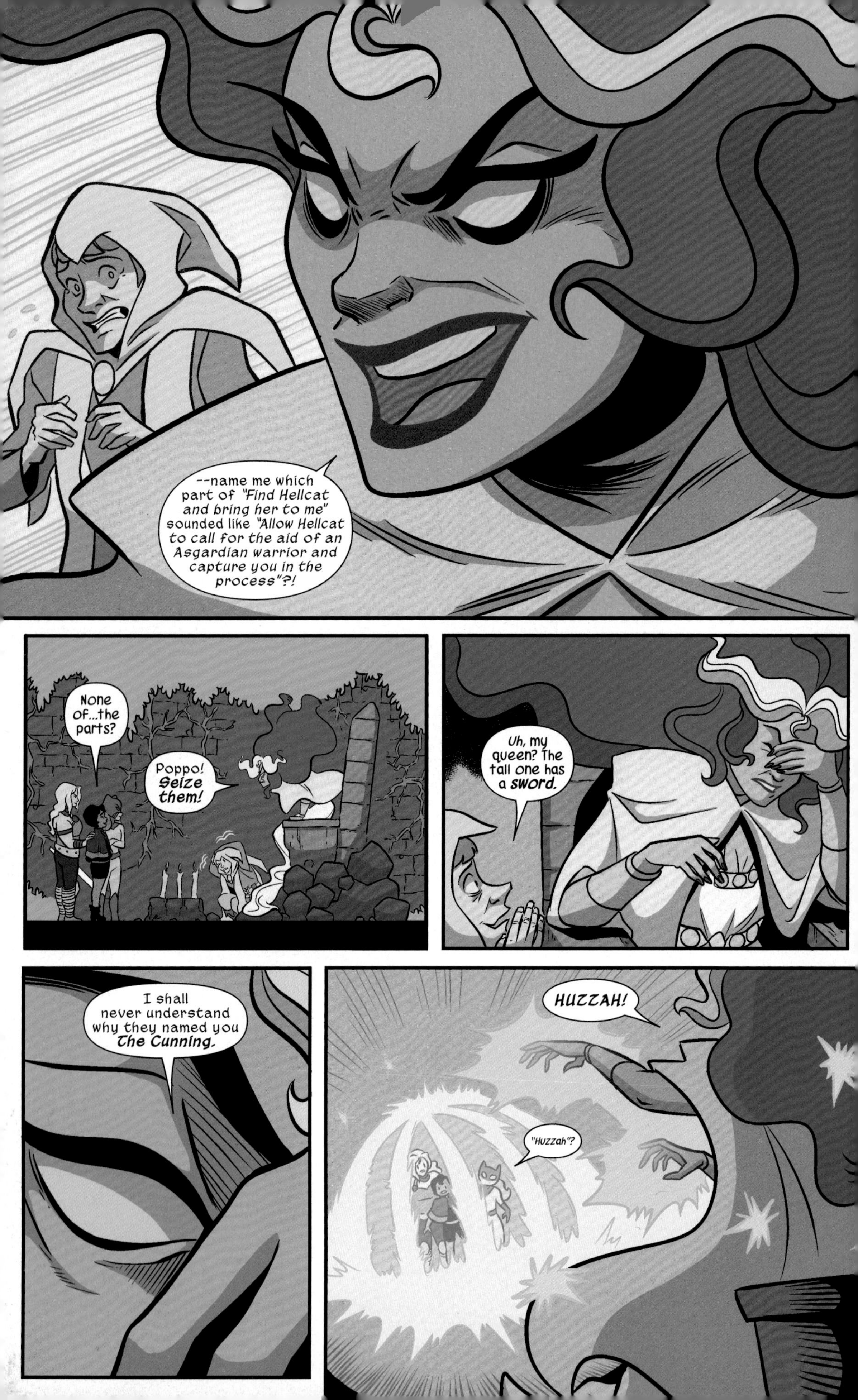
--name me which part of "Find Hellcat and bring her to me" sounded like "Allow Hellcat to call for the aid of an Asgardian warrior and capture you in the process"?!
None of...the parts?
Poppo! Seize them!
Uh, my queen? The tall one has a sword.
I shall never understand why they named you The Cunning.
HUZZAH!
"Huzzah"?

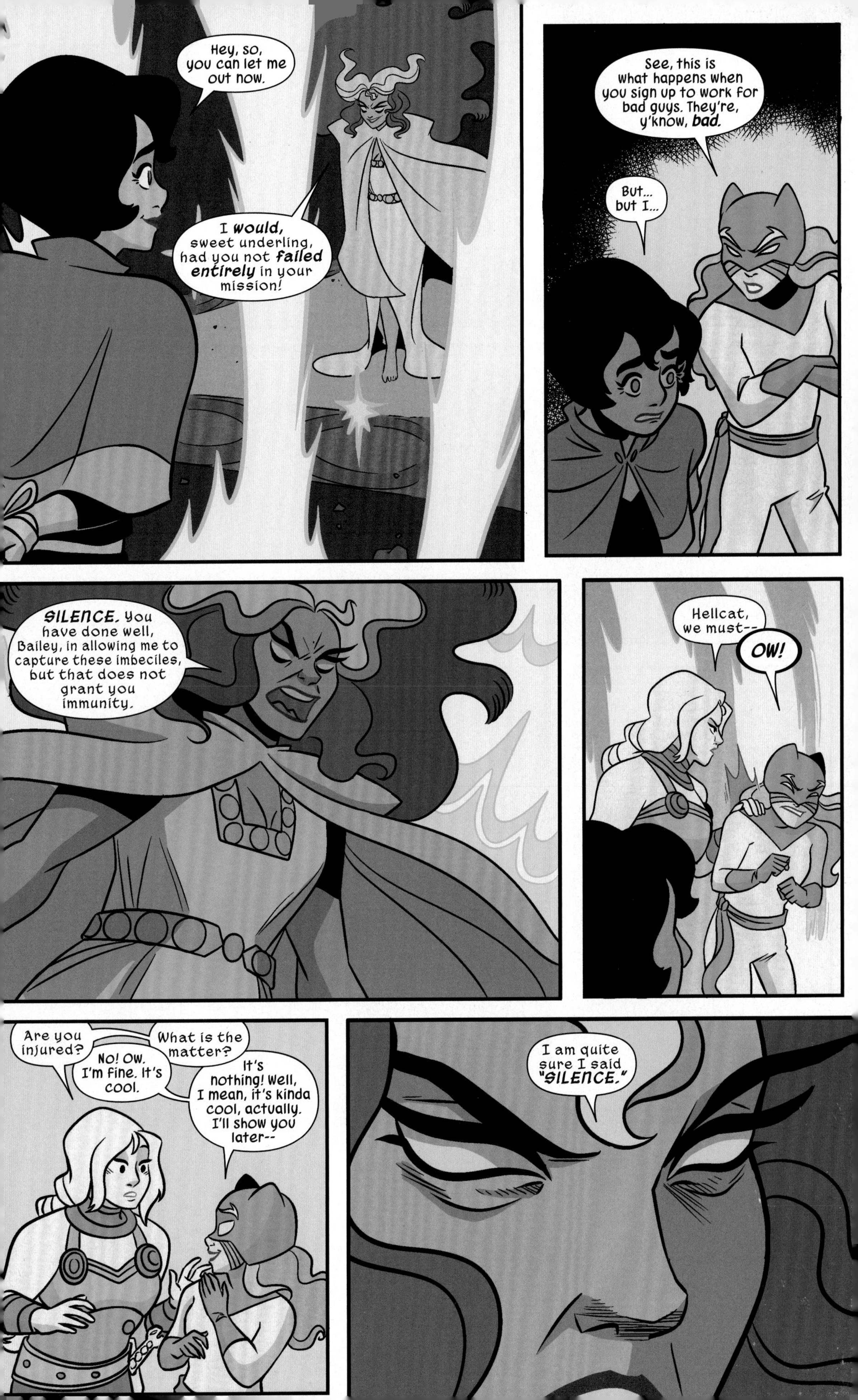
Hey, so, you can let me out now.
I *would,* sweet underling, had you not *failed entirely* in your mission!
See, this is what happens when you sign up to work for bad guys. They're, y'know, *bad.*
But... but I...
SILENCE. You have done well, Bailey, in allowing me to capture these imbeciles, but that does not grant you immunity.
Hellcat, we must--
OW!
Are you injured?
What is the matter?
No! Ow. I'm fine. It's cool.
It's nothing! Well, I mean, it's kinda cool, actually. I'll show you later--
I am quite sure I said *"SILENCE."*

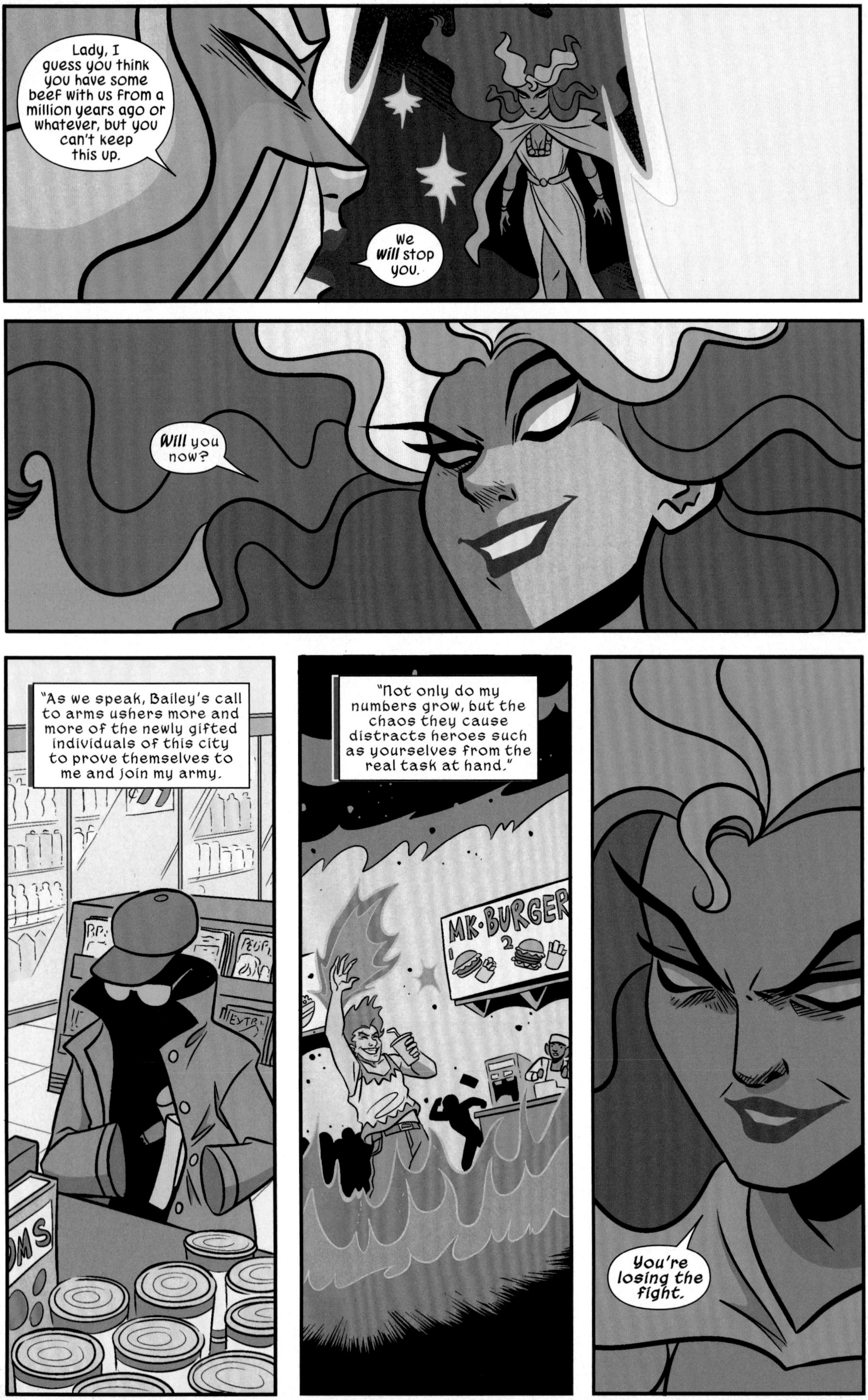
Lady, I guess you think you have some beef with us from a million years ago or whatever, but you can't keep this up.
We *Will* stop you.
Will you now?
"As we speak, Bailey's call to arms ushers more and more of the newly gifted individuals of this city to prove themselves to me and join my army.
"Not only do my numbers grow, but the chaos they cause distracts heroes such as yourselves from the real task at hand."
MK-BURGER
1
2
You're losing the fight.

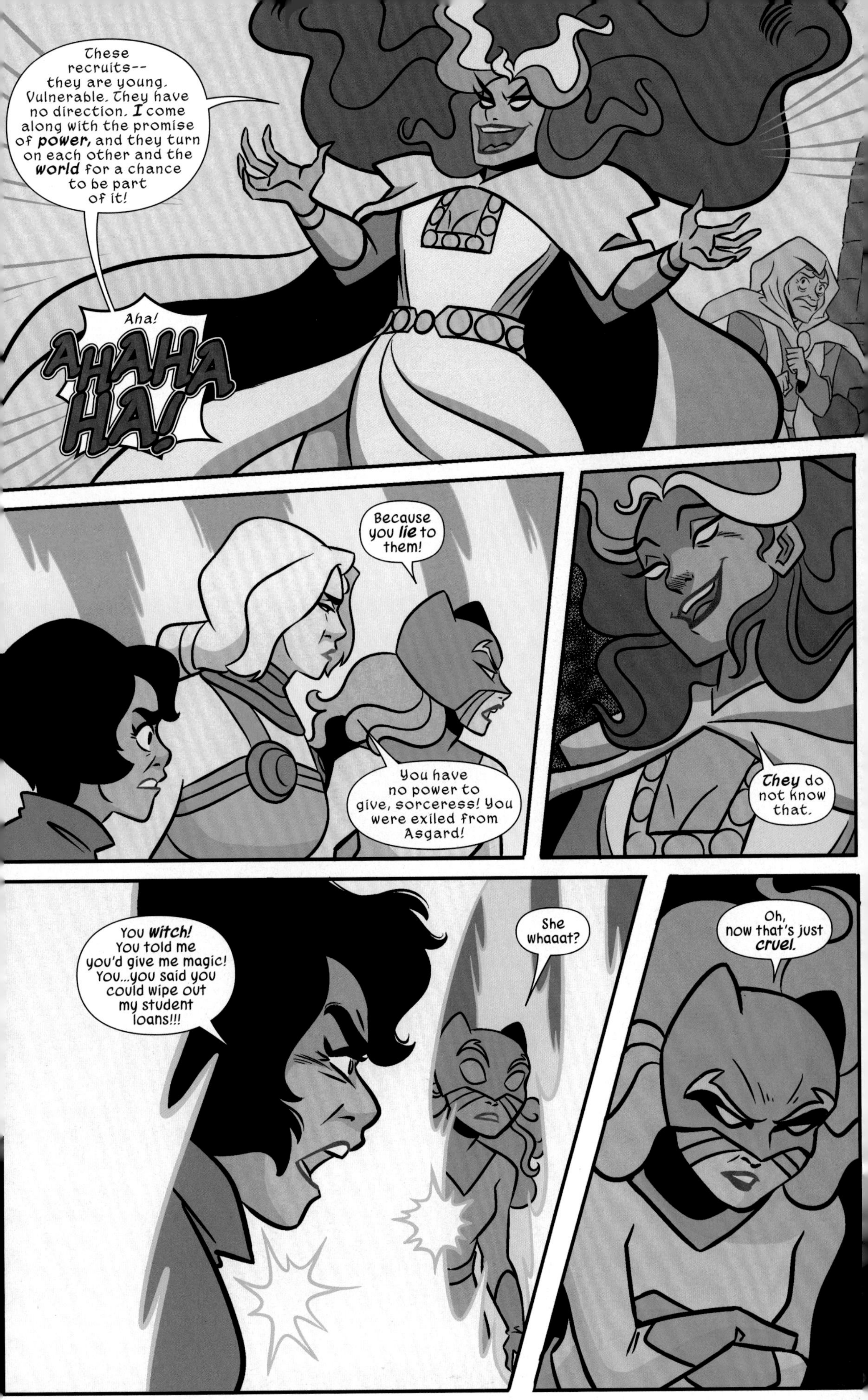
These recruits-- they are young. Vulnerable. They have no direction. I come along with the promise of power, and they turn on each other and the world for a chance to be part of it!
Aha!
AHAHA HA!
Because you lie to them!
You have no power to give, sorceress! You were exiled from Asgard!
They do not know that.
You witch! You told me you'd give me magic! You...you said you could wipe out my student loans!!!
She whaaat?
Oh, now that's just cruel.

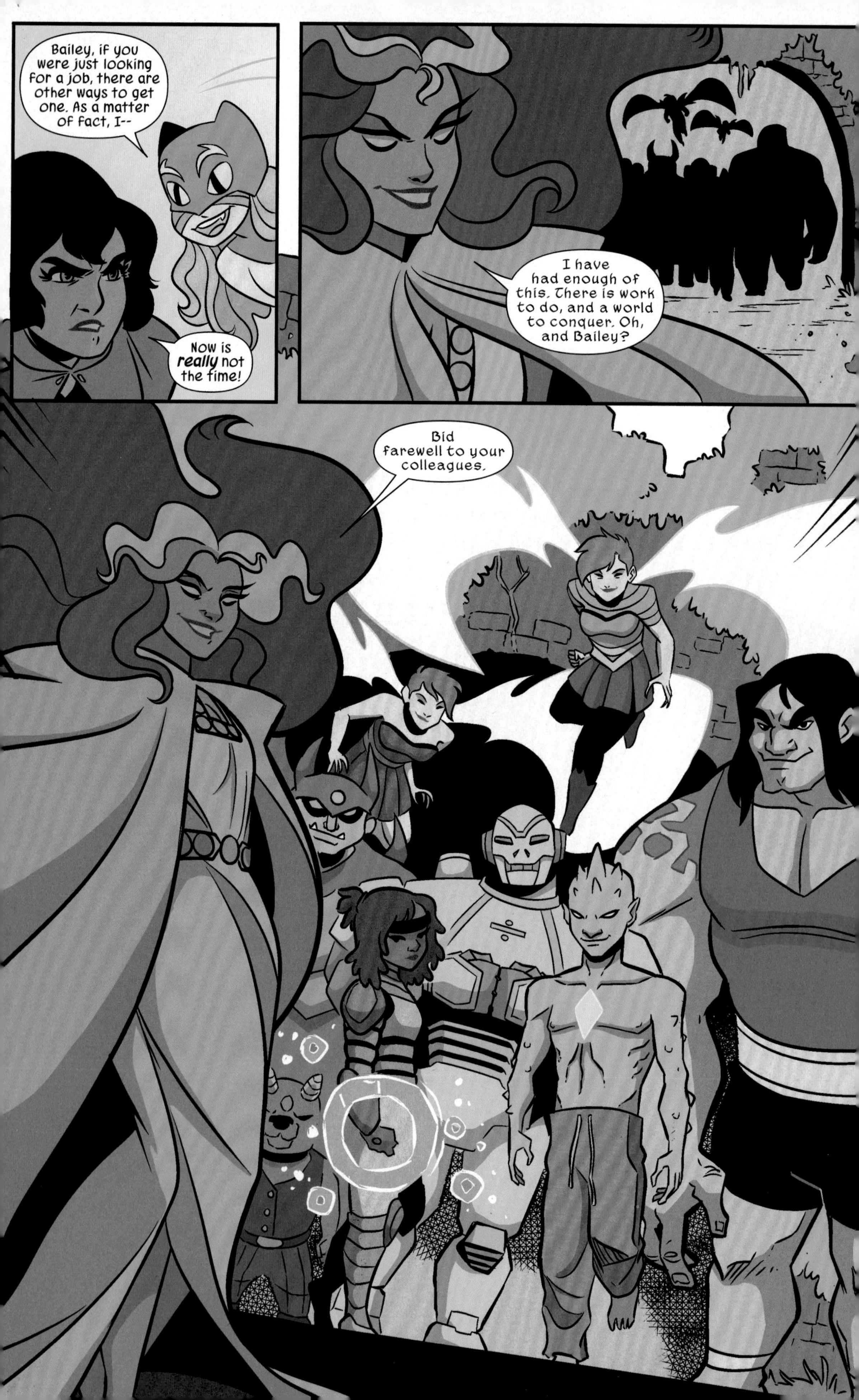
Bailey, if you were just looking for a job, there are other ways to get one. As a matter of fact, I--
Now is ***really*** not the time!
I have had enough of this. There is work to do, and a world to conquer. Oh, and Bailey?
Bid farewell to your colleagues.

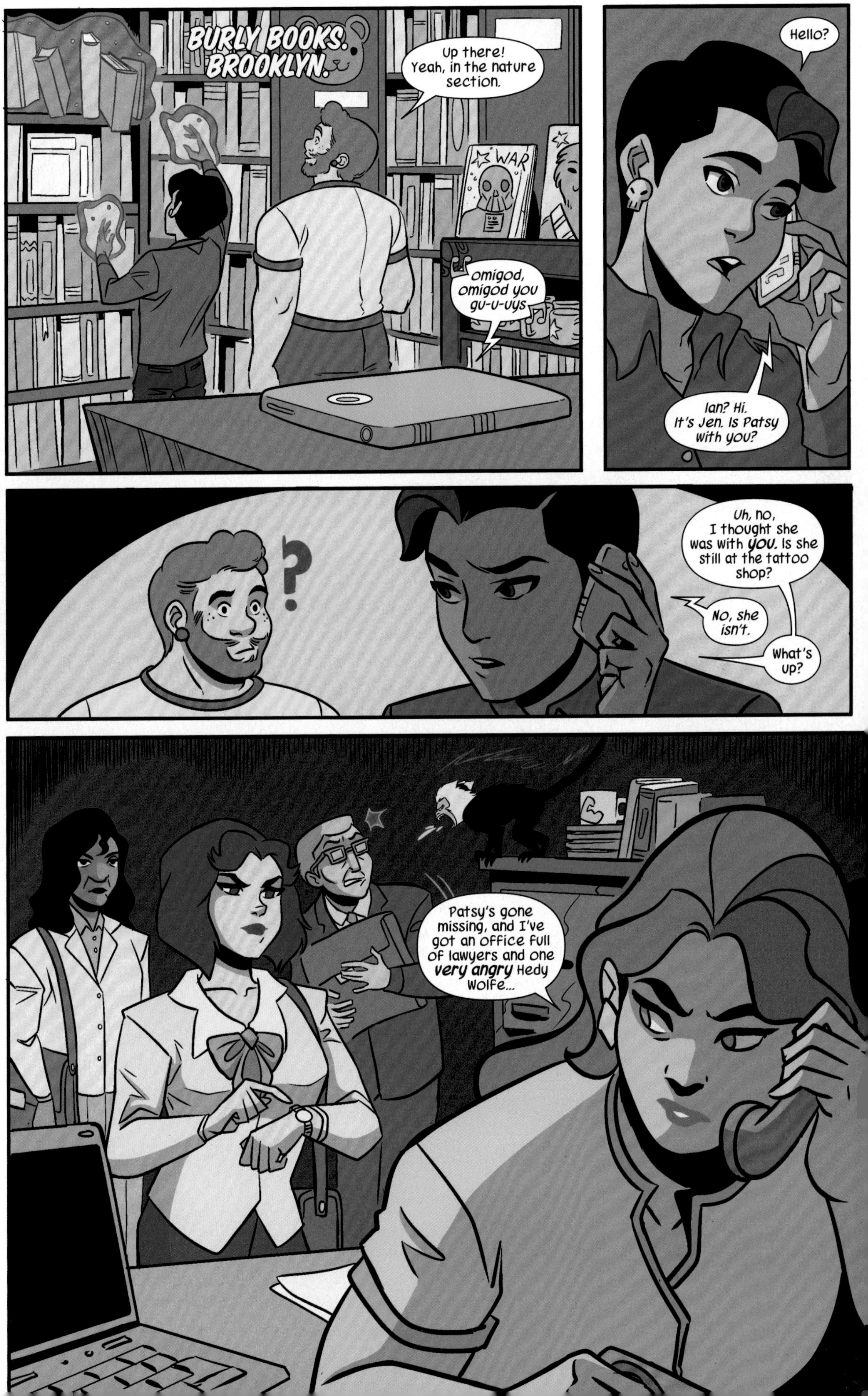
BURLY BOOKS. BROOKLYN.
Up there! Yeah, in the nature section.
omigod, omigod you gu-u-uys
WAR
Hello?
Ian? Hi. It's Jen. Is Patsy with you?
?
Uh, no, I thought she was with YOU. Is she still at the tattoo shop?
No, she isn't.
What's up?
Patsy's gone missing, and I've got an office full of lawyers and one very angry Hedy Wolfe...

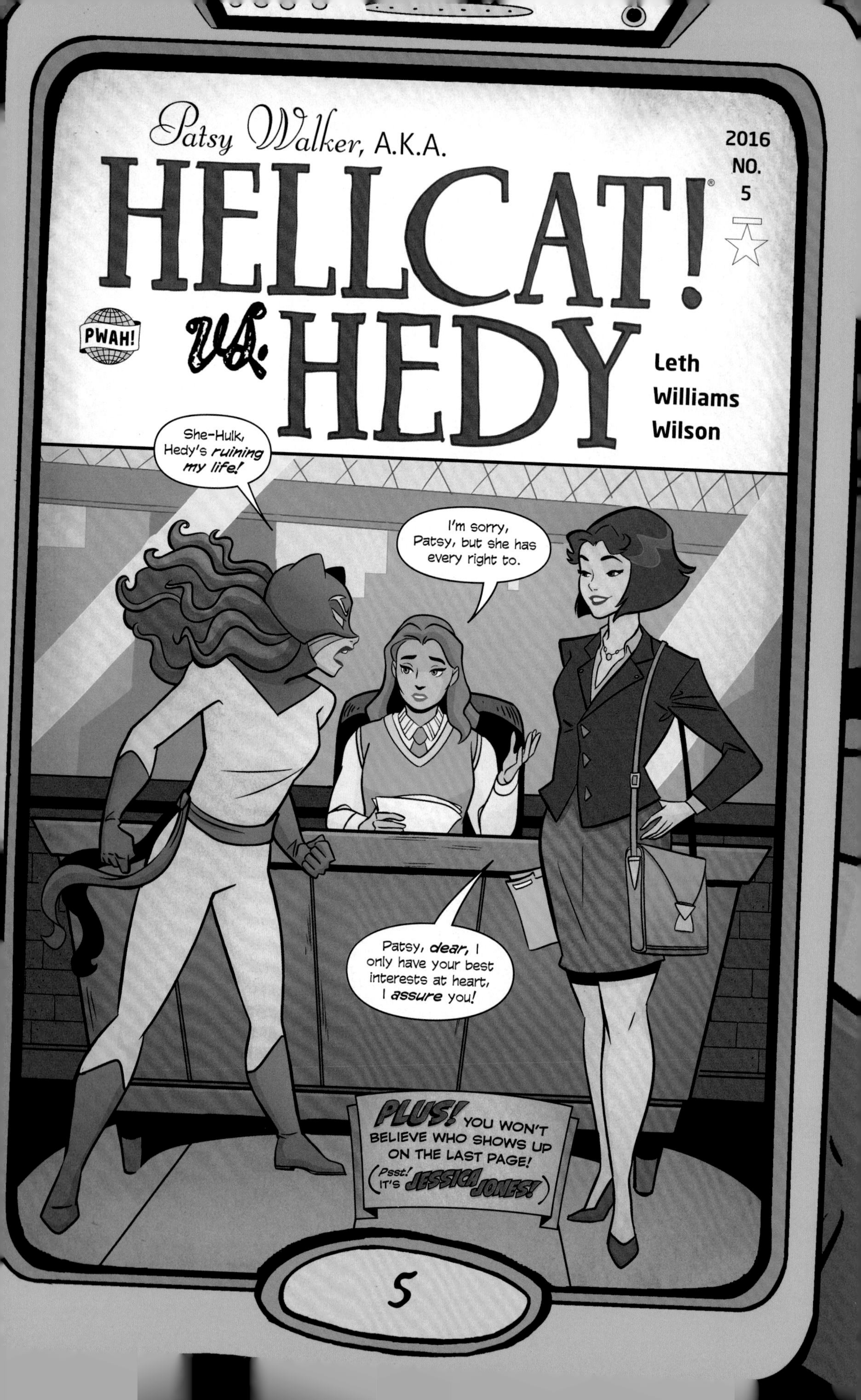

Patsy Walker, A.K.A.
HELLCAT!
2016
NO.
5
PWAH!
vs. HEDY
Leth
Williams
Wilson
She-Hulk, Hedy's ruining my life!
I'm sorry, Patsy, but she has every right to.
Patsy, dear, I only have your best interests at heart, I assure you!
PLUS! YOU WON'T BELIEVE WHO SHOWS UP ON THE LAST PAGE!
(Psst! IT'S JESSICA JONES!)
5

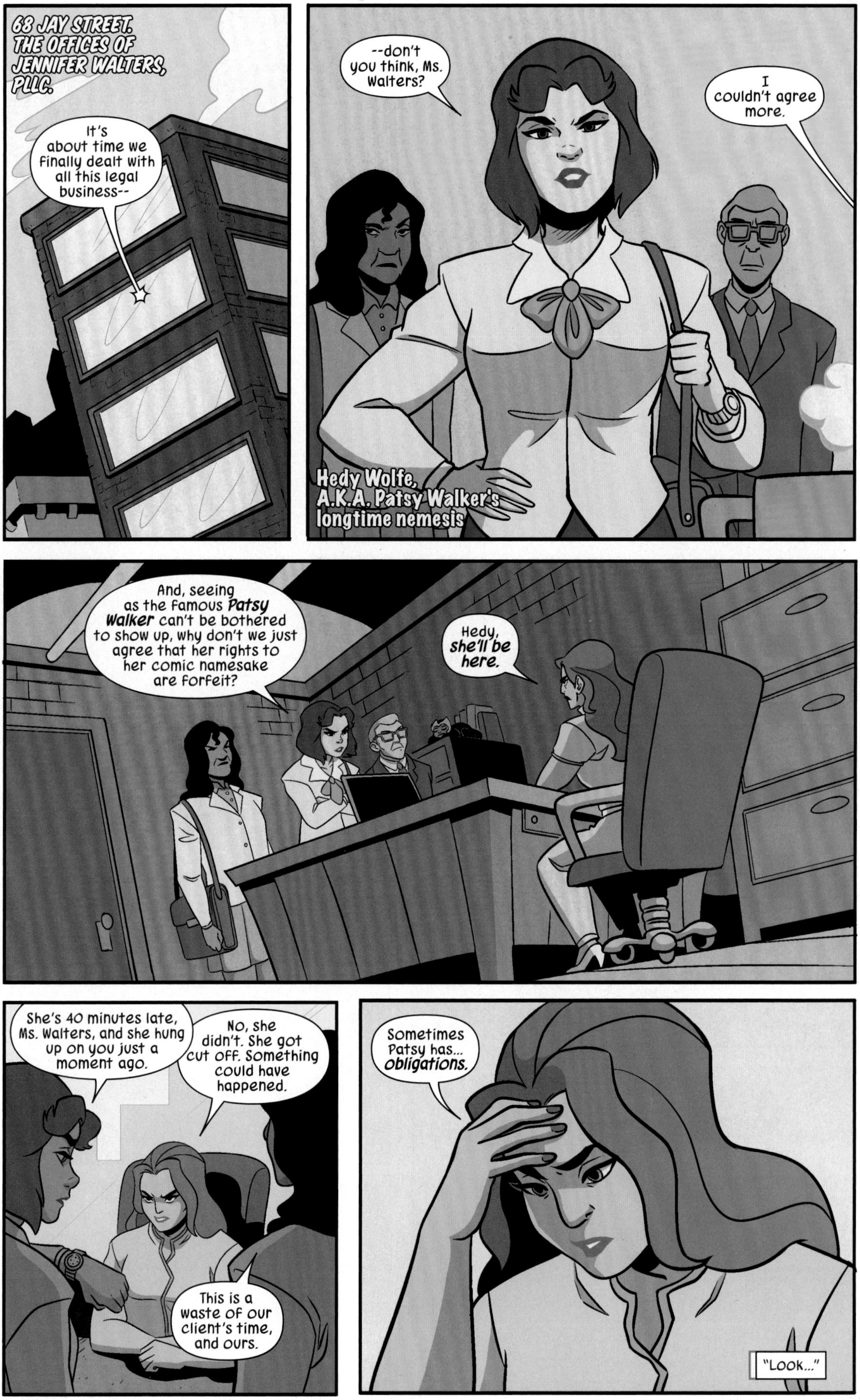
68 JAY STREET. THE OFFICES OF JENNIFER WALTERS, PLLC.
It's about time we finally dealt with all this legal business--
--don't you think, Ms. Walters?
I couldn't agree more.
Hedy Wolfe, A.K.A. Patsy Walker's longtime nemesis
And, seeing as the famous Patsy Walker can't be bothered to show up, why don't we just agree that her rights to her comic namesake are forfeit?
Hedy, she'll be here.
She's 40 minutes late, Ms. Walters, and she hung up on you just a moment ago.
No, she didn't. She got cut off. Something could have happened.
This is a waste of our client's time, and ours.
Sometimes Patsy has... obligations.
"LOOK..."

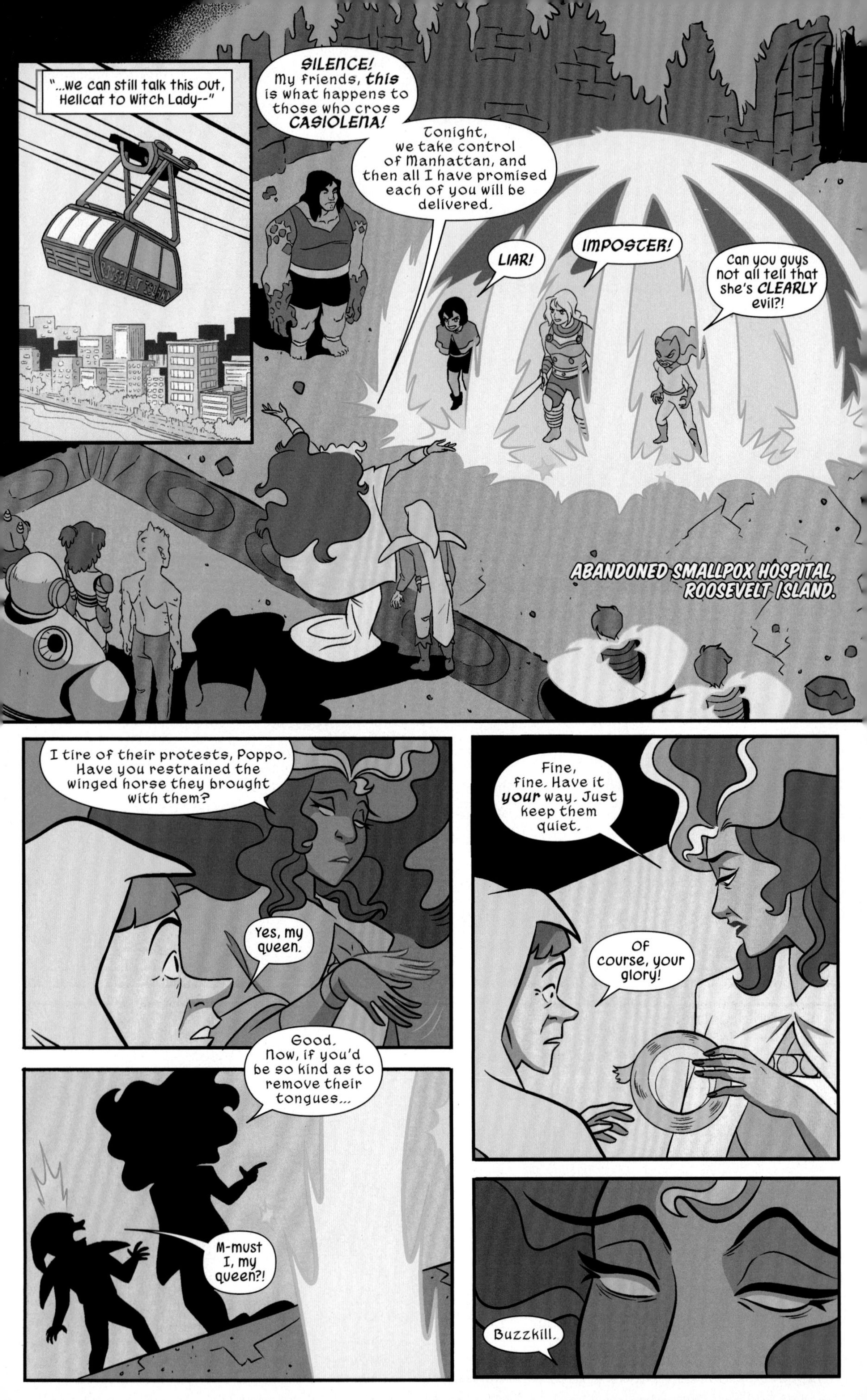
"...we can still talk this out, Hellcat to Witch Lady--"
SILENCE! My friends, this is what happens to those who cross CASIOLENA!
Tonight, we take control of Manhattan, and then all I have promised each of you will be delivered.
LIAR!
IMPOSTER!
Can you guys not all tell that she's CLEARLY evil?!
ABANDONED SMALLPOX HOSPITAL, ROOSEVELT ISLAND.
I tire of their protests, Poppo. Have you restrained the winged horse they brought with them?
Yes, my queen.
Good. Now, if you'd be so kind as to remove their tongues...
M-must I, my queen?!
Fine, fine. Have it your way. Just keep them quiet.
Of course, your glory!
Buzzkill.

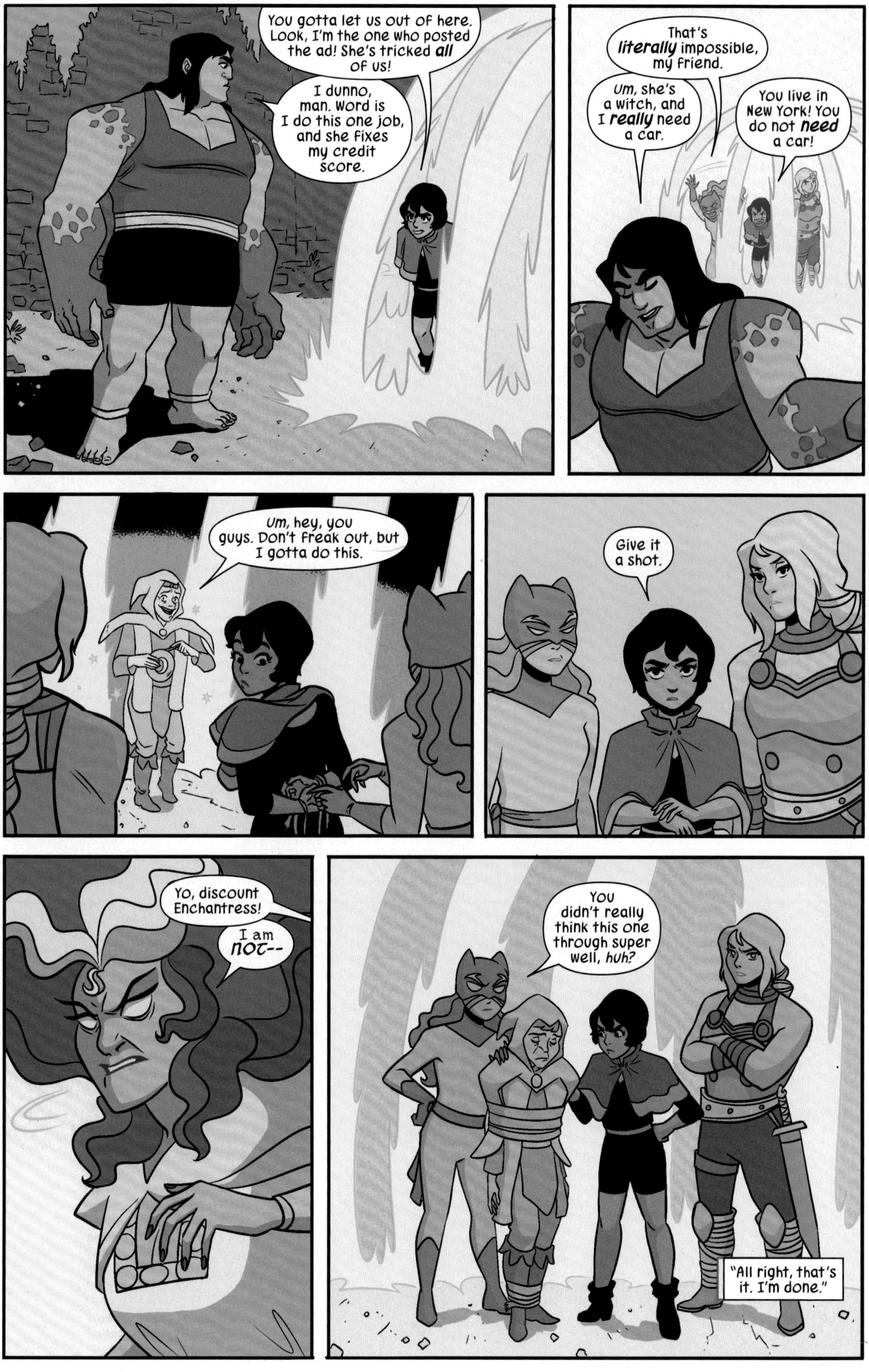
You gotta let us out of here. Look, I'm the one who posted the ad! She's tricked **all** of us!
I dunno, man. Word is I do this one job, and she fixes my credit score.
That's **literally** impossible, my friend.
Um, she's a witch, and I **really** need a car.
You live in New York! You do not **need** a car!
Um, hey, you guys. Don't freak out, but I gotta do this.
Give it a shot.
Yo, discount Enchantress!
I am **NOT**--
You didn't really think this one through super well, *huh?*
"All right, that's it. I'm done."

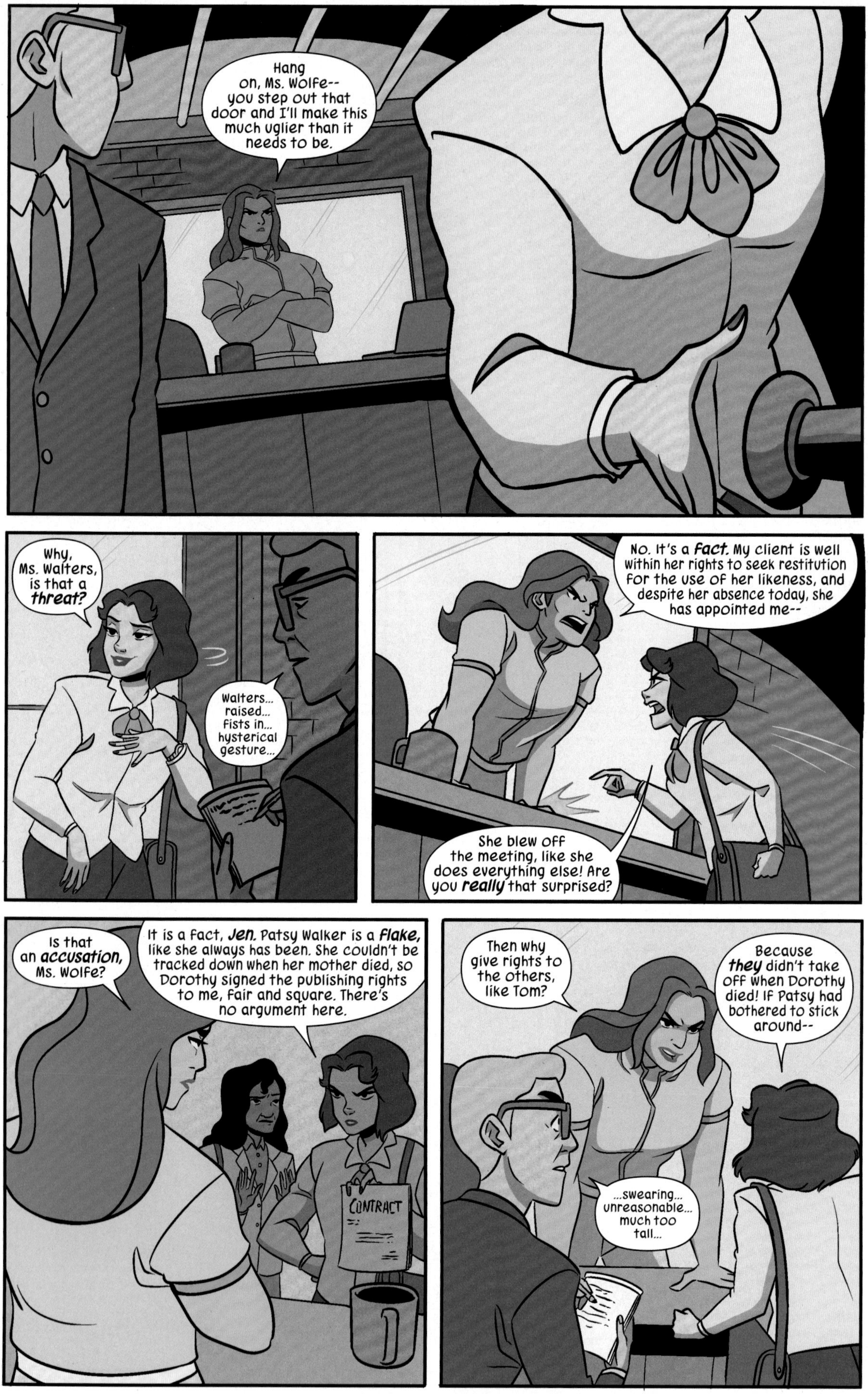
Hang on, Ms. Wolfe-- you step out that door and I'll make this much uglier than it needs to be.
Why, Ms. Walters, is that a *threat?*
Walters... raised... fists in... hysterical gesture...
No. It's a *fact.* My client is well within her rights to seek restitution for the use of her likeness, and despite her absence today, she has appointed me--
She blew off the meeting, like she does everything else! Are you *really* that surprised?
Is that an *accusation,* Ms. Wolfe?
It is a fact, *Jen.* Patsy Walker is a *flake,* like she always has been. She couldn't be tracked down when her mother died, so Dorothy signed the publishing rights to me, fair and square. There's no argument here.
CONTRACT
Then why give rights to the others, like Tom?
Because *they* didn't take off when Dorothy died! If Patsy had bothered to stick around--
...swearing... unreasonable... much too tall...

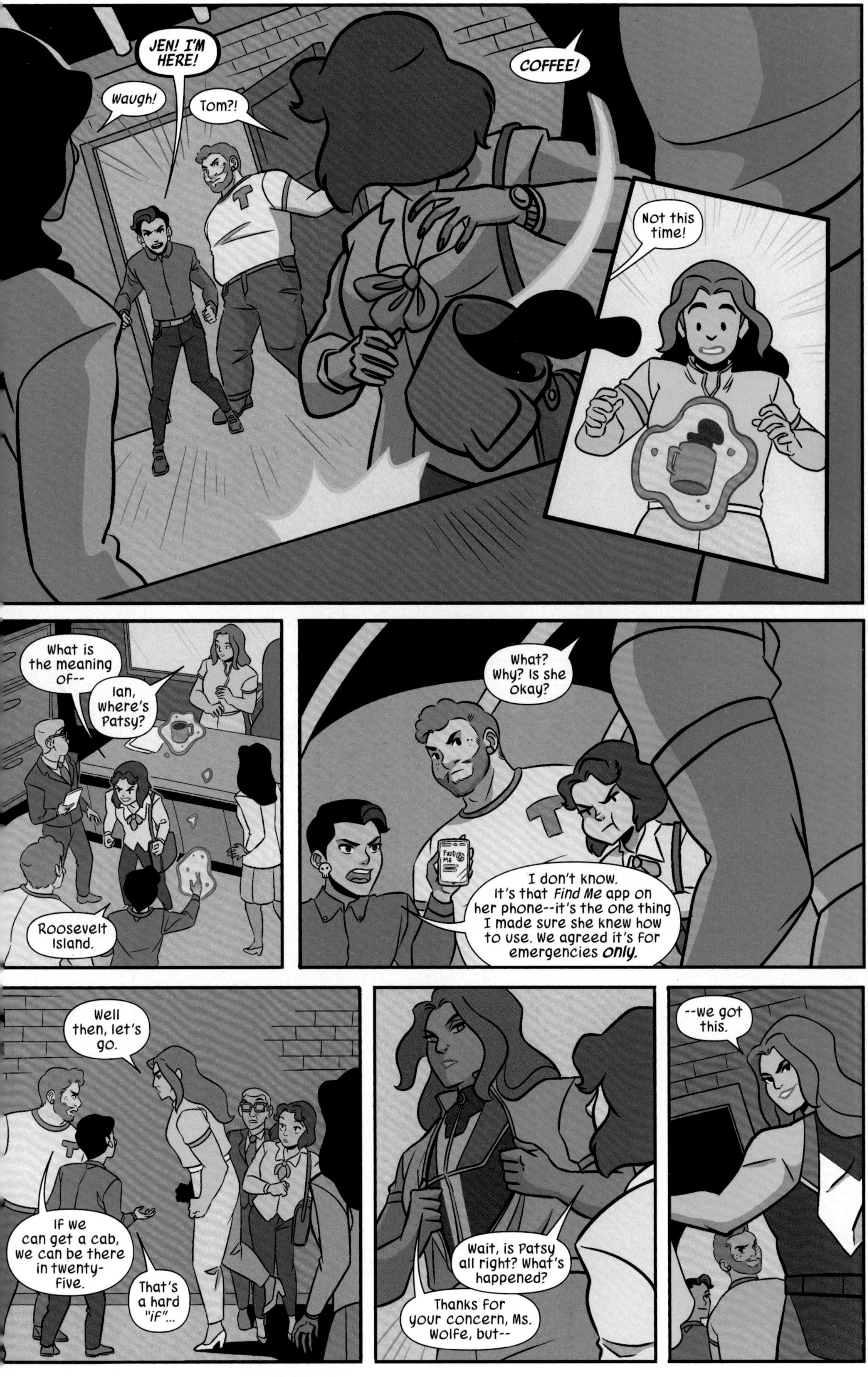
JEN! I'M HERE!
Waugh!
Tom?!
COFFEE!
Not this time!
What is the meaning of--
Ian, where's Patsy?
Roosevelt Island.
What? Why? Is she okay?
I don't know. It's that *Find Me* app on her phone--it's the one thing I made sure she knew how to use. We agreed it's for emergencies ***only.***
FIND ME
Well then, let's go.
If we can get a cab, we can be there in twenty-five.
That's a hard "*if*"...
Wait, is Patsy all right? What's happened?
Thanks for your concern, Ms. Wolfe, but--
--we got this.

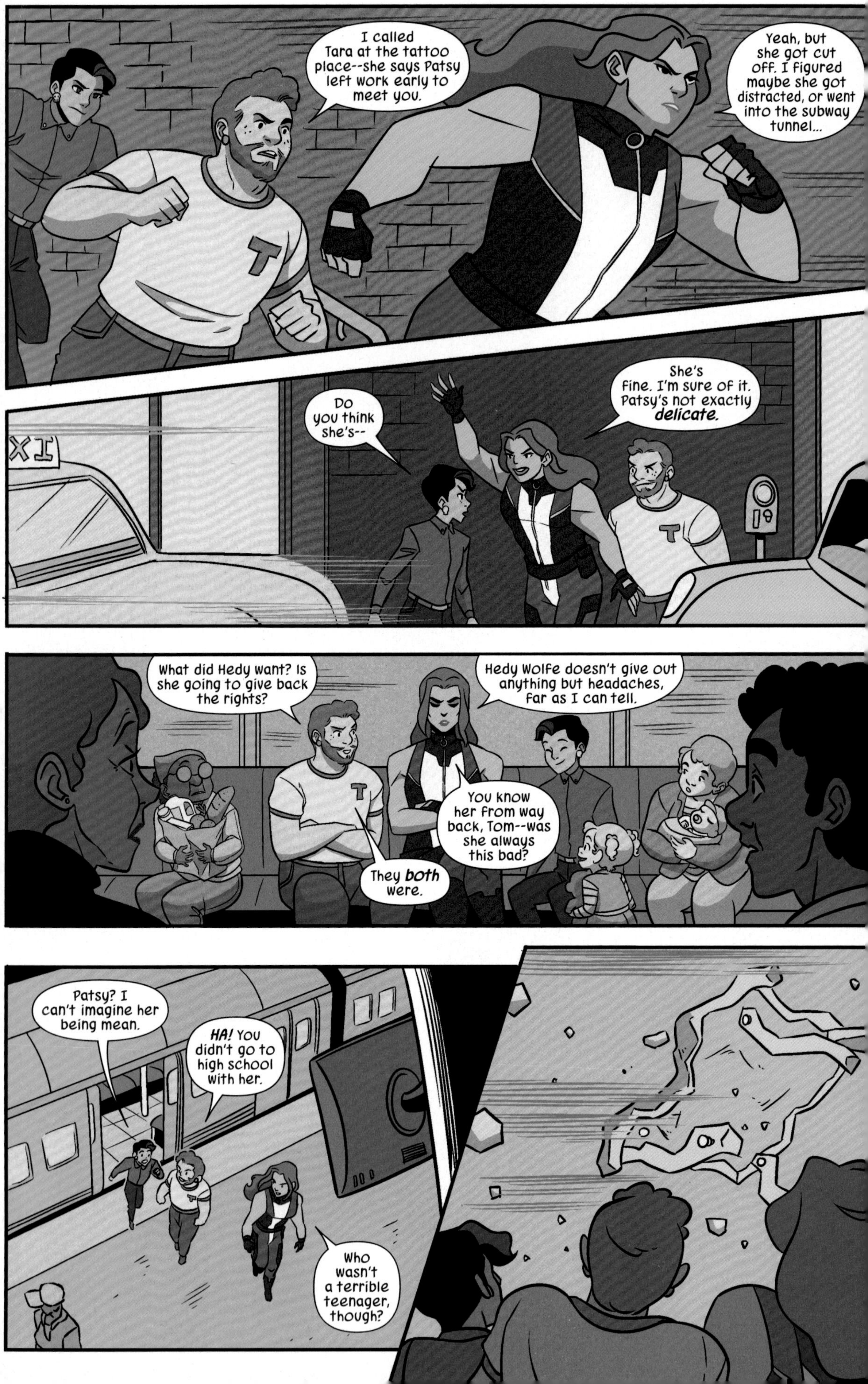
I called Tara at the tattoo place--she says Patsy left work early to meet you.
Yeah, but she got cut off. I figured maybe she got distracted, or went into the subway tunnel...
Do you think she's--
She's fine. I'm sure of it. Patsy's not exactly *delicate.*
What did Hedy want? Is she going to give back the rights?
Hedy Wolfe doesn't give out anything but headaches, far as I can tell.
You know her from way back, Tom--was she always this bad?
They *both* were.
Patsy? I can't imagine her being mean.
HA! You didn't go to high school with her.
Who wasn't a terrible teenager, though?

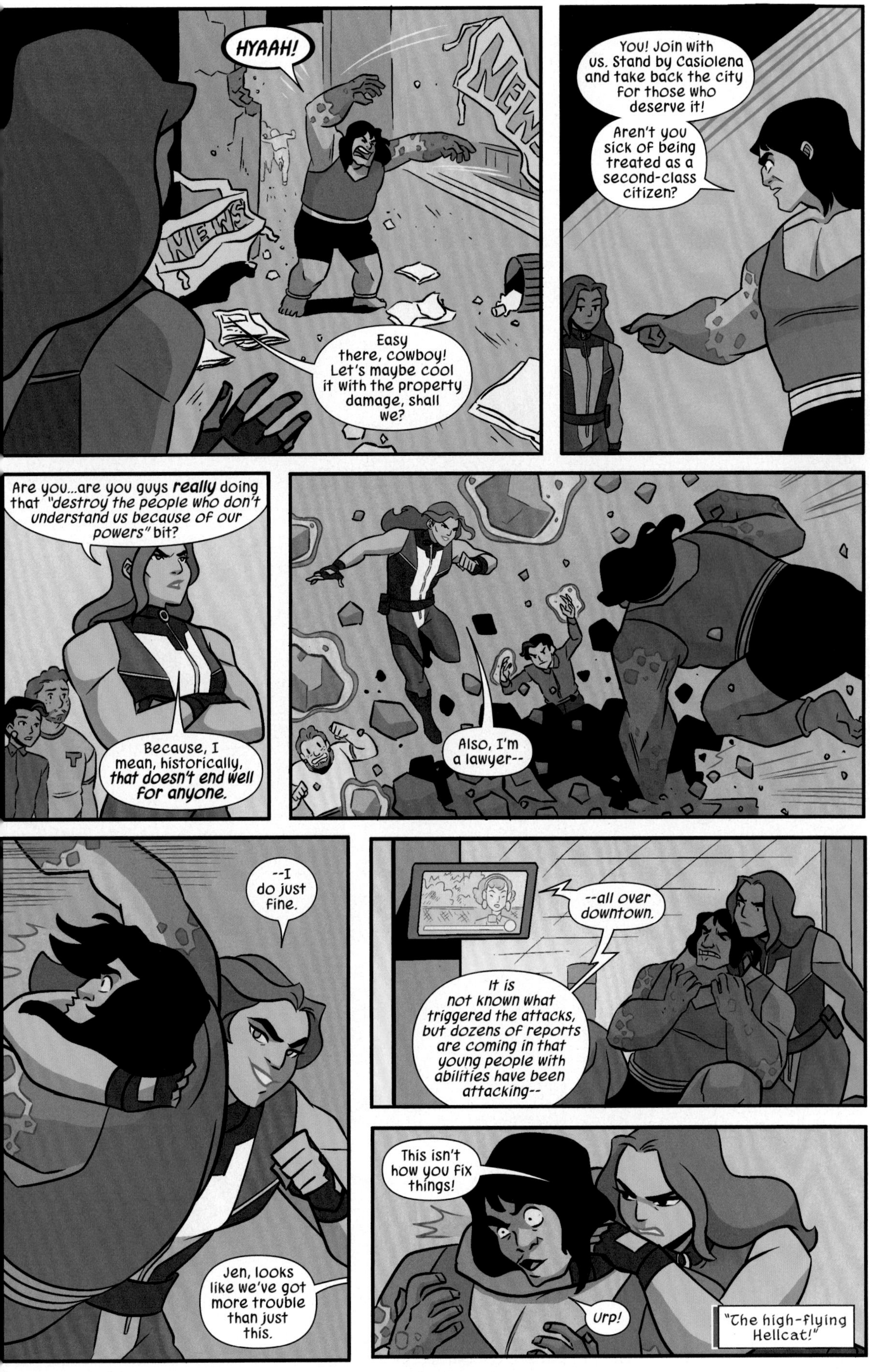
HYAAH!
NEWS
NEWS
Easy there, cowboy! Let's maybe cool it with the property damage, shall we?
You! Join with us. Stand by Casiolena and take back the city for those who deserve it!
Aren't you sick of being treated as a second-class citizen?
Are you...are you guys **really** doing that *"destroy the people who don't understand us because of our powers"* bit?
Because, I mean, historically, **that doesn't end well for anyone.**
Also, I'm a lawyer--
--I do just fine.
Jen, looks like we've got more trouble than just this.
--all over downtown.
It is not known what triggered the attacks, but dozens of reports are coming in that young people with abilities have been attacking--
This isn't how you fix things!
Urp!
"The high-flying Hellcat!"

Not to mention the leader of the Valkyrior herself. Tell me, both of you, how does it feel to watch the city you protect come to ruin?

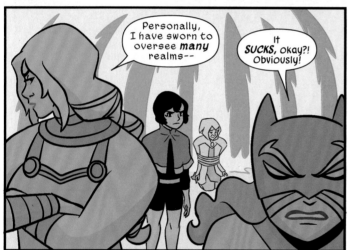

Personally, I have sworn to oversee **many** realms--

It **SUCKS**, okay?! Obviously!

My queen, I hate to interrupt, but might you consider freeing me?

You got yourself captured, Poppo. That was **your** decision.

I bet **Enchantress** doesn't treat her lackeys this way...

What did you say?

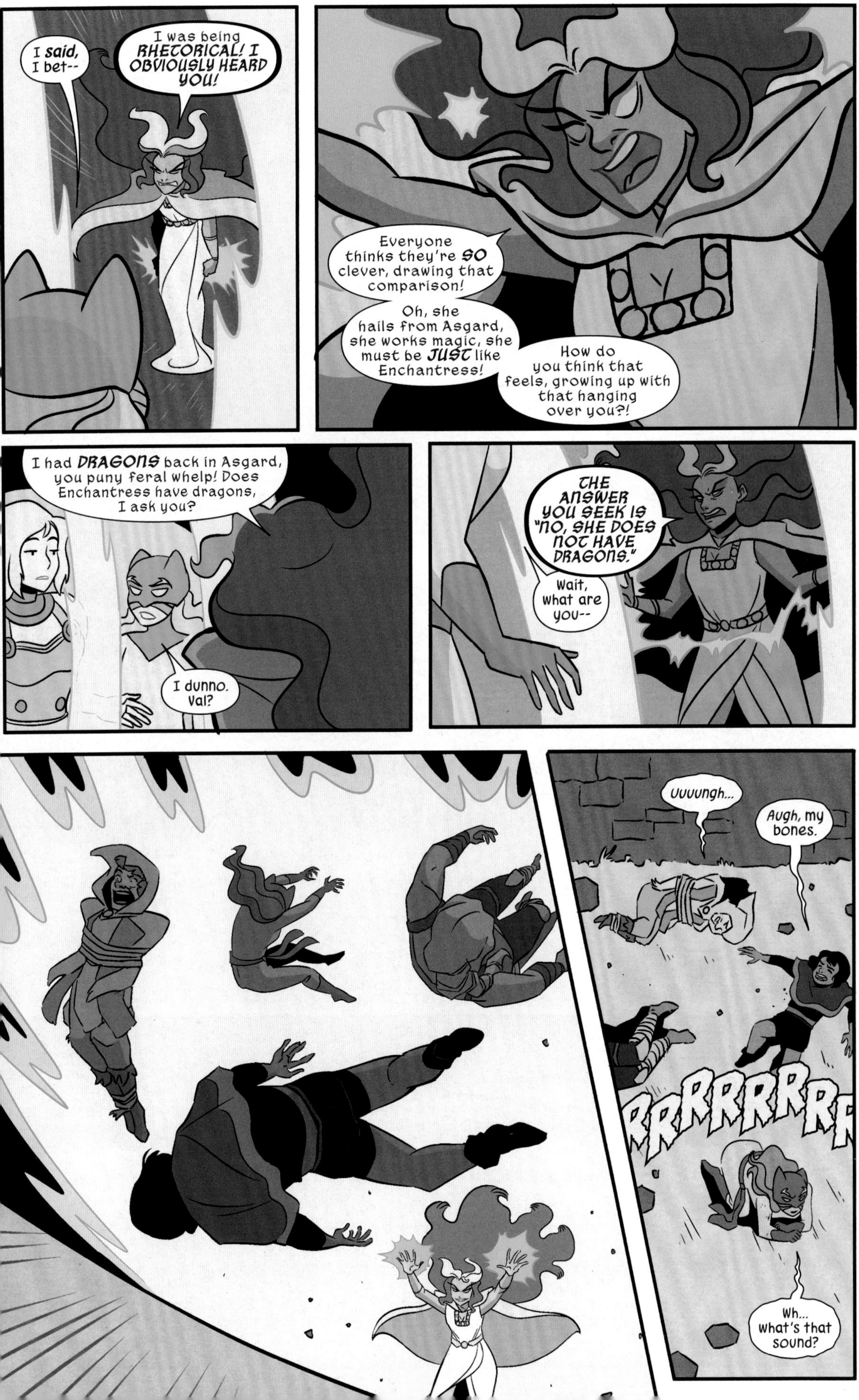
I said, I bet--
I was being RHETORICAL! I OBVIOUSLY HEARD YOU!
Everyone thinks they're SO clever, drawing that comparison!
Oh, she hails from Asgard, she works magic, she must be JUST like Enchantress!
How do you think that feels, growing up with that hanging over you?!
I had DRAGONS back in Asgard, you puny feral whelp! Does Enchantress have dragons, I ask you?
I dunno. Val?
THE ANSWER YOU SEEK IS "NO, SHE DOES NOT HAVE DRAGONS."
Wait, what are you--
Uuuungh...
Augh, my bones.
RRRRRRRRR
Wh... what's that sound?

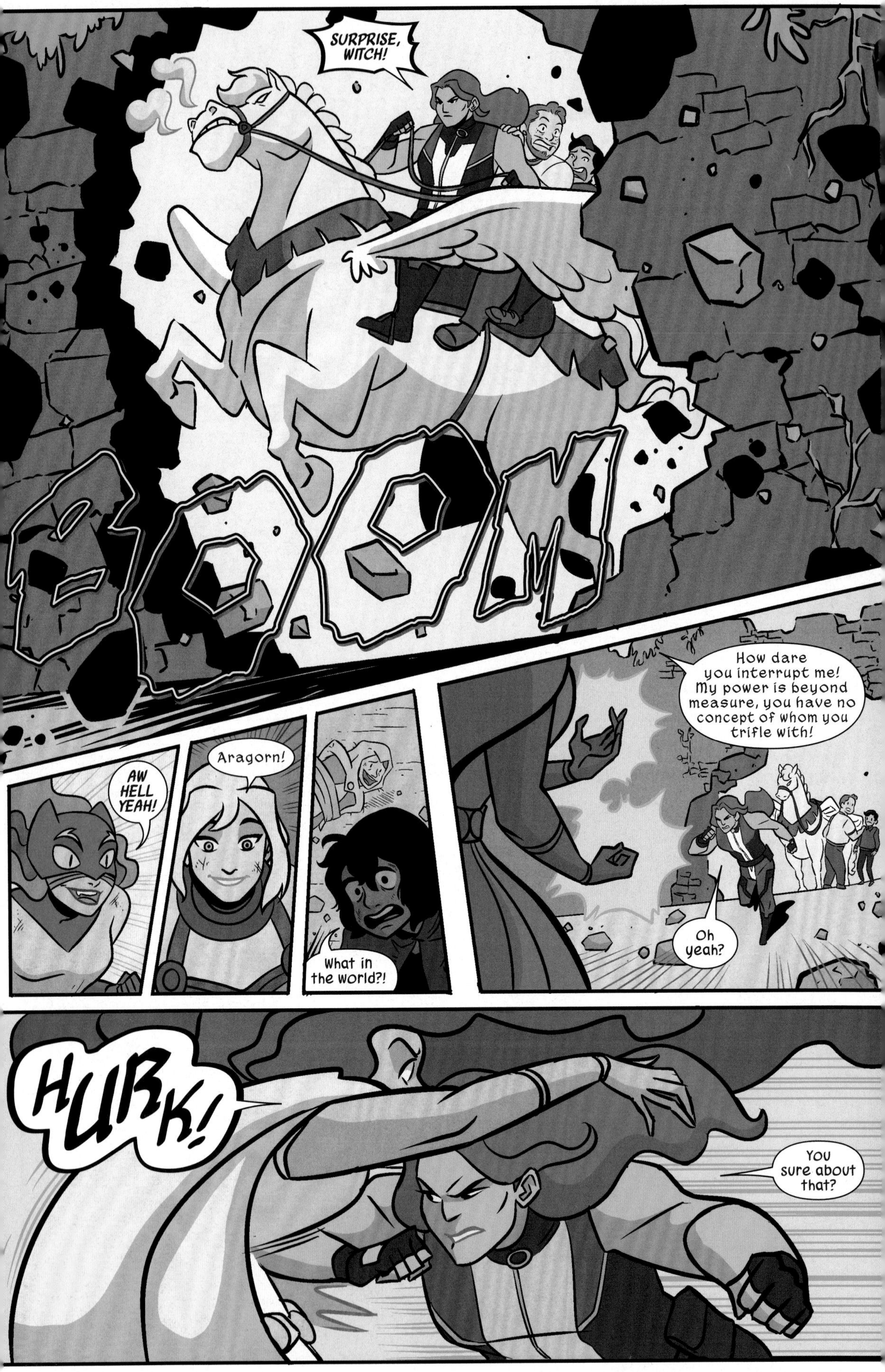
SURPRISE, WITCH!
BOOM
AW HELL YEAH!
Aragorn!
What in the world?!
How dare you interrupt me! My power is beyond measure, you have no concept of whom you trifle with!
Oh yeah?
HURK!
You sure about that?

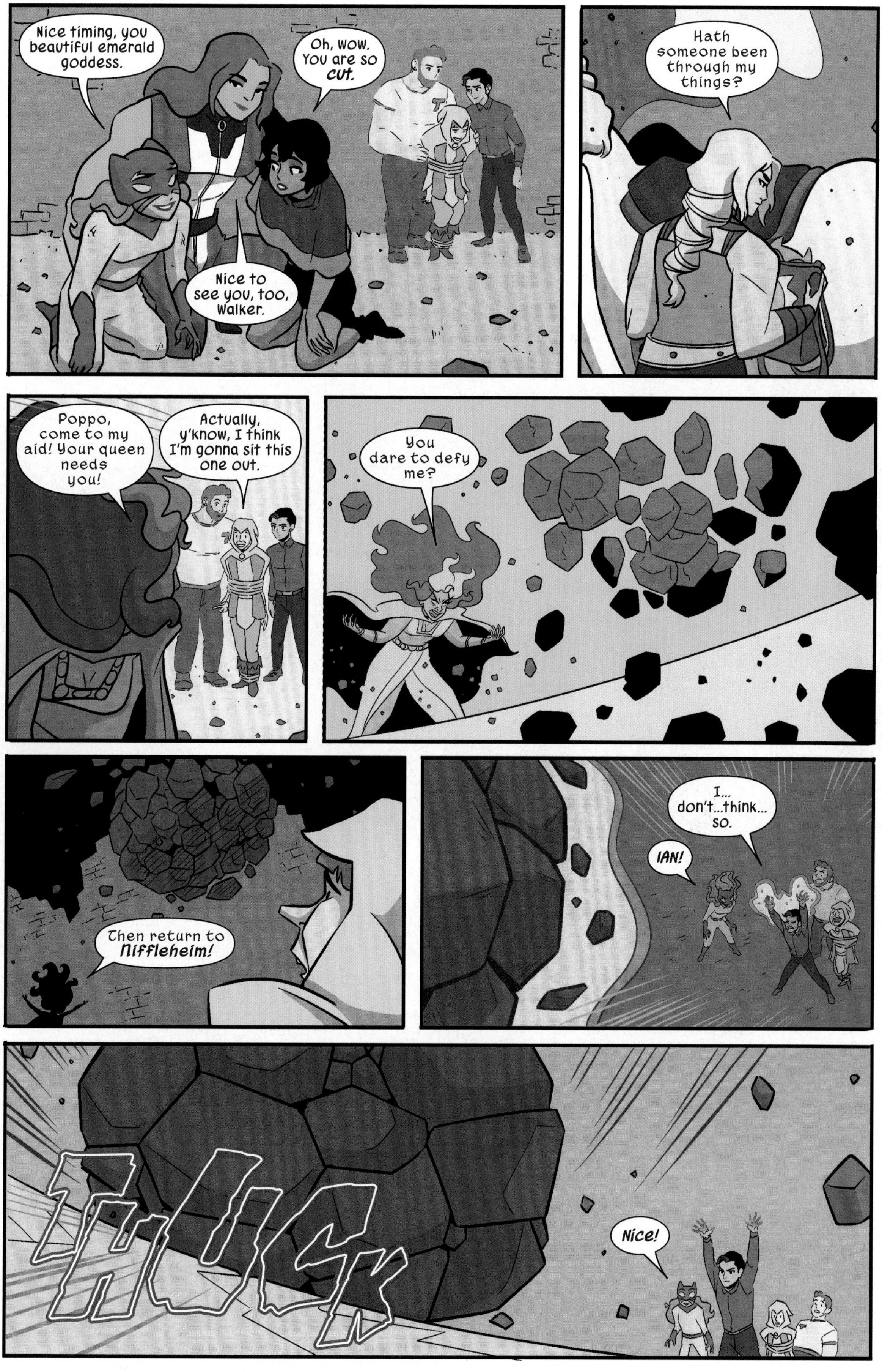

Nice timing, you beautiful emerald goddess.
Oh, wow. You are so cut.
Nice to see you, too, Walker.
Hath someone been through my things?
Poppo, come to my aid! Your queen needs you!
Actually, y'know, I think I'm gonna sit this one out.
You dare to defy me?
Then return to Niffleheim!
I... don't...think... so.
IAN!
THUCK
Nice!

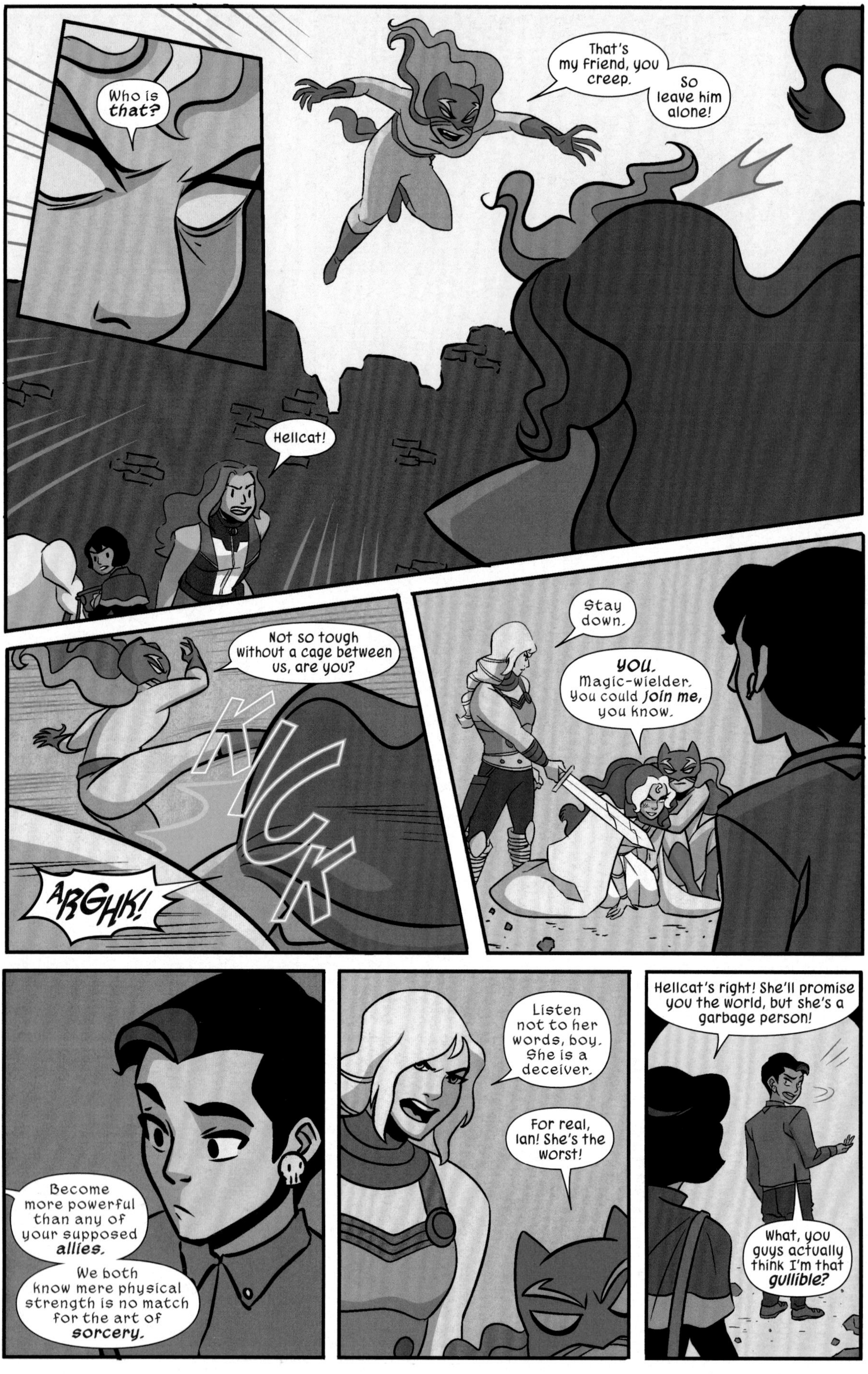
Who is that?
That's my friend, you creep.
So leave him alone!
Hellcat!
Not so tough without a cage between us, are you?
KICK
ARGHK!
Stay down.
YOU. Magic-wielder. You could join me, you know.
Become more powerful than any of your supposed allies.
We both know mere physical strength is no match for the art of sorcery.
Listen not to her words, boy. She is a deceiver.
For real, Ian! She's the worst!
Hellcat's right! She'll promise you the world, but she's a garbage person!
What, you guys actually think I'm that gullible?

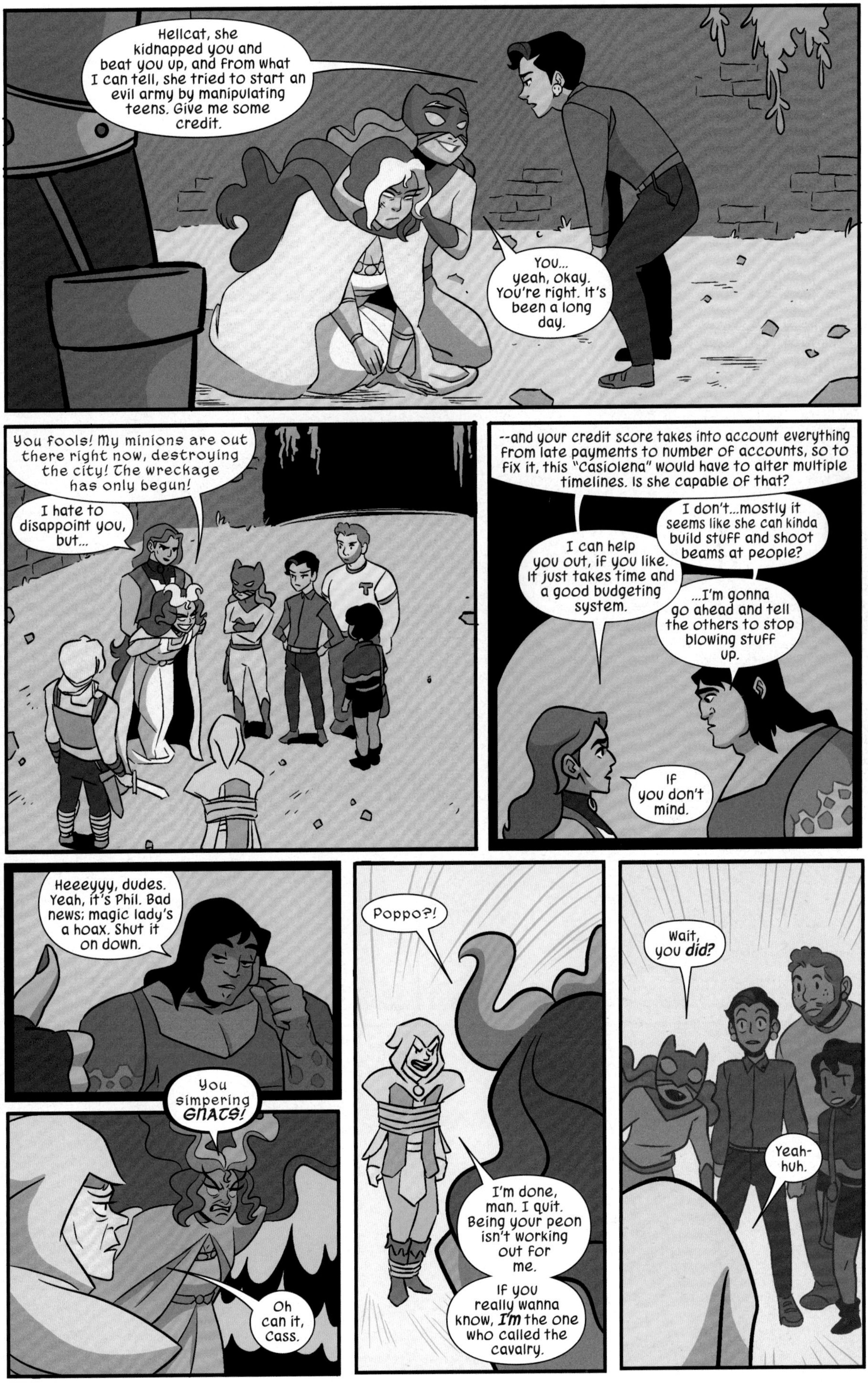
Hellcat, she kidnapped you and beat you up, and from what I can tell, she tried to start an evil army by manipulating teens. Give me some credit.
You... yeah, okay. You're right. It's been a long day.
You fools! My minions are out there right now, destroying the city! The wreckage has only begun!
I hate to disappoint you, but...
--and your credit score takes into account everything from late payments to number of accounts, so to fix it, this "Casiolena" would have to alter multiple timelines. Is she capable of that?
I don't...mostly it seems like she can kinda build stuff and shoot beams at people?
I can help you out, if you like. It just takes time and a good budgeting system.
...I'm gonna go ahead and tell the others to stop blowing stuff up.
If you don't mind.
Heeeyyy, dudes. Yeah, it's Phil. Bad news; magic lady's a hoax. Shut it on down.
You simpering GNATS!
Oh can it, Cass.
Poppo?!
I'm done, man. I quit. Being your peon isn't working out for me.
If you really wanna know, I'm the one who called the cavalry.
Wait, you did?
Yeah-huh.

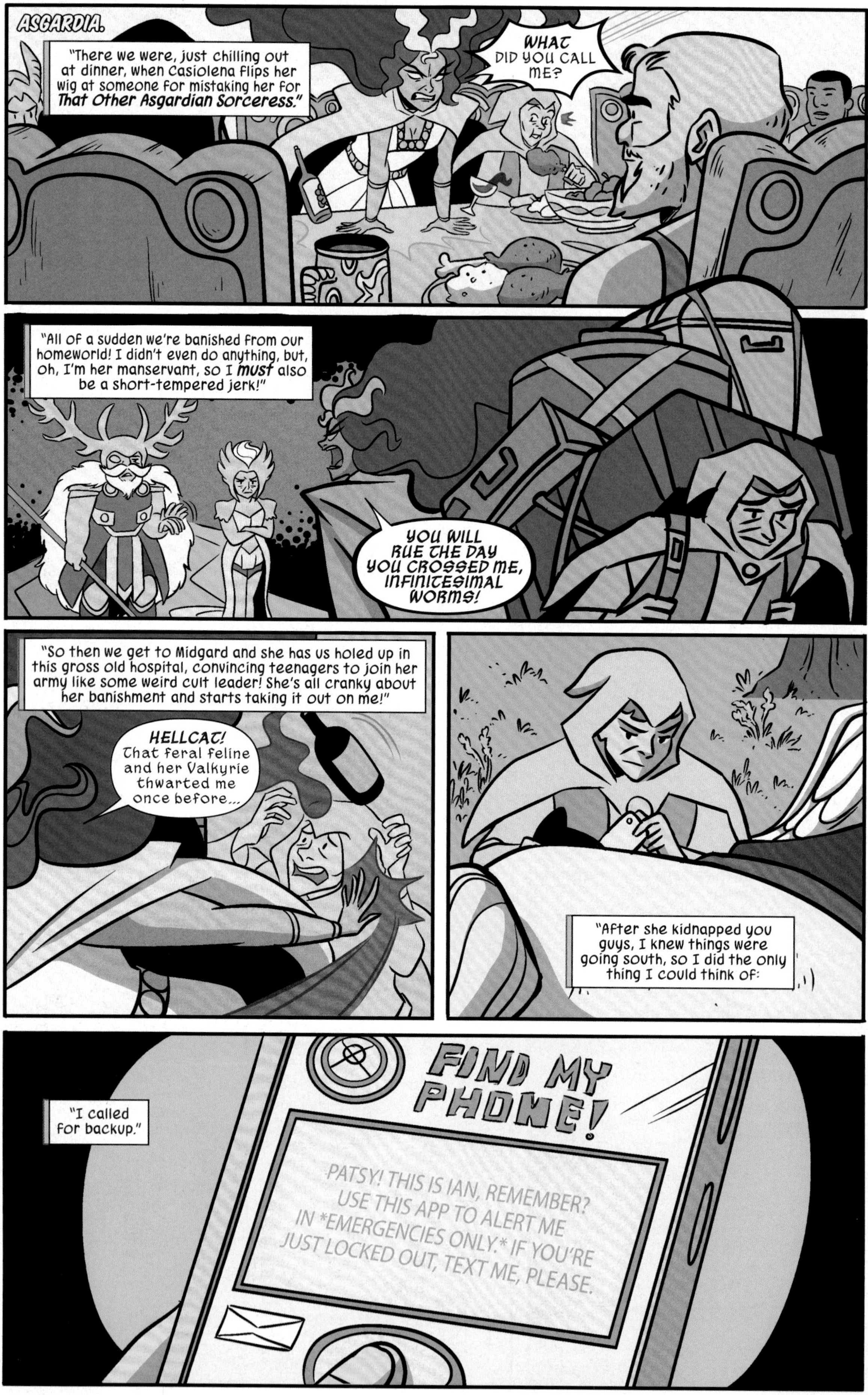

ASGARDIA.
"There we were, just chilling out at dinner, when Casiolena flips her wig at someone for mistaking her for *That Other Asgardian Sorceress.*"
WHAT DID YOU CALL ME?
"All of a sudden we're banished from our homeworld! I didn't even do anything, but, oh, I'm her manservant, so I *must* also be a short-tempered jerk!"
YOU WILL RUE THE DAY YOU CROSSED ME, INFINITESIMAL WORMS!
"So then we get to Midgard and she has us holed up in this gross old hospital, convincing teenagers to join her army like some weird cult leader! She's all cranky about her banishment and starts taking it out on me!"
HELLCAT! That feral feline and her Valkyrie thwarted me once before...
"After she kidnapped you guys, I knew things were going south, so I did the only thing I could think of:
"I called for backup."
FIND MY PHONE!
PATSY! THIS IS IAN, REMEMBER? USE THIS APP TO ALERT ME IN *EMERGENCIES ONLY.* IF YOU'RE JUST LOCKED OUT, TEXT ME, PLEASE.

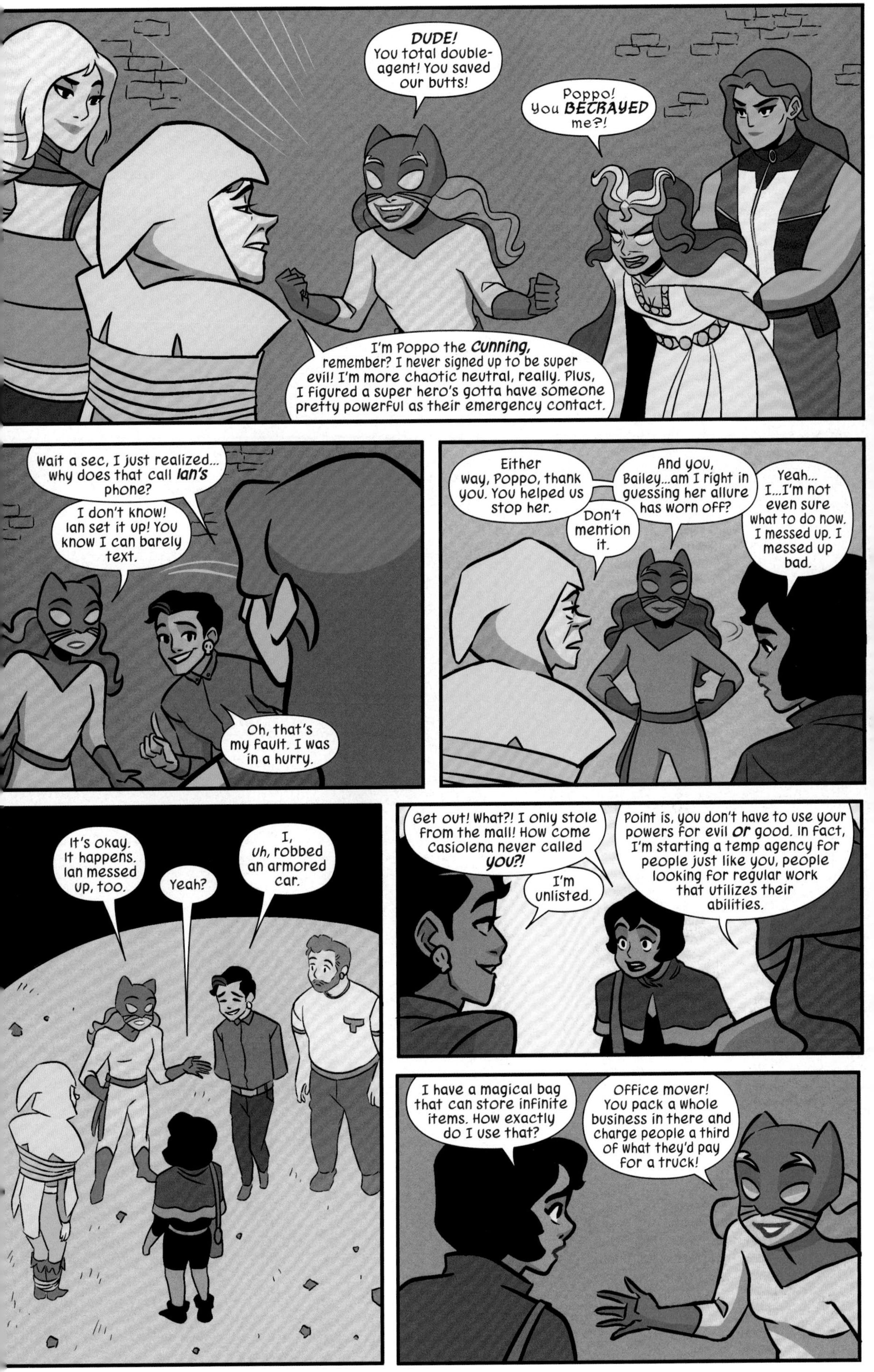
DUDE! You total double-agent! You saved our butts!
Poppo! You BETRAYED me?!
I'm Poppo the Cunning, remember? I never signed up to be super evil! I'm more chaotic neutral, really. Plus, I figured a super hero's gotta have someone pretty powerful as their emergency contact.
Wait a sec, I just realized... why does that call Ian's phone?
I don't know! Ian set it up! You know I can barely text.
Oh, that's my fault. I was in a hurry.
Either way, Poppo, thank you. You helped us stop her.
Don't mention it.
And you, Bailey...am I right in guessing her allure has worn off?
Yeah... I...I'm not even sure what to do now. I messed up. I messed up bad.
It's okay. It happens. Ian messed up, too.
Yeah?
I, uh, robbed an armored car.
Get out! What?! I only stole from the mall! How come Casiolena never called YOU?!
I'm unlisted.
Point is, you don't have to use your powers for evil OR good. In fact, I'm starting a temp agency for people just like you, people looking for regular work that utilizes their abilities.
I have a magical bag that can store infinite items. How exactly do I use that?
Office mover! You pack a whole business in there and charge people a third of what they'd pay for a truck!

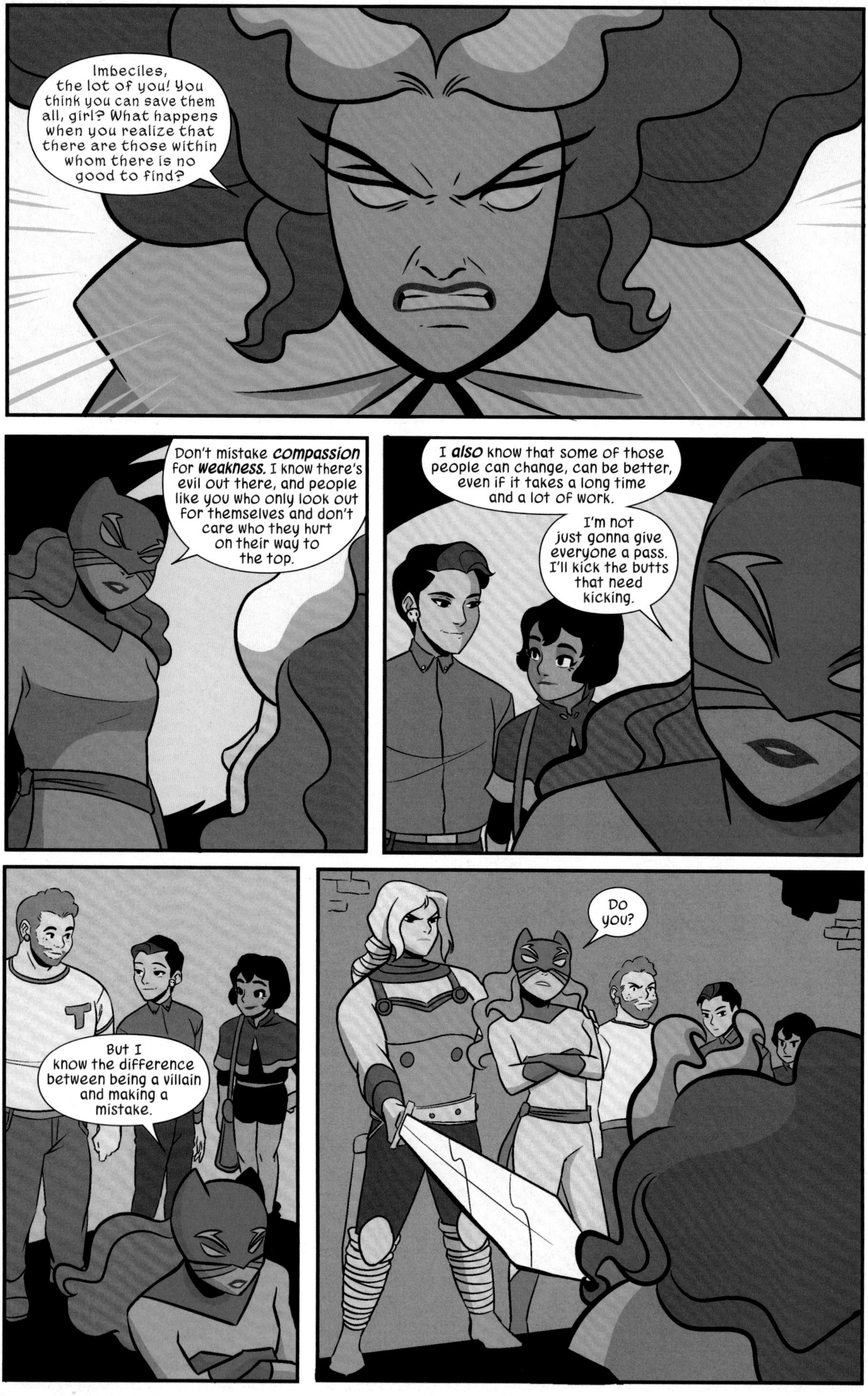
Imbeciles, the lot of you! You think you can save them all, girl? What happens when you realize that there are those within whom there is no good to find?
Don't mistake *compassion* for *weakness.* I know there's evil out there, and people like you who only look out for themselves and don't care who they hurt on their way to the top.
I *also* know that some of those people can change, can be better, even if it takes a long time and a lot of work.
I'm not just gonna give everyone a pass. I'll kick the butts that need kicking.
But I know the difference between being a villain and making a mistake.
Do you?

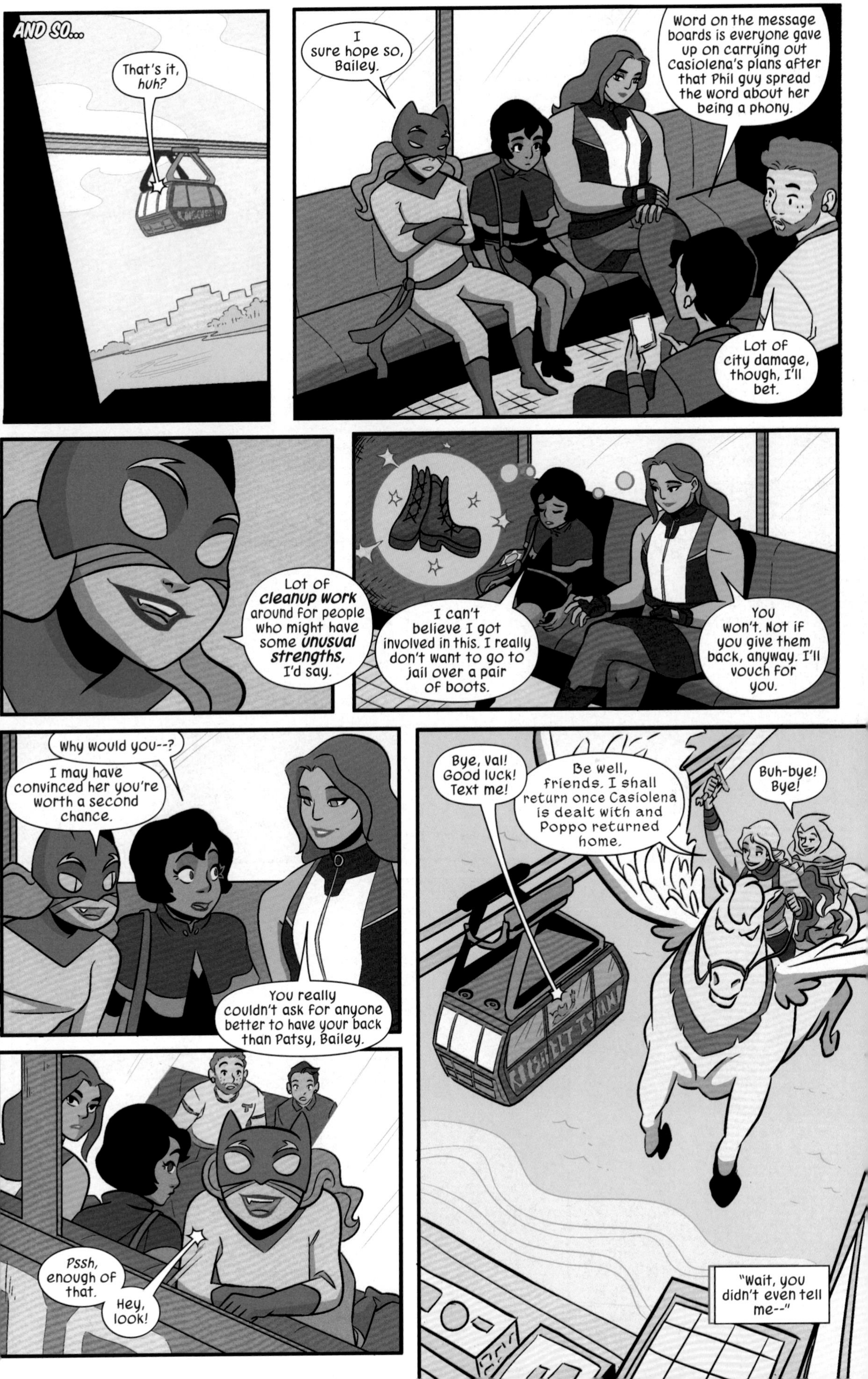
AND SO...
That's it, huh?
I sure hope so, Bailey.
Word on the message boards is everyone gave up on carrying out Casiolena's plans after that Phil guy spread the word about her being a phony.
Lot of city damage, though, I'll bet.
Lot of cleanup work around for people who might have some unusual strengths, I'd say.
I can't believe I got involved in this. I really don't want to go to jail over a pair of boots.
You won't. Not if you give them back, anyway. I'll vouch for you.
Why would you--?
I may have convinced her you're worth a second chance.
You really couldn't ask for anyone better to have your back than Patsy, Bailey.
Pssh, enough of that.
Hey, look!
Bye, Val! Good luck! Text me!
Be well, friends. I shall return once Casiolena is dealt with and Poppo returned home.
Buh-bye! Bye!
"Wait, you didn't even tell me--"

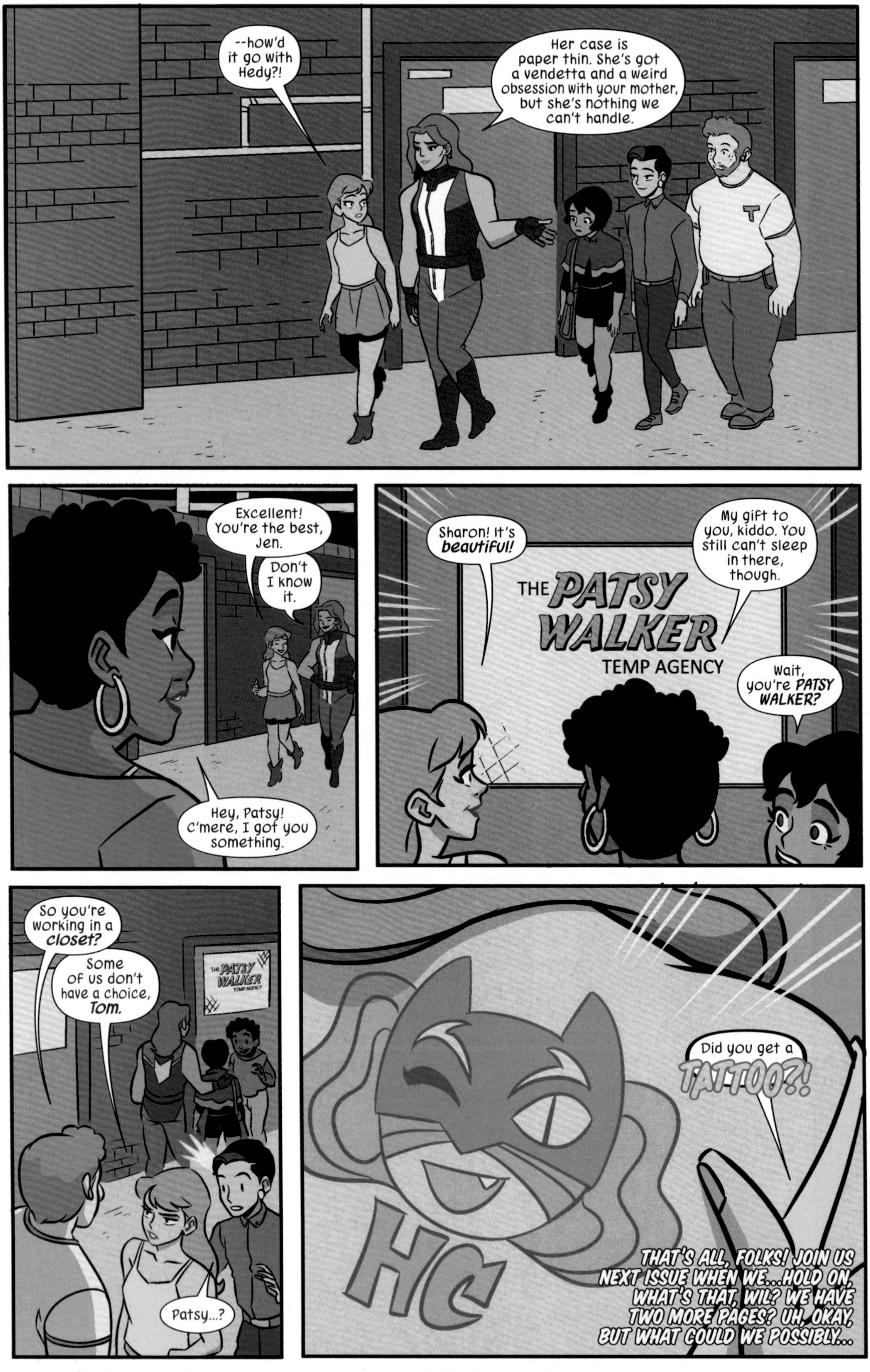
--how'd it go with Hedy?!
Her case is paper thin. She's got a vendetta and a weird obsession with your mother, but she's nothing we can't handle.
T
Excellent! You're the best, Jen.
Don't I know it.
Hey, Patsy! C'mere, I got you something.
Sharon! It's *beautiful!*
THE PATSY WALKER TEMP AGENCY
My gift to you, kiddo. You still can't sleep in there, though.
Wait, you're PATSY WALKER?
So you're working in a *closet?*
Some of us don't have a choice, *Tom.*
THE PATSY WALKER TEMP AGENCY
Patsy...?
Did you get a TATTOO?!
HC
THAT'S ALL, FOLKS! JOIN US NEXT ISSUE WHEN WE...HOLD ON, WHAT'S THAT, WIL? WE HAVE TWO MORE PAGES? UH, OKAY, BUT WHAT COULD WE POSSIBLY...

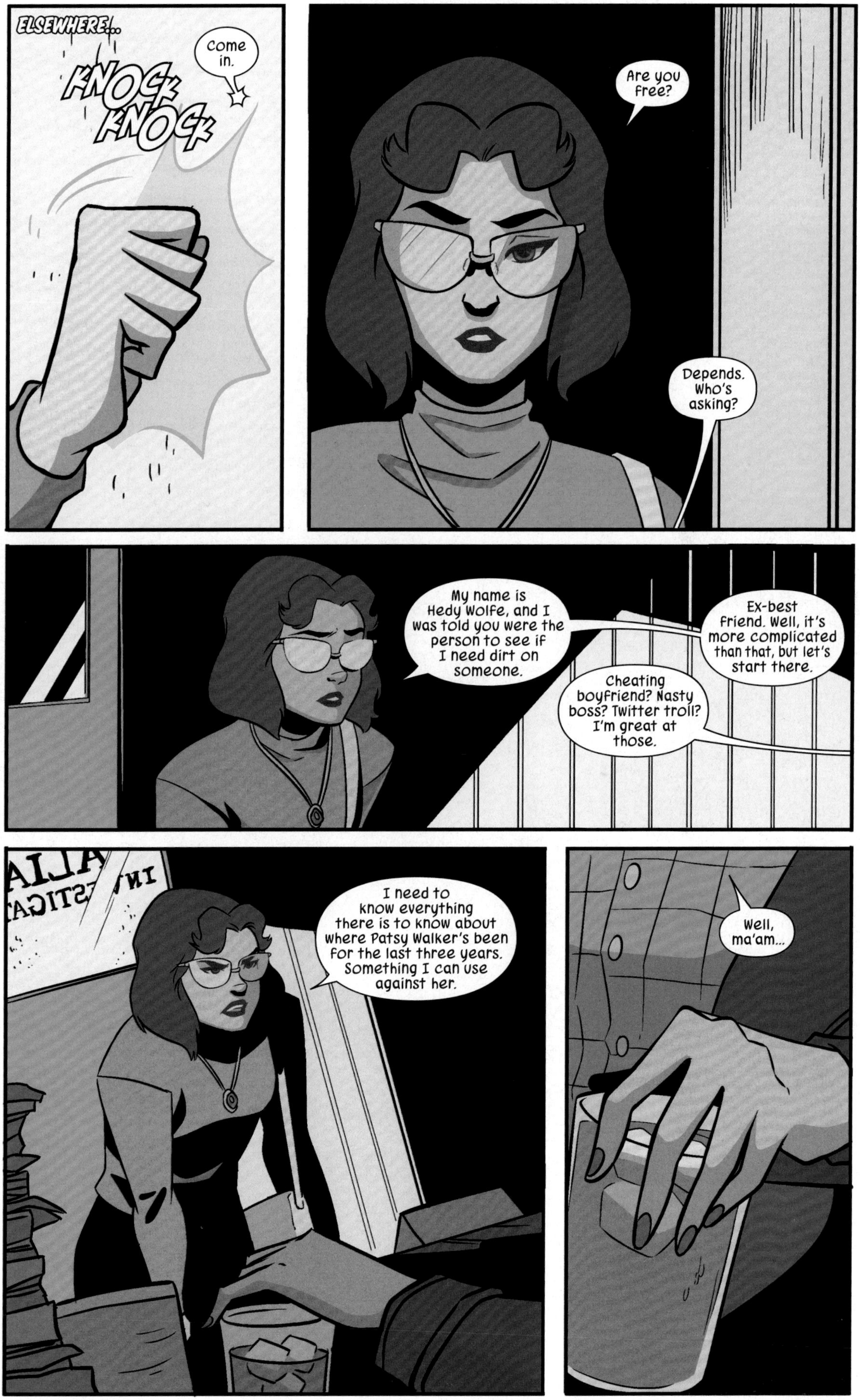
ELSEWHERE...
KNOCK KNOCK
Come in.
Are you free?
Depends. Who's asking?
My name is Hedy Wolfe, and I was told you were the person to see if I need dirt on someone.
Cheating boyfriend? Nasty boss? Twitter troll? I'm great at those.
Ex-best friend. Well, it's more complicated than that, but let's start there.
I need to know everything there is to know about where Patsy Walker's been for the last three years. Something I can use against her.
Well, ma'am...

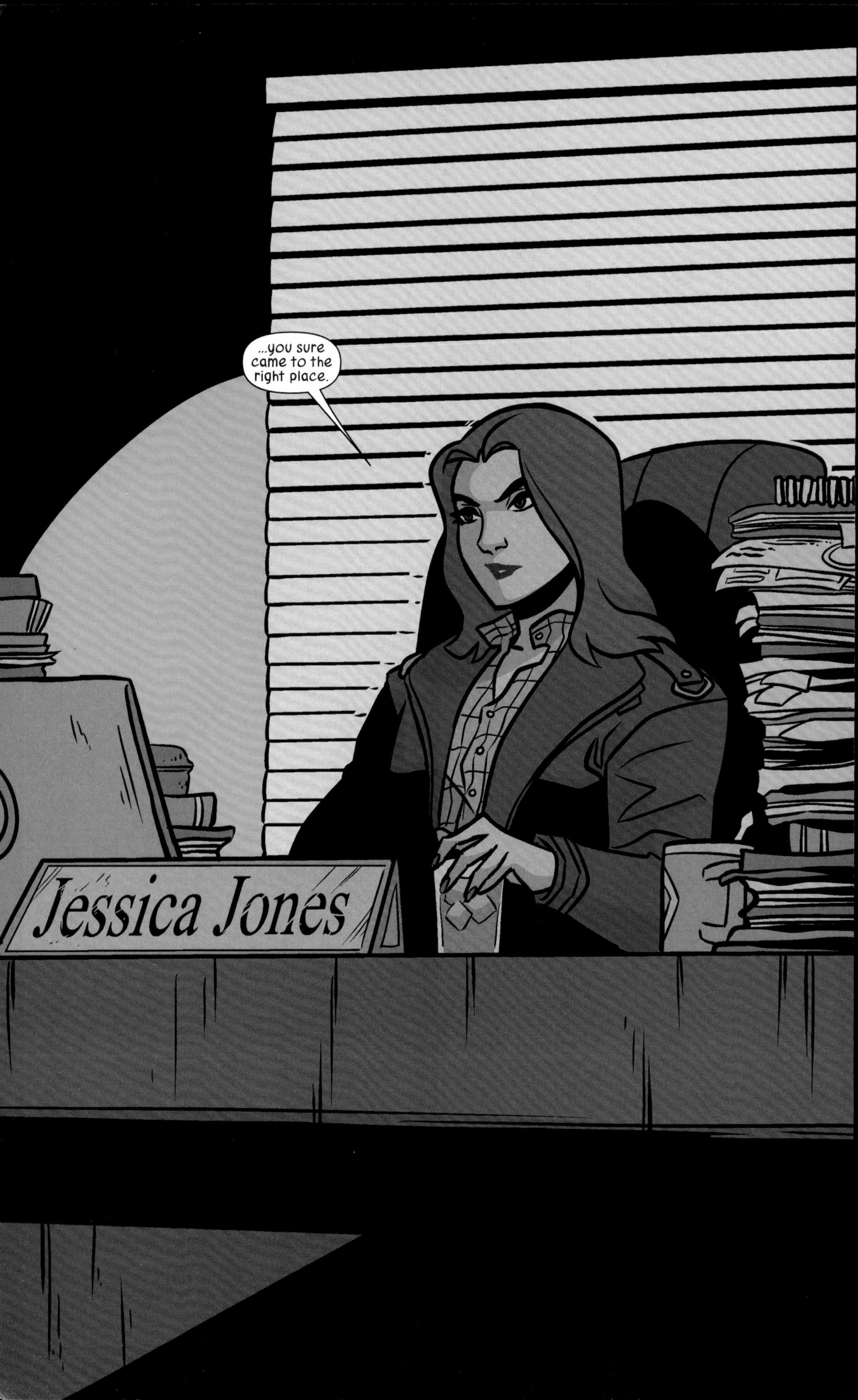
...you sure came to the right place.
Jessica Jones

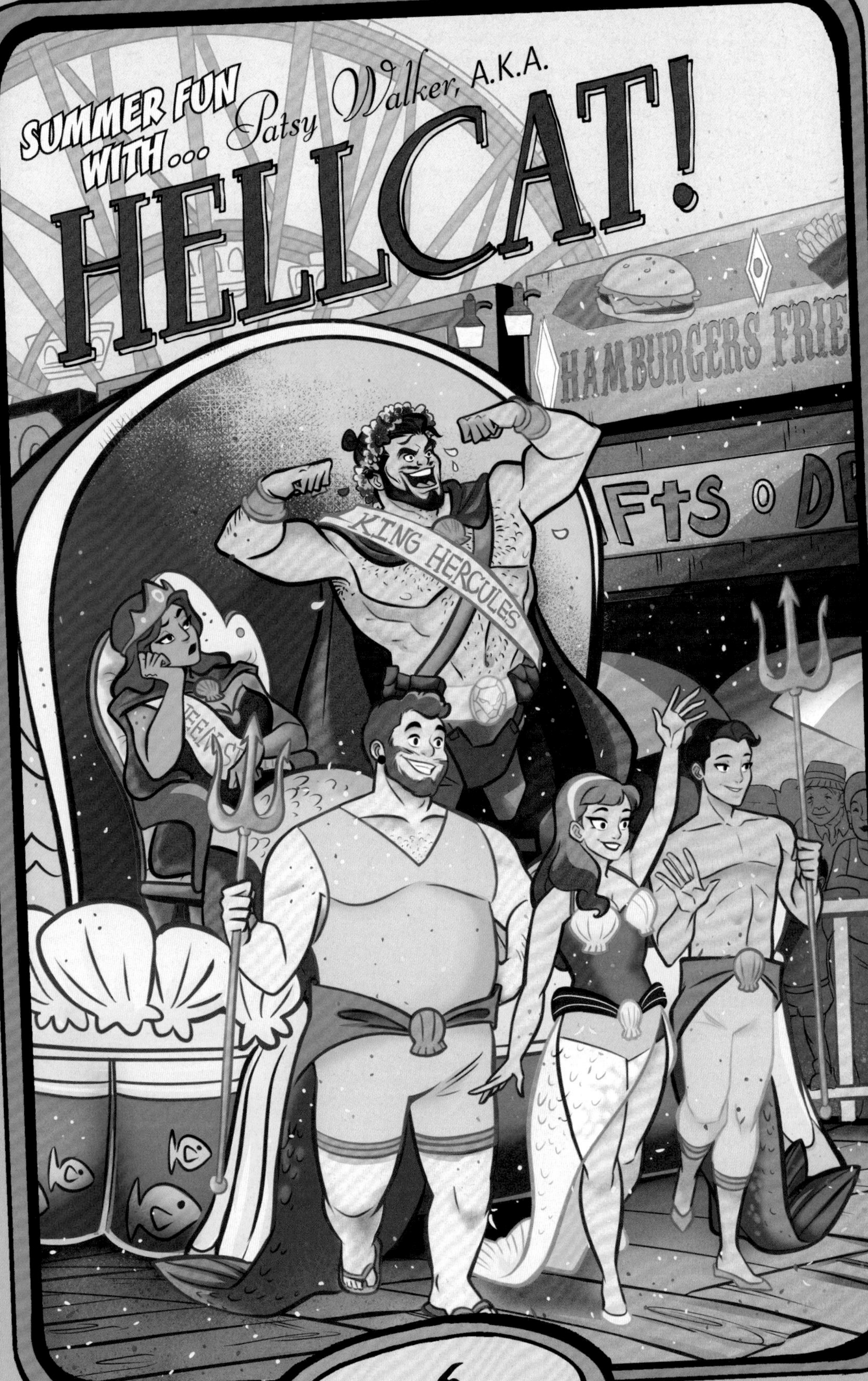
SUMMER FUN WITH... Patsy Walker, A.K.A.
HELLCAT!
HAMBURGERS
KING HERCULES

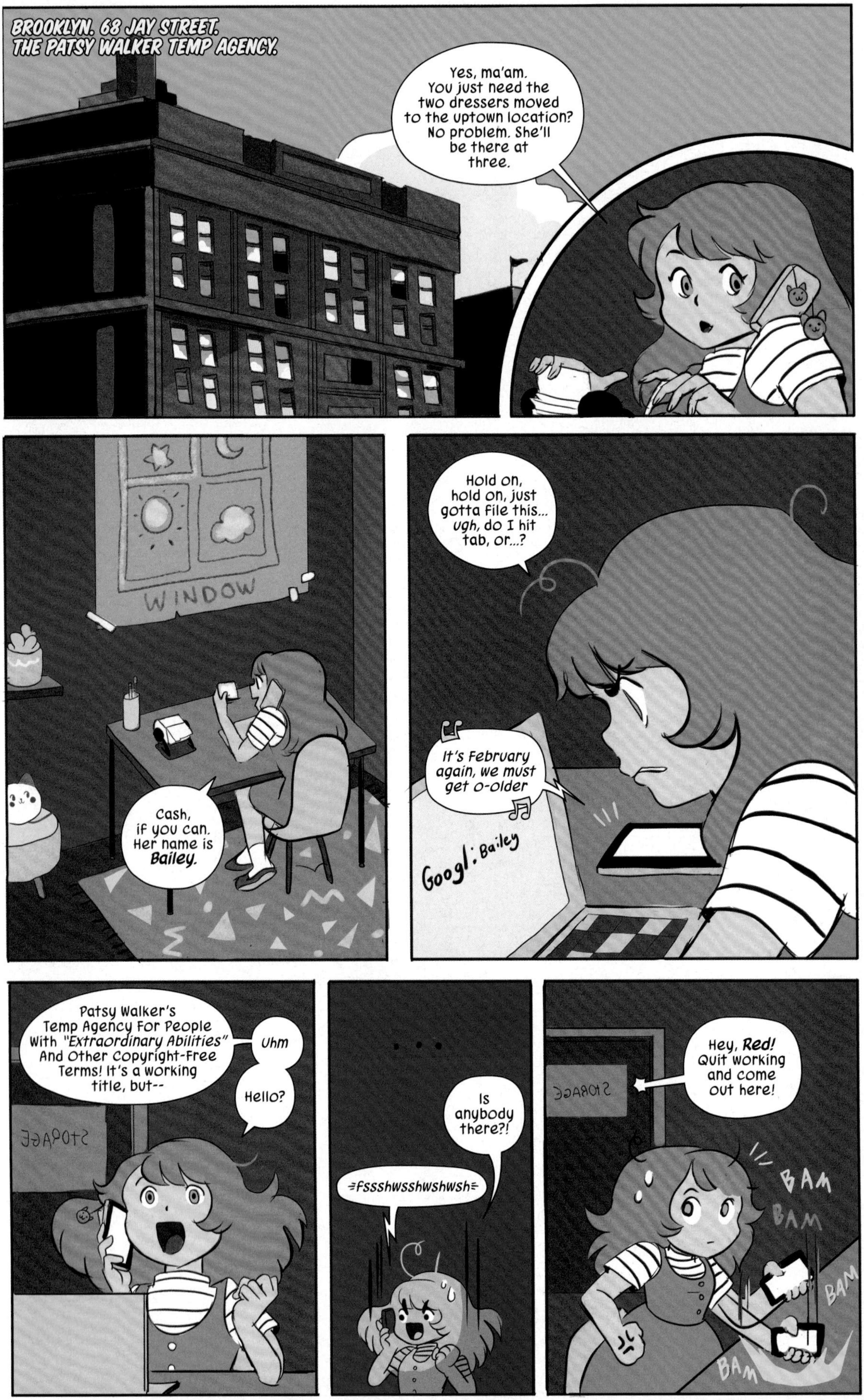
BROOKLYN. 68 JAY STREET.
THE PATSY WALKER TEMP AGENCY.
Yes, ma'am. You just need the two dressers moved to the uptown location? No problem. She'll be there at three.
WINDOW
Cash, if you can. Her name is *Bailey.*
Hold on, hold on, just gotta file this... *ugh,* do I hit tab, or...?
It's February again, we must get o-older
Googl: Bailey
Patsy Walker's Temp Agency For People With *"Extraordinary Abilities"* And Other Copyright-Free Terms! It's a working title, but--
Uhm
Hello?
STORAGE
...
Is anybody there?!
=fssshwsshwshwsh=
Hey, *Red!* Quit working and come out here!
STORAGE
BAM
BAM
BAM
BAM

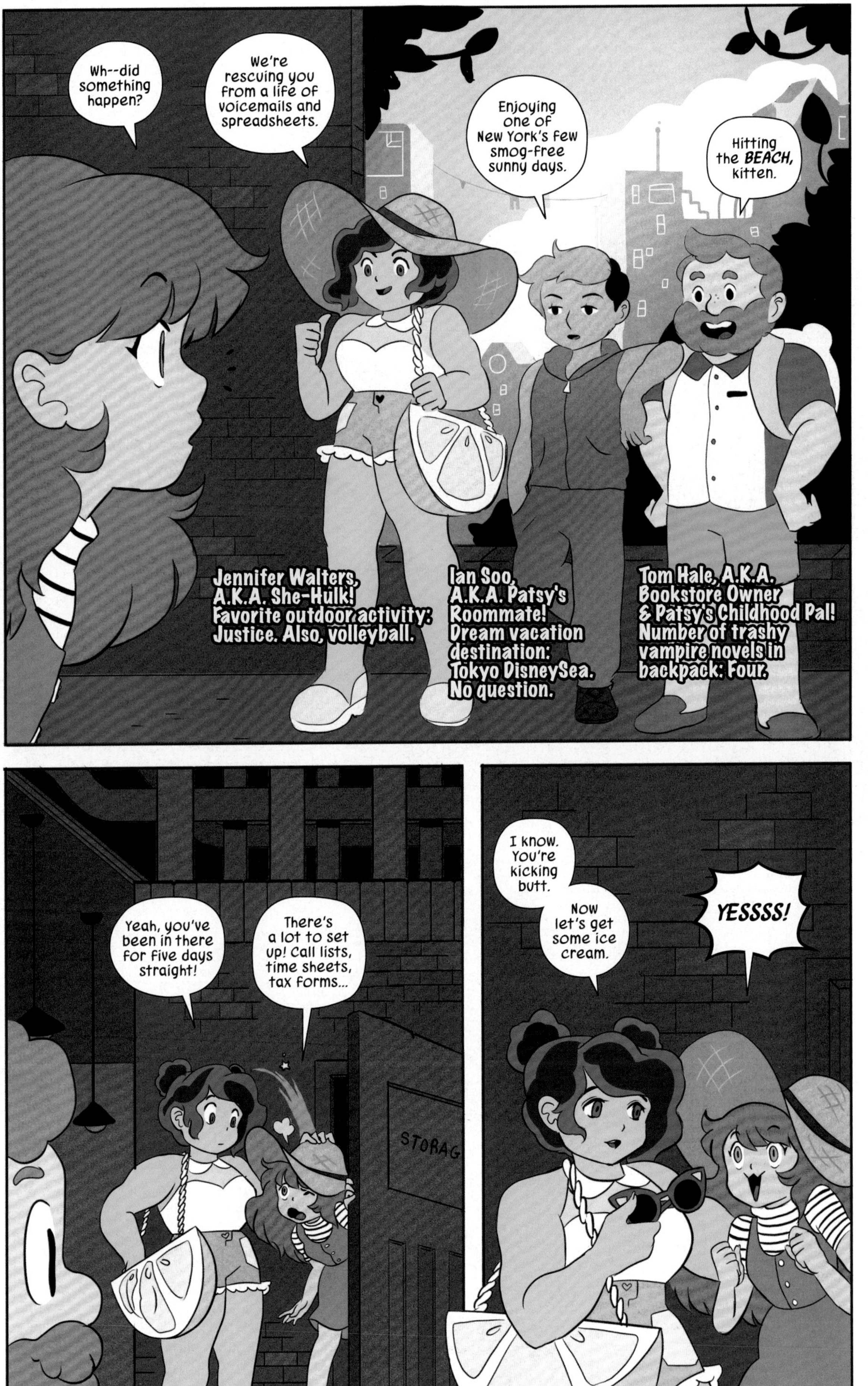
Wh--did something happen?
We're rescuing you from a life of voicemails and spreadsheets.
Enjoying one of New York's few smog-free sunny days.
Hitting the BEACH, kitten.
Jennifer Walters, A.K.A. She-Hulk! Favorite outdoor activity: Justice. Also, volleyball.
Ian Soo, A.K.A. Patsy's Roommate! Dream vacation destination: Tokyo DisneySea. No question.
Tom Hale, A.K.A. Bookstore Owner & Patsy's Childhood Pal! Number of trashy vampire novels in backpack: Four.
Yeah, you've been in there for five days straight!
There's a lot to set up! Call lists, time sheets, tax forms...
STORAG
I know. You're kicking butt.
Now let's get some ice cream.
YESSSS!

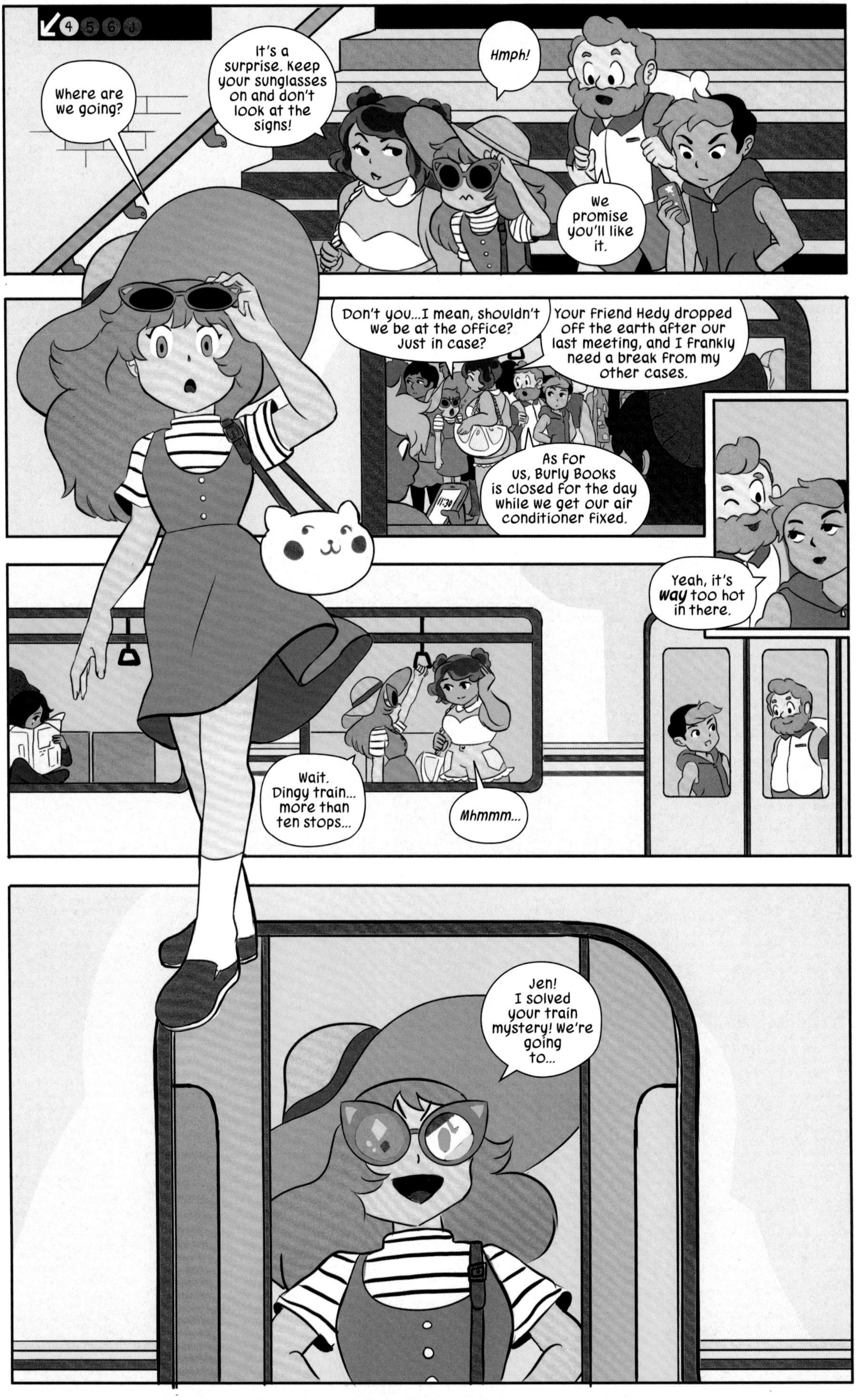

Where are we going?
It's a surprise. Keep your sunglasses on and don't look at the signs!
Hmph!
We promise you'll like it.
Don't you...I mean, shouldn't we be at the office? Just in case?
Your friend Hedy dropped off the earth after our last meeting, and I frankly need a break from my other cases.
As for us, Burly Books is closed for the day while we get our air conditioner fixed.
Yeah, it's **way** too hot in there.
Wait. Dingy train... more than ten stops...
Mhmmm...
Jen! I solved your train mystery! We're going to...

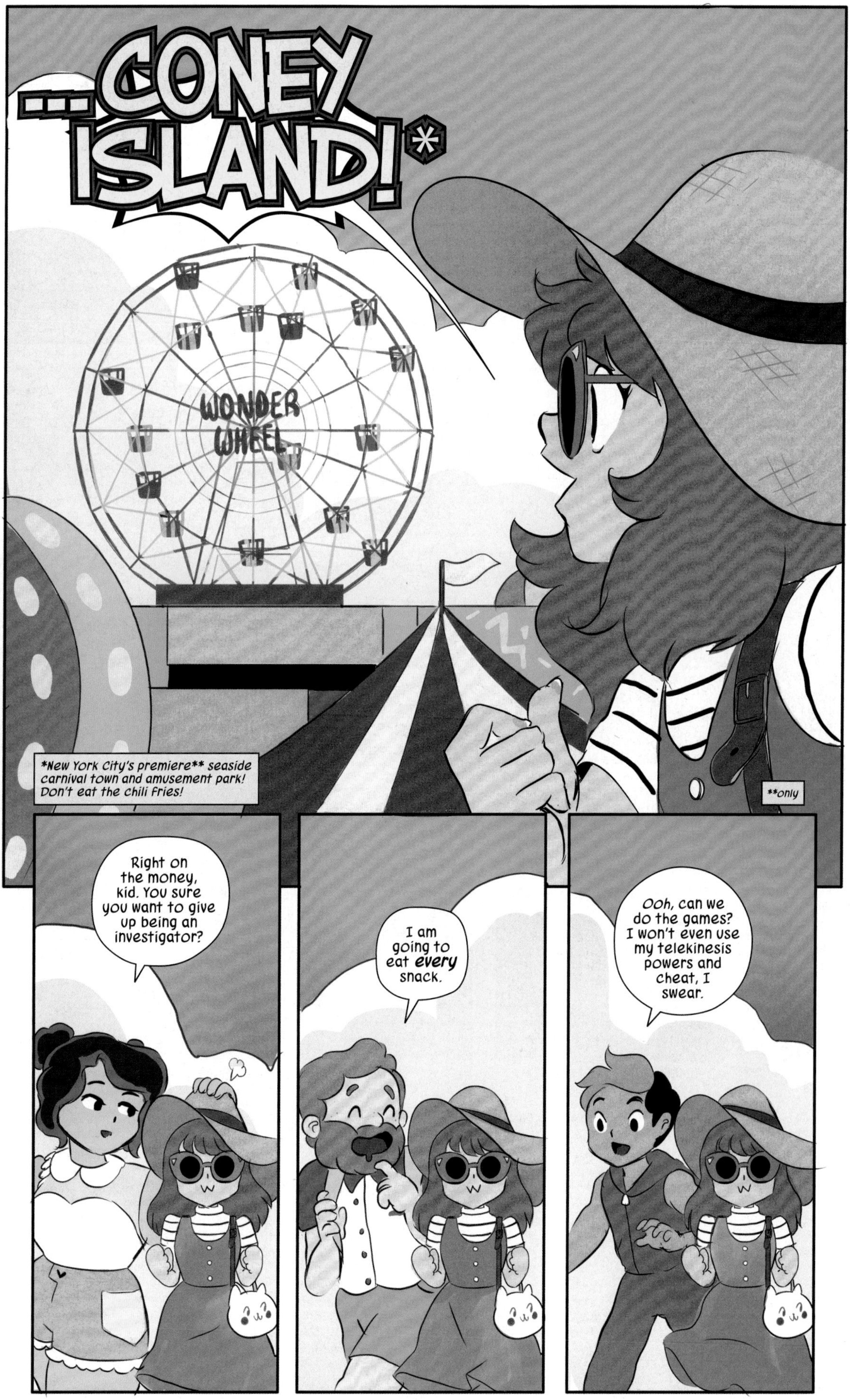
...CONEY ISLAND!*
WONDER WHEEL
*New York City's premiere** seaside carnival town and amusement park! Don't eat the chili fries!
**only
Right on the money, kid. You sure you want to give up being an investigator?
I am going to eat *every* snack.
Ooh, can we do the games? I won't even use my telekinesis powers and cheat, I swear.

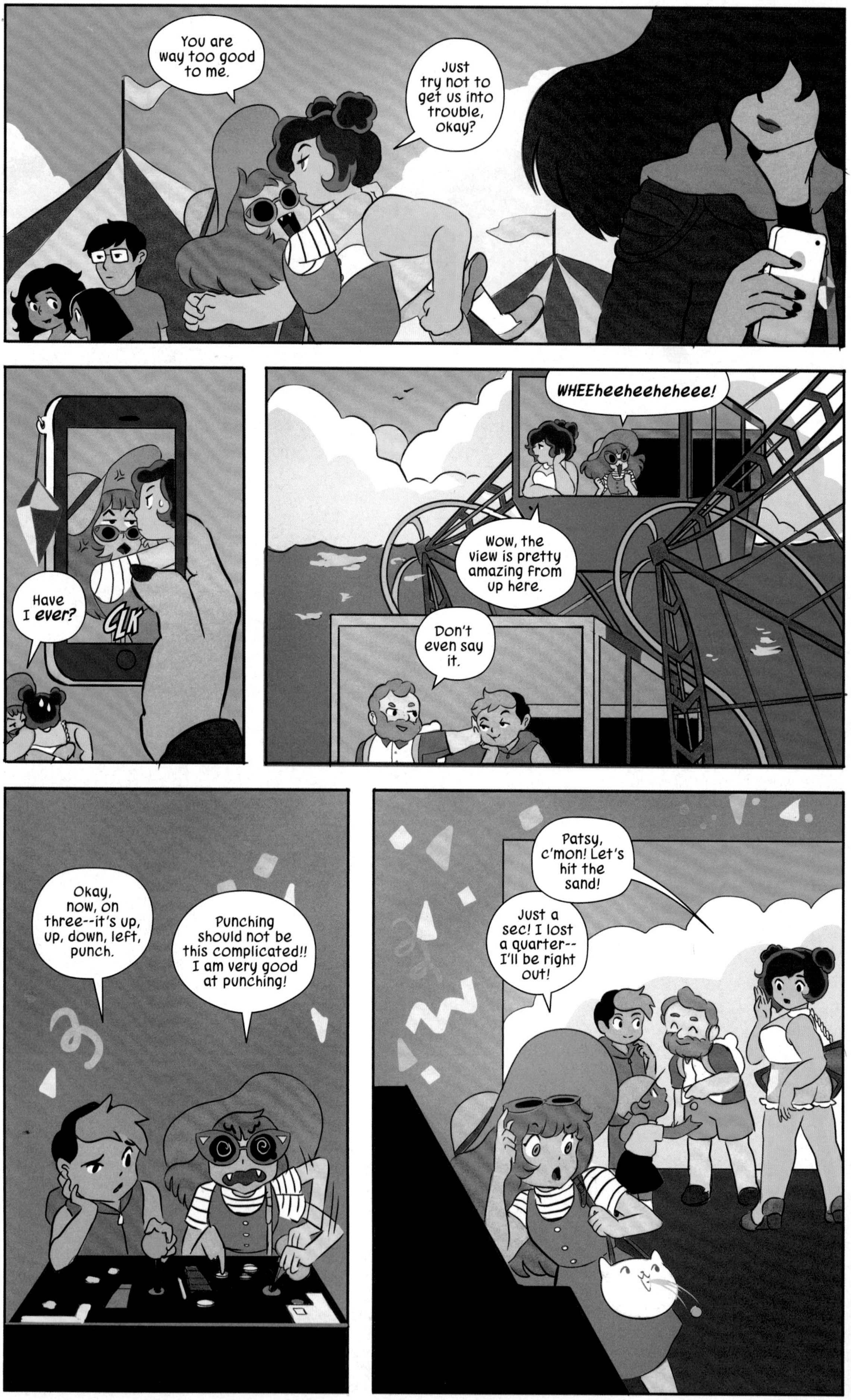
You are way too good to me.
Just try not to get us into trouble, okay?
Have I ever?
CLK
WHEEheeheeheheee!
Wow, the view is pretty amazing from up here.
Don't even say it.
Okay, now, on three--it's up, up, down, left, punch.
Punching should not be this complicated!! I am very good at punching!
Patsy, c'mon! Let's hit the sand!
Just a sec! I lost a quarter-- I'll be right out!

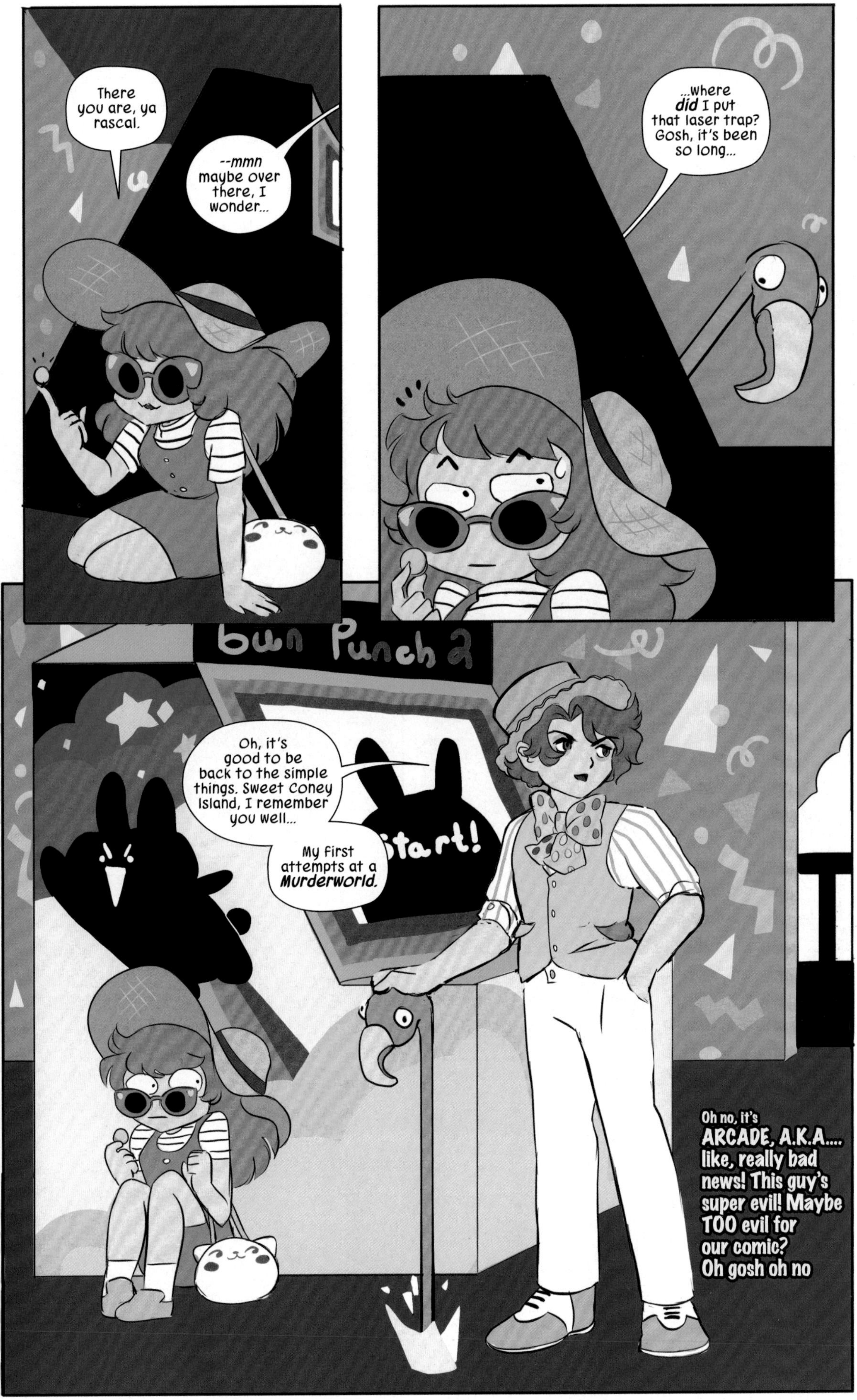
There you are, ya rascal.
--mmn maybe over there, I wonder...
...where *did* I put that laser trap? Gosh, it's been so long...
bun Punch 2
Start!
Oh, it's good to be back to the simple things. Sweet Coney Island, I remember you well...
My first attempts at a *Murderworld.*
Oh no, it's **ARCADE, A.K.A....** like, really bad news! This guy's super evil! Maybe TOO evil for our comic? Oh gosh oh no

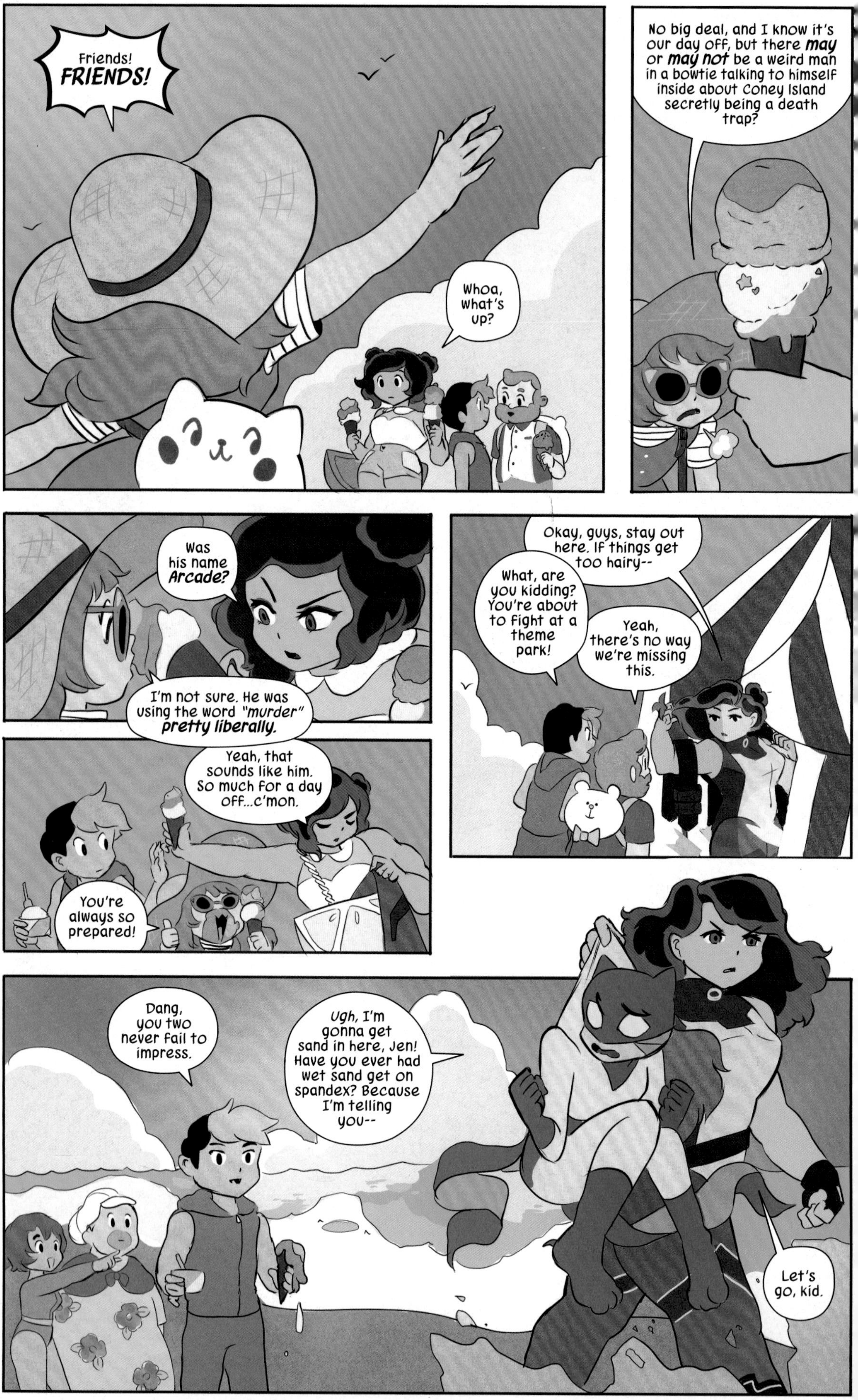
Friends! FRIENDS!
Whoa, what's up?
No big deal, and I know it's our day off, but there may or may not be a weird man in a bowtie talking to himself inside about Coney Island secretly being a death trap?
Was his name Arcade?
I'm not sure. He was using the word "murder" pretty liberally.
Yeah, that sounds like him. So much for a day off...c'mon.
You're always so prepared!
Okay, guys, stay out here. If things get too hairy--
What, are you kidding? You're about to fight at a theme park!
Yeah, there's no way we're missing this.
Dang, you two never fail to impress.
Ugh, I'm gonna get sand in here, Jen! Have you ever had wet sand get on spandex? Because I'm telling you--
Let's go, kid.

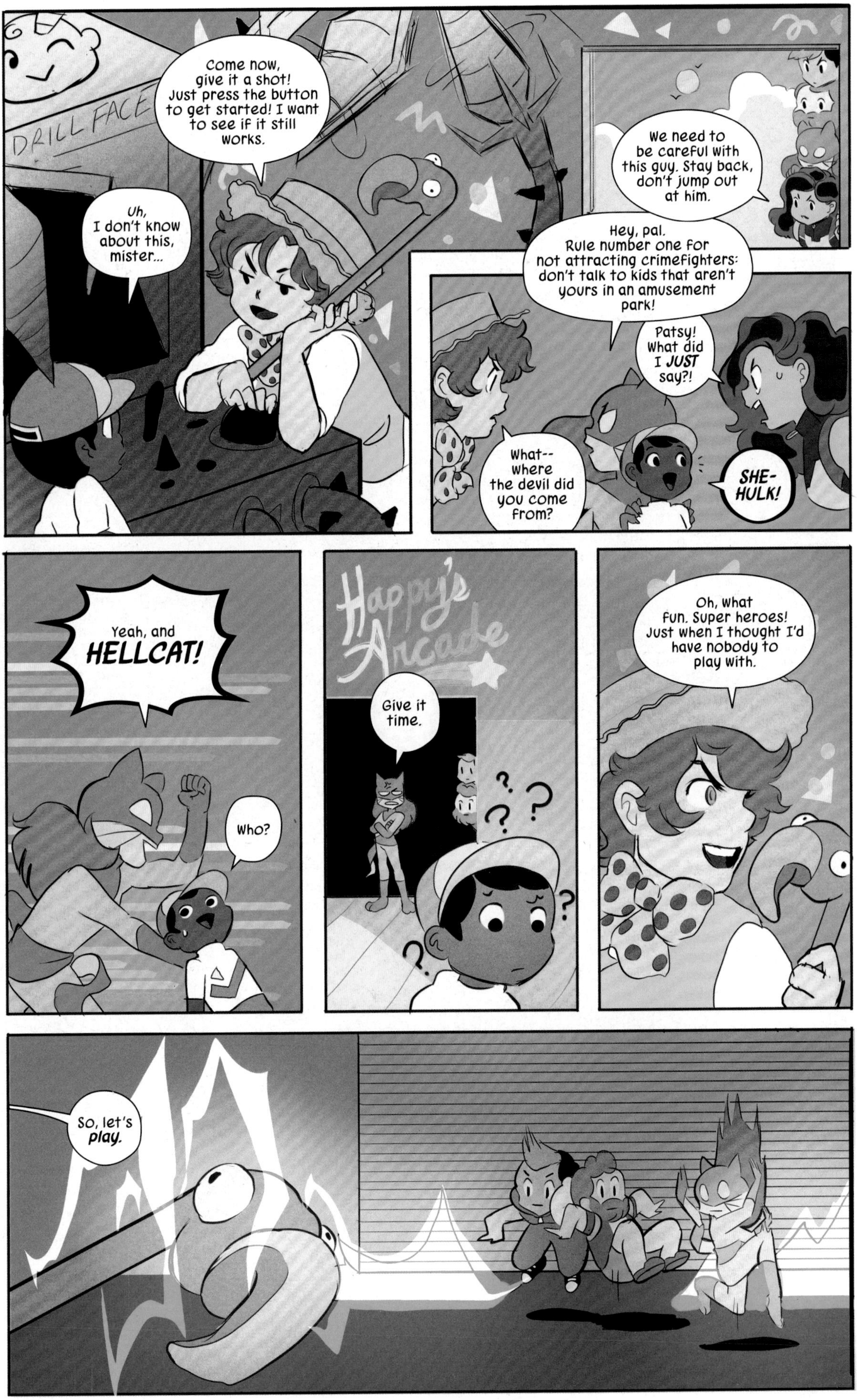
Come now, give it a shot! Just press the button to get started! I want to see if it still works.
DRILL FACE
Uh, I don't know about this, mister...
We need to be careful with this guy. Stay back, don't jump out at him.
Hey, pal. Rule number one for not attracting crimefighters: don't talk to kids that aren't yours in an amusement park!
Patsy! What did I JUST say?!
What-- where the devil did you come from?
SHE-HULK!
Yeah, and HELLCAT!
Who?
Happy's Arcade
Give it time.
Oh, what fun. Super heroes! Just when I thought I'd have nobody to play with.
So, let's play.

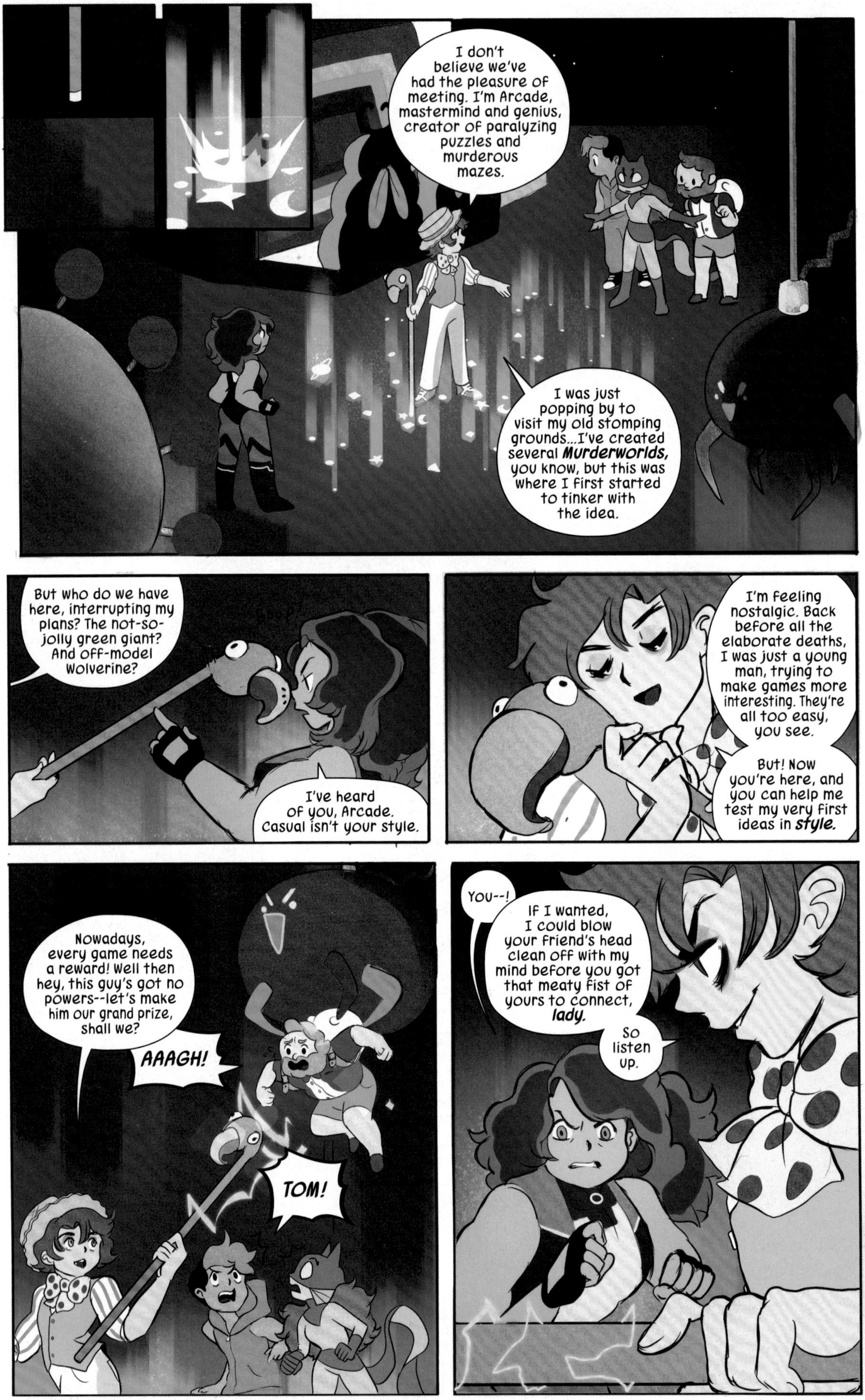
I don't believe we've had the pleasure of meeting. I'm Arcade, mastermind and genius, creator of paralyzing puzzles and murderous mazes.
I was just popping by to visit my old stomping grounds...I've created several **Murderworlds,** you know, but this was where I first started to tinker with the idea.
But who do we have here, interrupting my plans? The not-so-jolly green giant? And off-model Wolverine?
I've heard of you, Arcade. Casual isn't your style.
I'm feeling nostalgic. Back before all the elaborate deaths, I was just a young man, trying to make games more interesting. They're all too easy, you see.
But! Now you're here, and you can help me test my very first ideas in **style.**
Nowadays, every game needs a reward! Well then hey, this guy's got no powers--let's make him our grand prize, shall we?
AAAGH!
TOM!
YOU--!
If I wanted, I could blow your friend's head clean off with my mind before you got that meaty fist of yours to connect, **lady.**
So listen up.

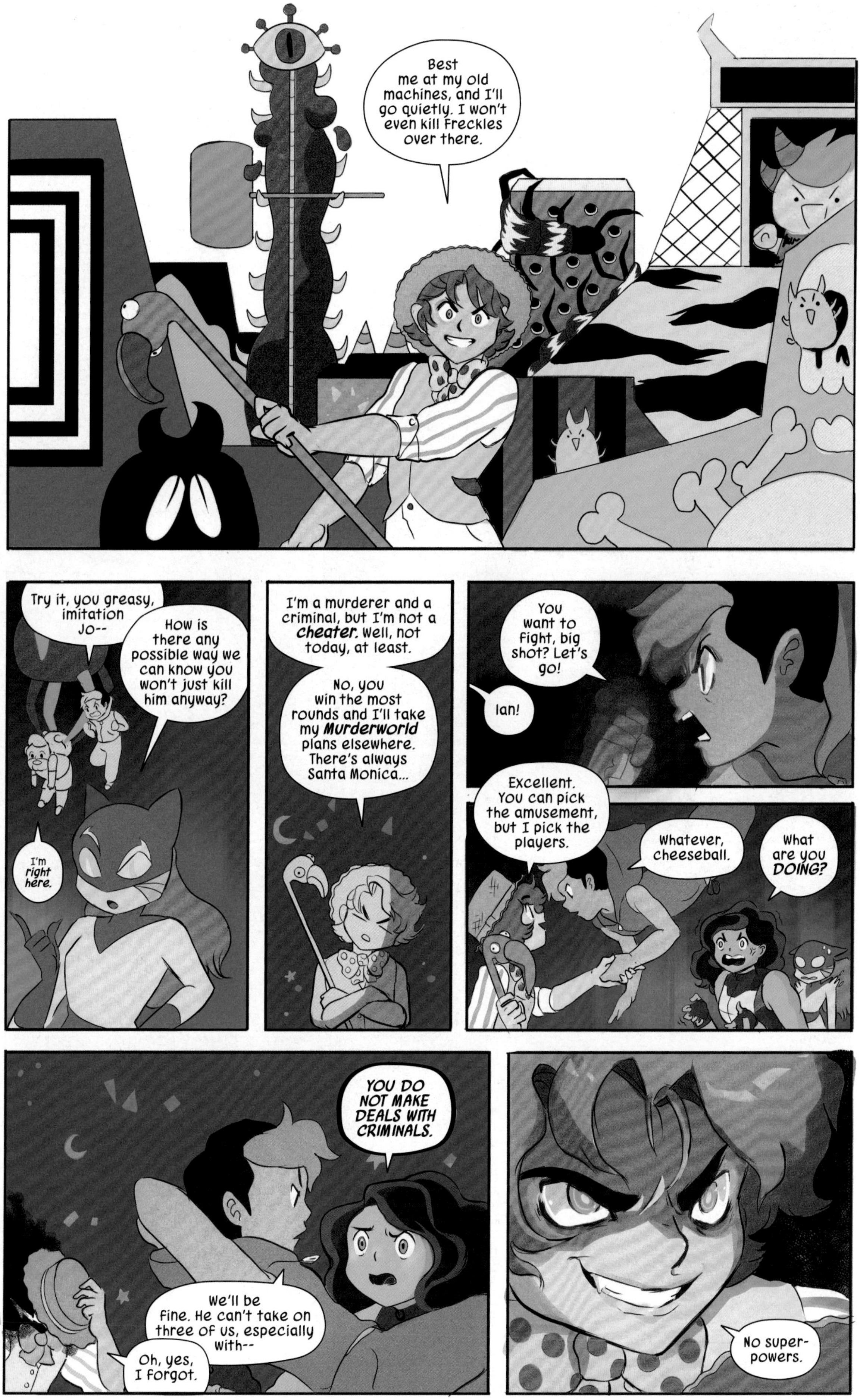
Best me at my old machines, and I'll go quietly. I won't even kill Freckles over there.
Try it, you greasy, imitation Jo--
How is there any possible way we can know you won't just kill him anyway?
I'm right here.
I'm a murderer and a criminal, but I'm not a cheater. Well, not today, at least.
No, you win the most rounds and I'll take my Murderworld plans elsewhere. There's always Santa Monica...
You want to fight, big shot? Let's go!
Ian!
Excellent. You can pick the amusement, but I pick the players.
Whatever, cheeseball.
What are you DOING?
YOU DO NOT MAKE DEALS WITH CRIMINALS.
We'll be fine. He can't take on three of us, especially with--
Oh, yes, I forgot.
No superpowers.

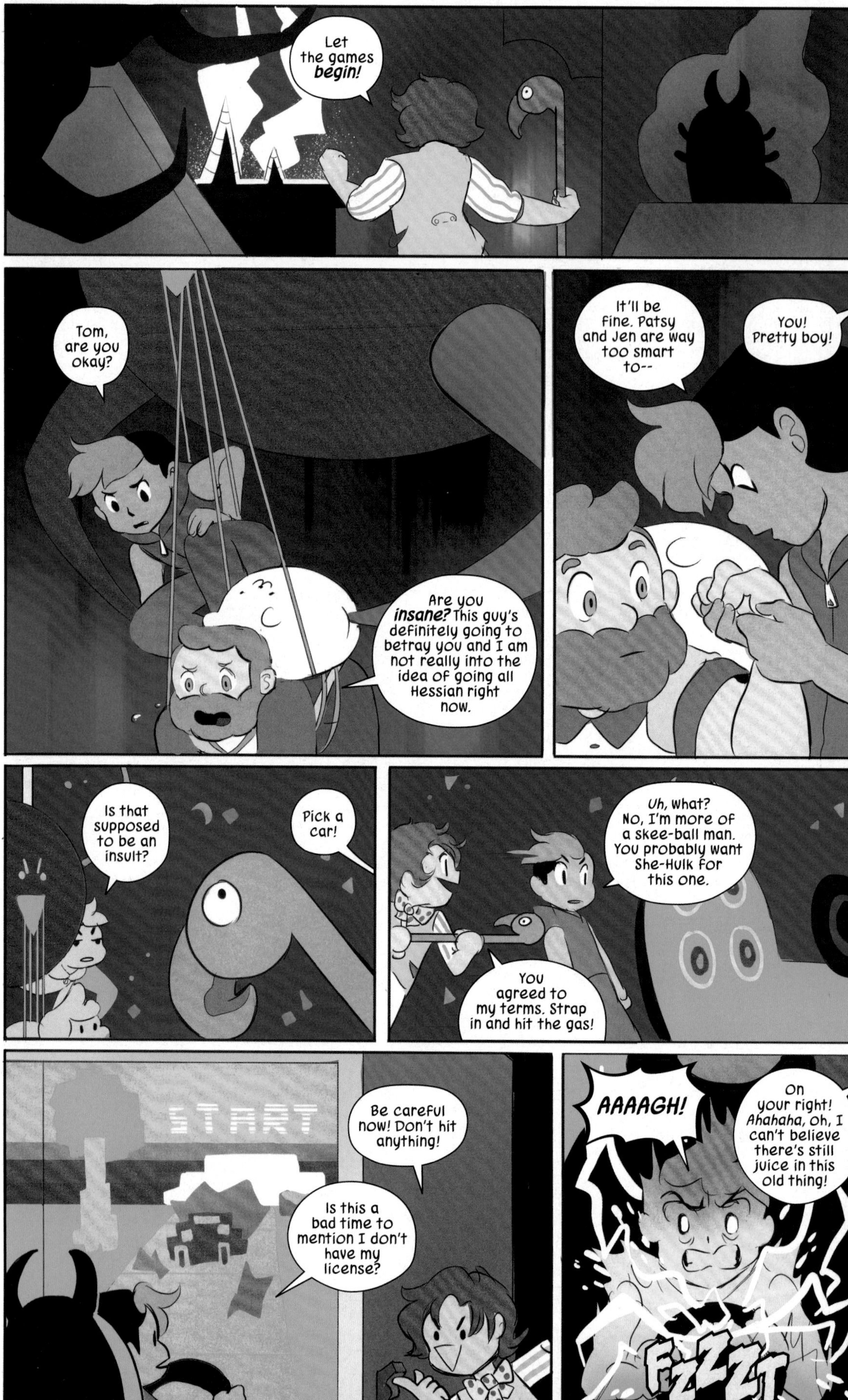
Let the games *begin!*
Tom, are you okay?
Are you *insane?* This guy's definitely going to betray you and I am not really into the idea of going all Hessian right now.
It'll be fine. Patsy and Jen are way too smart to--
You! Pretty boy!
Is that supposed to be an insult?
Pick a car!
Uh, What? No, I'm more of a skee-ball man. You probably want She-Hulk for this one.
You agreed to my terms. Strap in and hit the gas!
START
Be careful now! Don't hit anything!
Is this a bad time to mention I don't have my license?
AAAAGH!
On your right! *Ahahaha,* Oh, I can't believe there's still juice in this old thing!
FZZZT

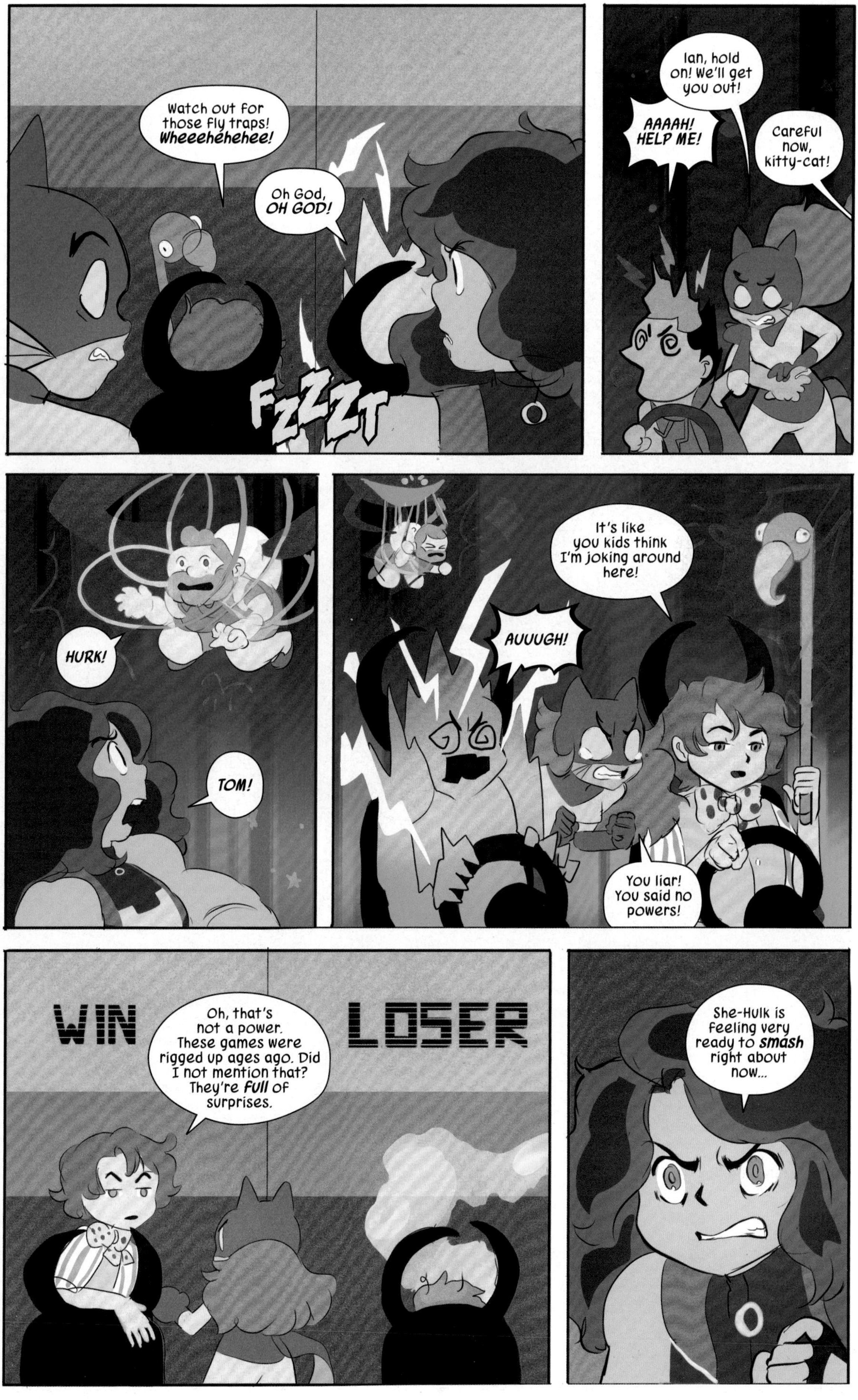
Watch out for those fly traps! Wheeehehehee!
Oh God, OH GOD!
FZZZT
Ian, hold on! We'll get you out!
AAAAH! HELP ME!
Careful now, kitty-cat!
HURK!
TOM!
It's like you kids think I'm joking around here!
AUUUGH!
You liar! You said no powers!
WIN
LOSER
Oh, that's not a power. These games were rigged up ages ago. Did I not mention that? They're full of surprises.
She-Hulk is feeling very ready to smash right about now...

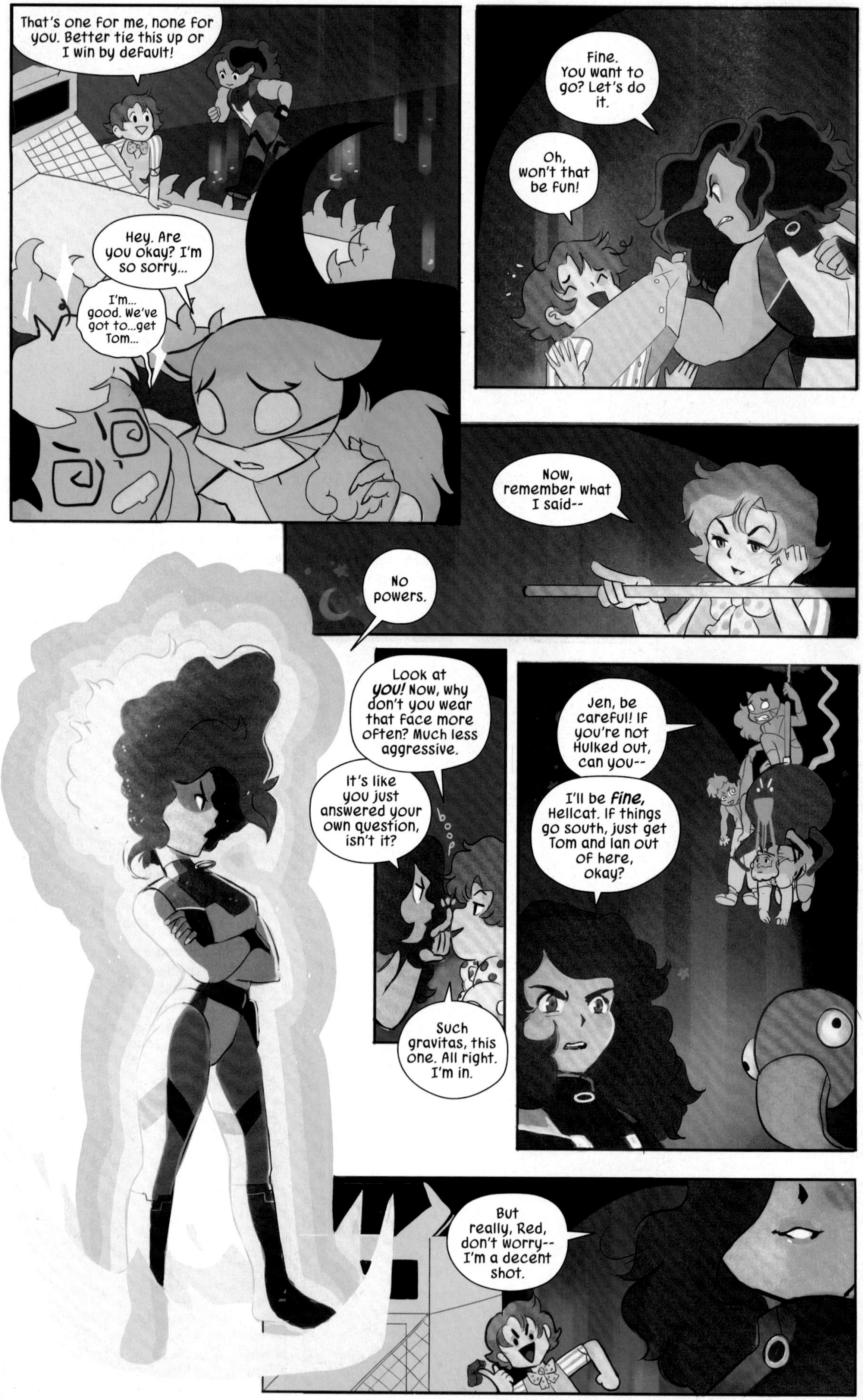
That's one for me, none for you. Better tie this up or I win by default!
Hey. Are you okay? I'm so sorry...
I'm... good. We've got to...get Tom...
Fine. You want to go? Let's do it.
Oh, won't that be fun!
Now, remember what I said--
No powers.
Look at YOU! Now, why don't you wear that face more often? Much less aggressive.
It's like you just answered your own question, isn't it?
boop
Such gravitas, this one. All right. I'm in.
Jen, be careful! If you're not Hulked out, can you--
I'll be fine, Hellcat. If things go south, just get Tom and Ian out of here, okay?
But really, Red, don't worry-- I'm a decent shot.

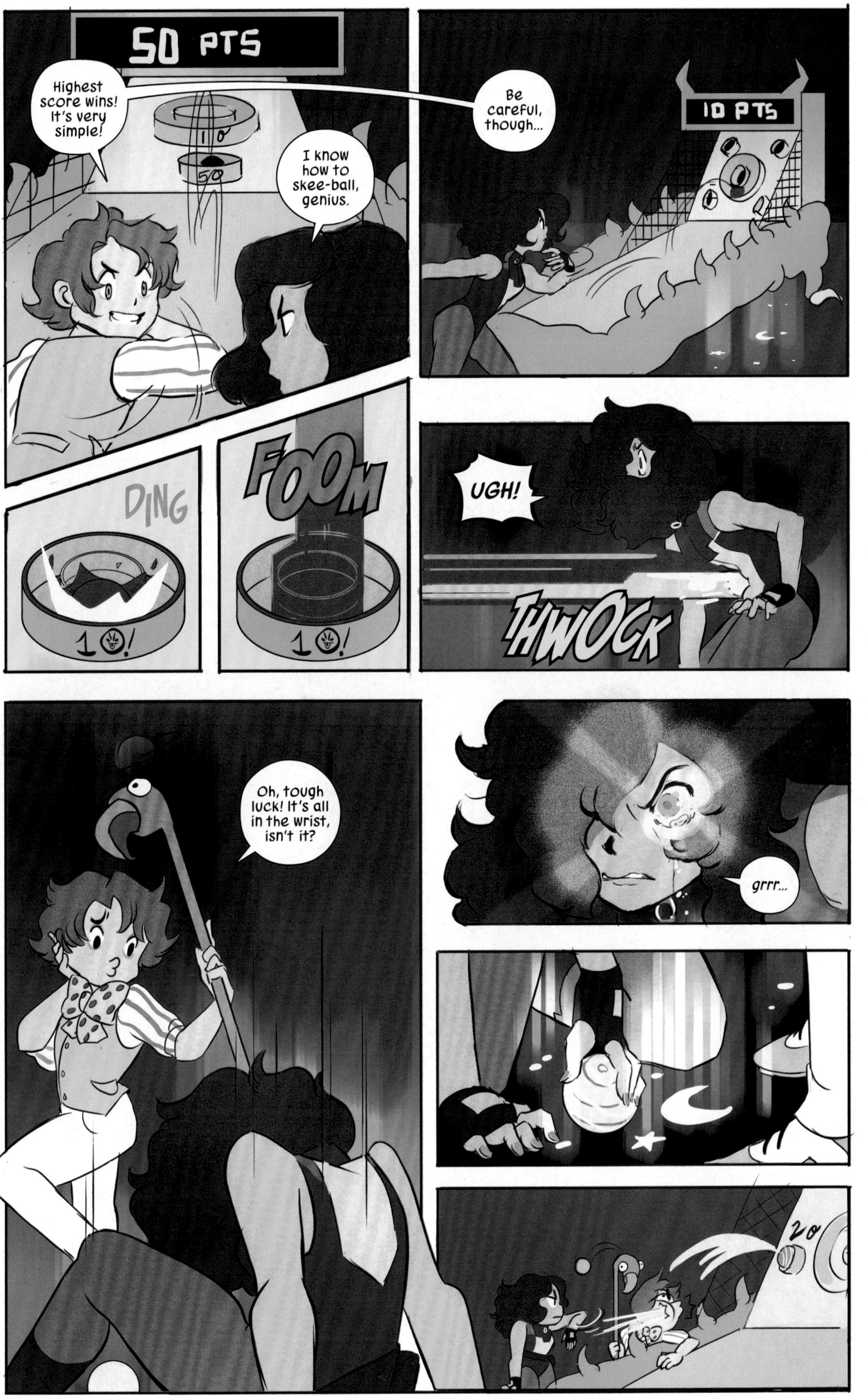
50 PTS
Highest score wins! It's very simple!
Be careful, though...
I know how to skee-ball, genius.
10 PTS
DING
10!
FOOM
10!
UGH!
THWOCK
Oh, tough luck! It's all in the wrist, isn't it?
grrr...
20

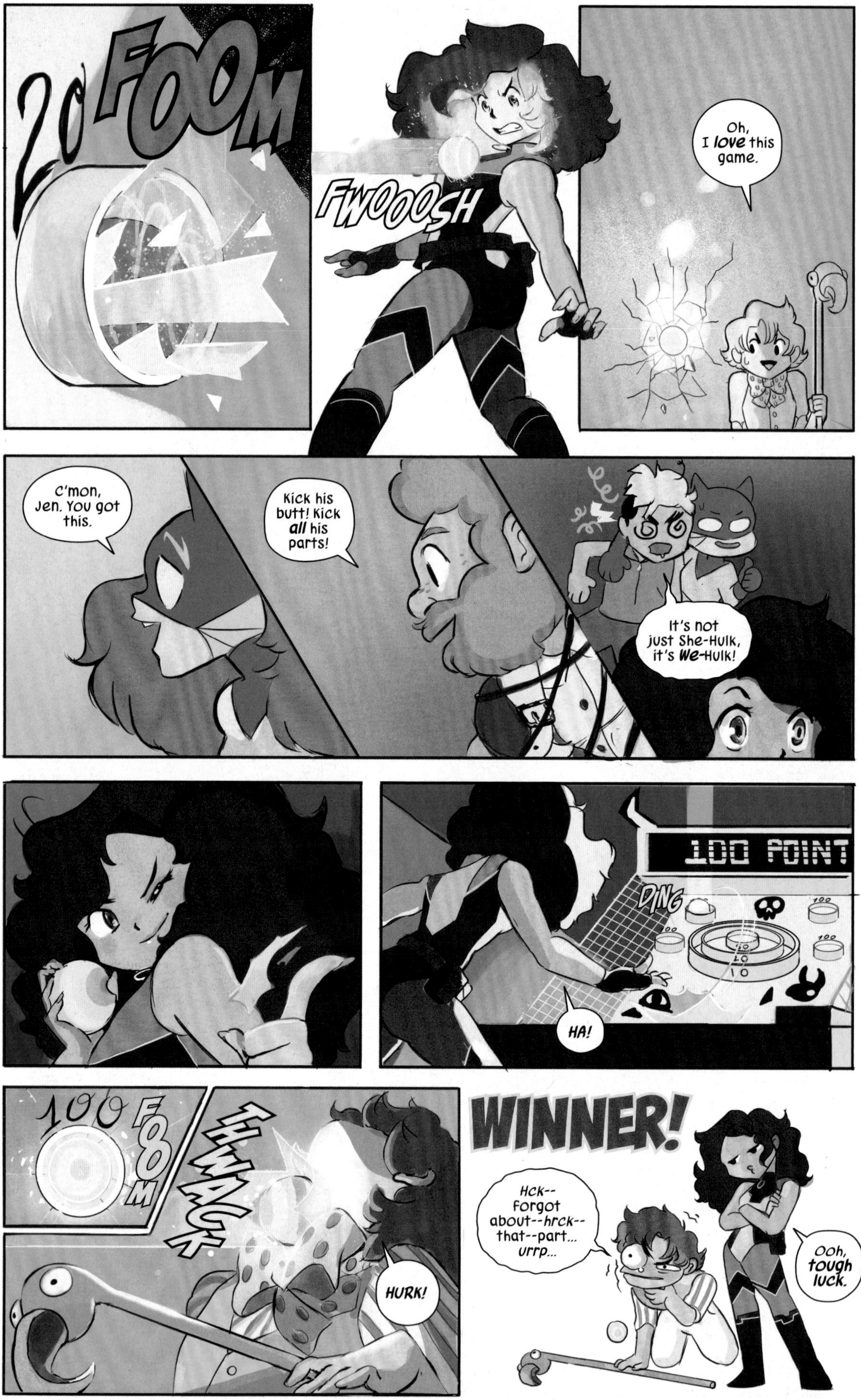
20
FOOM
FWOOOSH
Oh, I love this game.
C'mon, Jen. You got this.
Kick his butt! Kick all his parts!
It's not just She-Hulk, it's We-Hulk!
100 POINT
DING
HA!
100
FOOM
THWACK
HURK!
WINNER!
Hck-- forgot about--hrck-- that--part... urrp...
Ooh, tough luck.

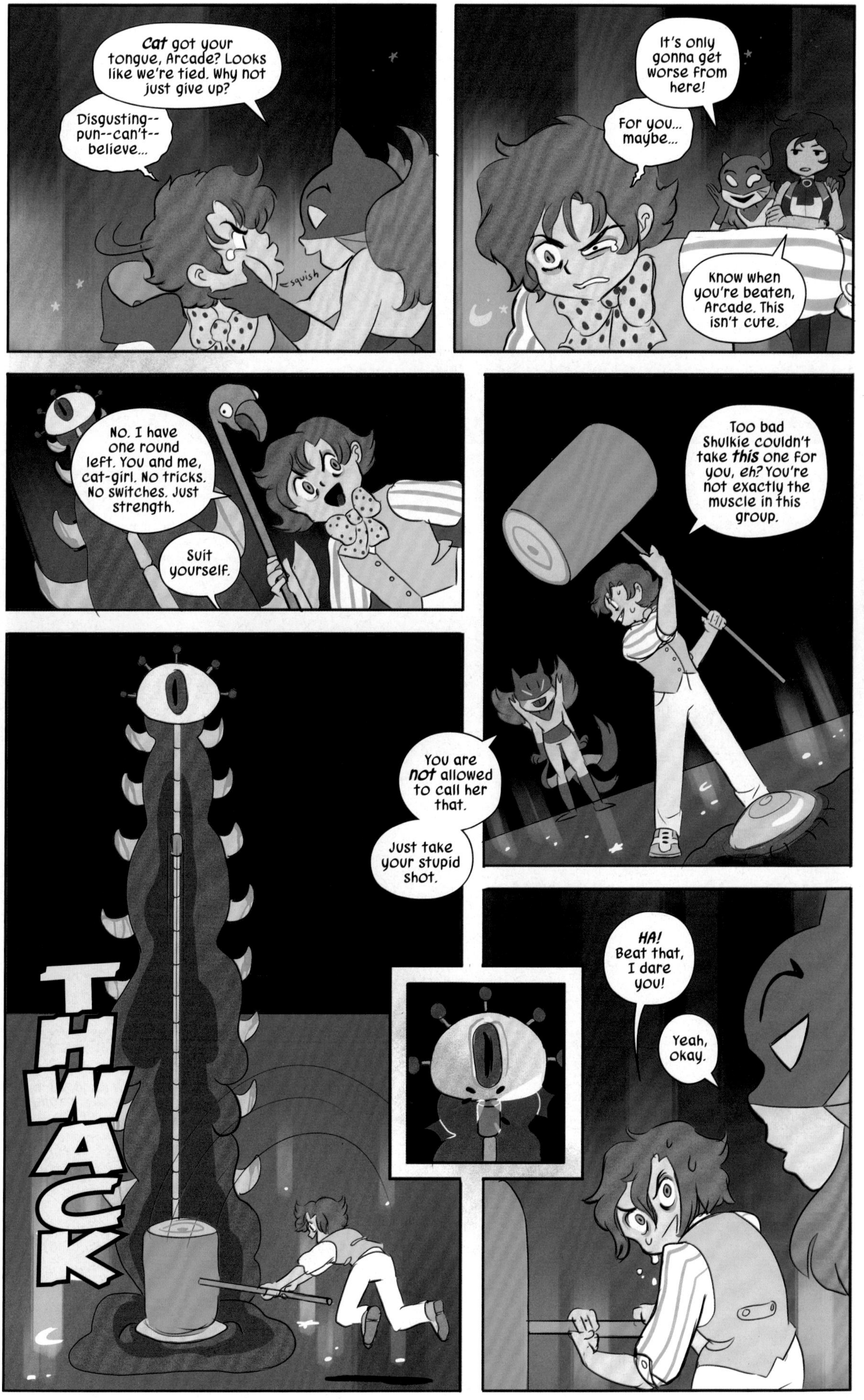

Cat got your tongue, Arcade? Looks like we're tied. Why not just give up?
Disgusting--pun--can't--believe...
squish
It's only gonna get worse from here!
For you... maybe...
Know when you're beaten, Arcade. This isn't cute.
No. I have one round left. You and me, cat-girl. No tricks. No switches. Just strength.
Suit yourself.
Too bad Shulkie couldn't take *this* one for you, eh? You're not exactly the muscle in this group.
You are *not* allowed to call her that.
Just take your stupid shot.
THWACK
HA! Beat that, I dare you!
Yeah, okay.

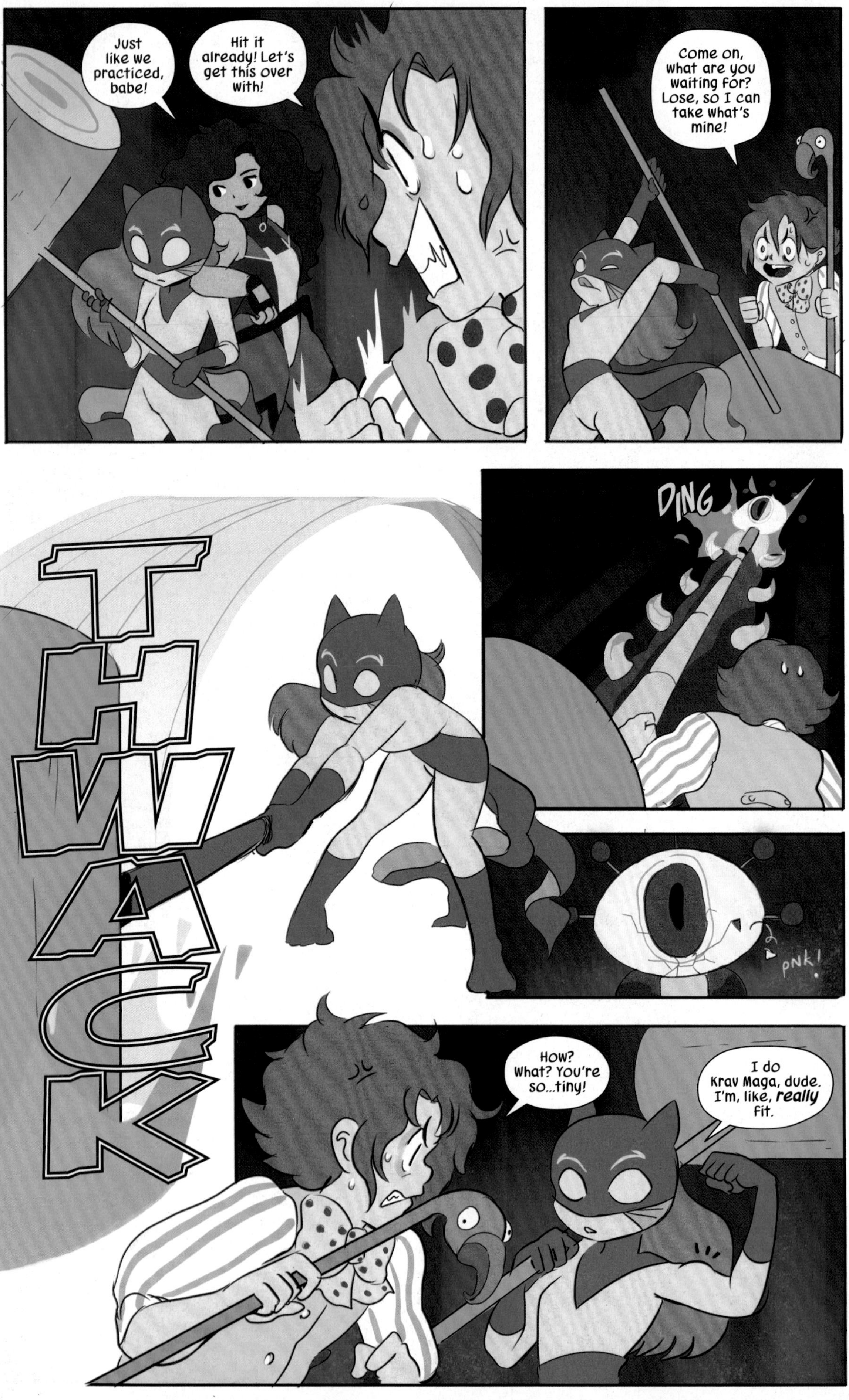

Just like we practiced, babe!
Hit it already! Let's get this over with!
Come on, what are you waiting for? Lose, so I can take what's mine!
THWACK
DING
pNK!
How? What? You're so...tiny!
I do Krav Maga, dude. I'm, like, *really* fit.

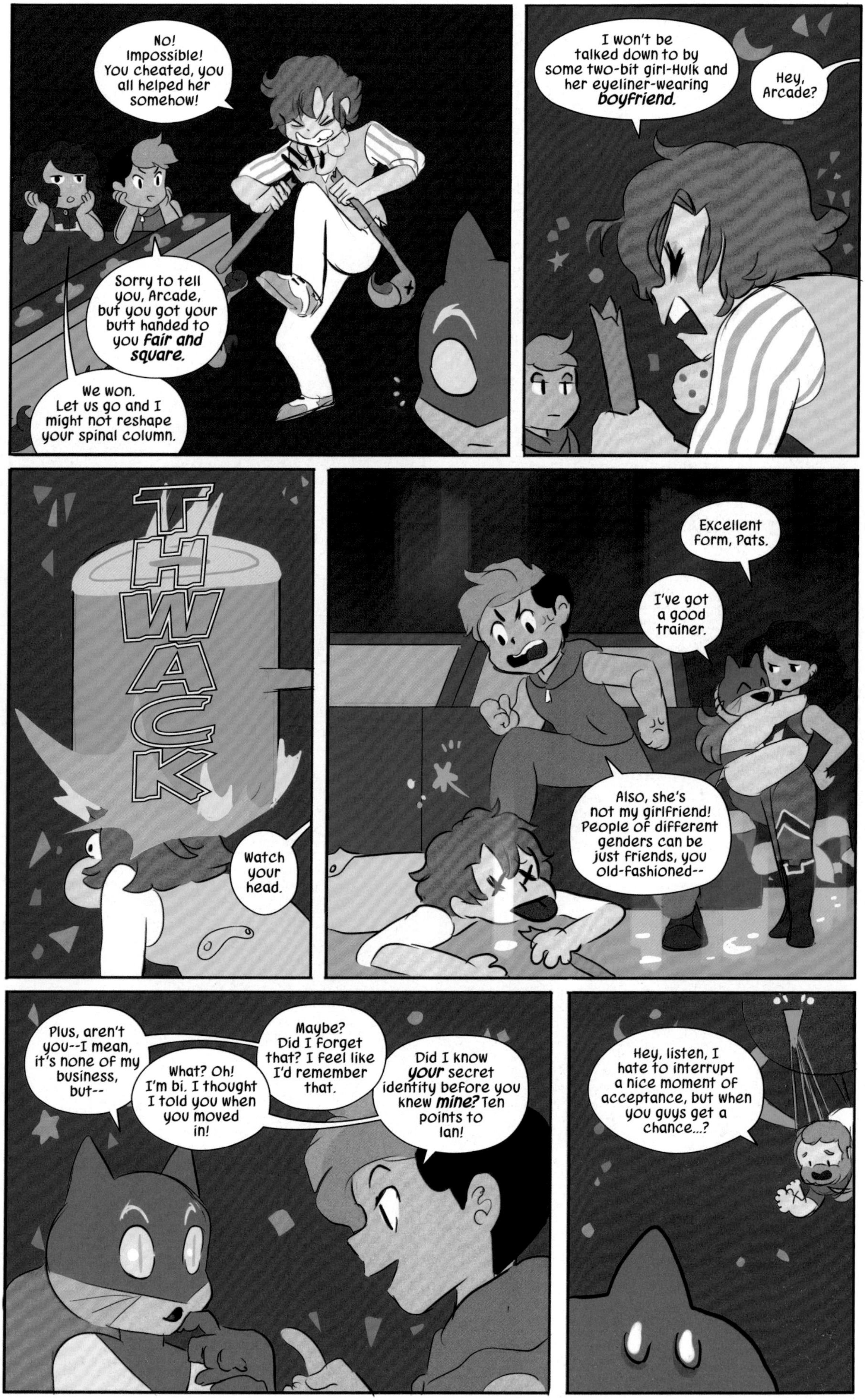
No! Impossible! You cheated, you all helped her somehow!
Sorry to tell you, Arcade, but you got your butt handed to you fair and square.
We won. Let us go and I might not reshape your spinal column.
I won't be talked down to by some two-bit girl-Hulk and her eyeliner-wearing boyfriend.
Hey, Arcade?
THWACK
Watch your head.
Excellent form, Pats.
I've got a good trainer.
Also, she's not my girlfriend! People of different genders can be just friends, you old-fashioned--
Plus, aren't you--I mean, it's none of my business, but--
What? Oh! I'm bi. I thought I told you when you moved in!
Maybe? Did I forget that? I feel like I'd remember that.
Did I know your secret identity before you knew mine? Ten points to Ian!
Hey, listen, I hate to interrupt a nice moment of acceptance, but when you guys get a chance...?

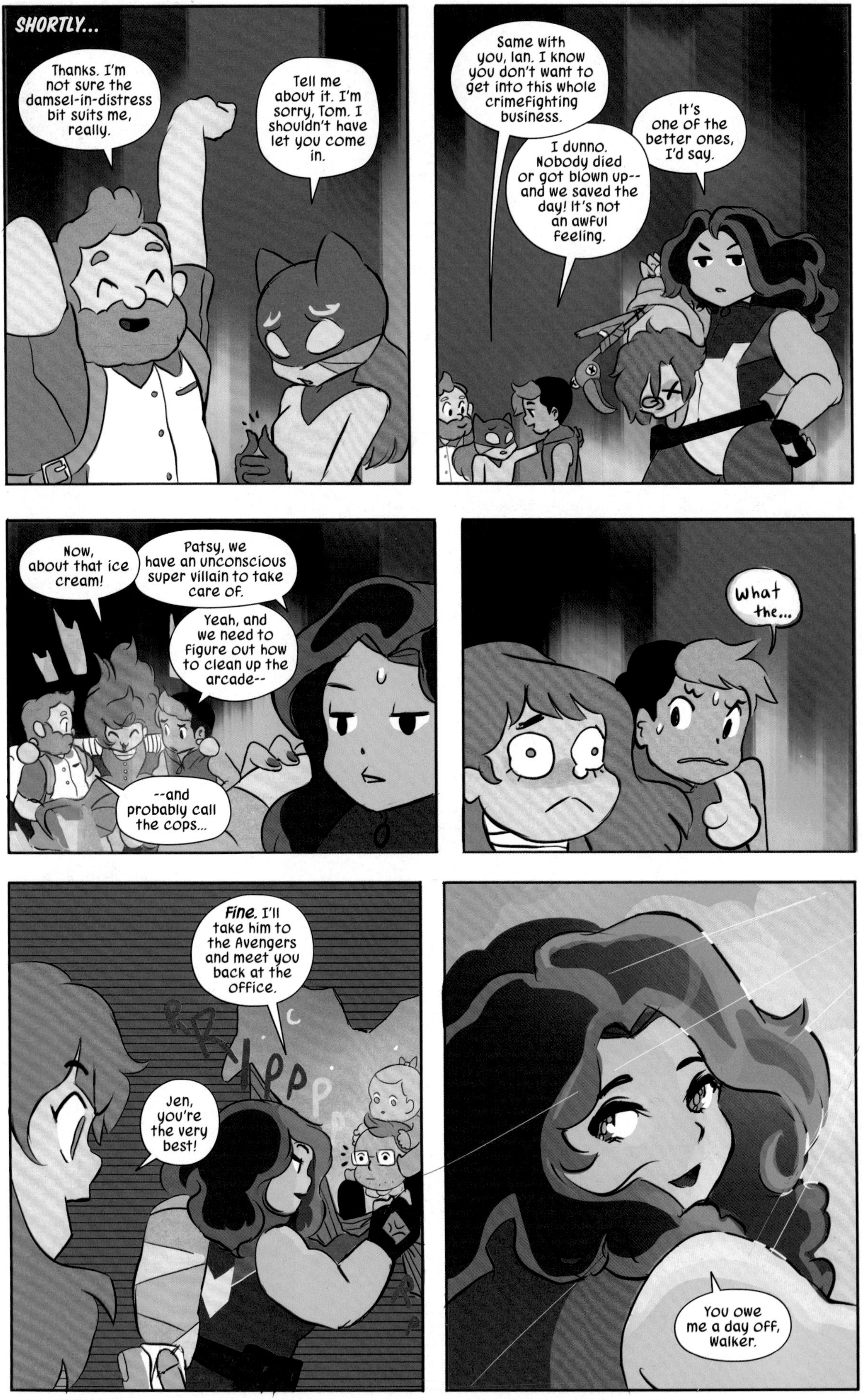
SHORTLY...
Thanks. I'm not sure the damsel-in-distress bit suits me, really.
Tell me about it. I'm sorry, Tom. I shouldn't have let you come in.
Same with you, Ian. I know you don't want to get into this whole crimefighting business.
I dunno. Nobody died or got blown up-- and we saved the day! It's not an awful feeling.
It's one of the better ones, I'd say.
Now, about that ice cream!
Patsy, we have an unconscious super villain to take care of.
Yeah, and we need to figure out how to clean up the arcade--
--and probably call the cops...
What the...
Fine. I'll take him to the Avengers and meet you back at the office.
Jen, you're the very best!
RRIPPP
You owe me a day off, Walker.

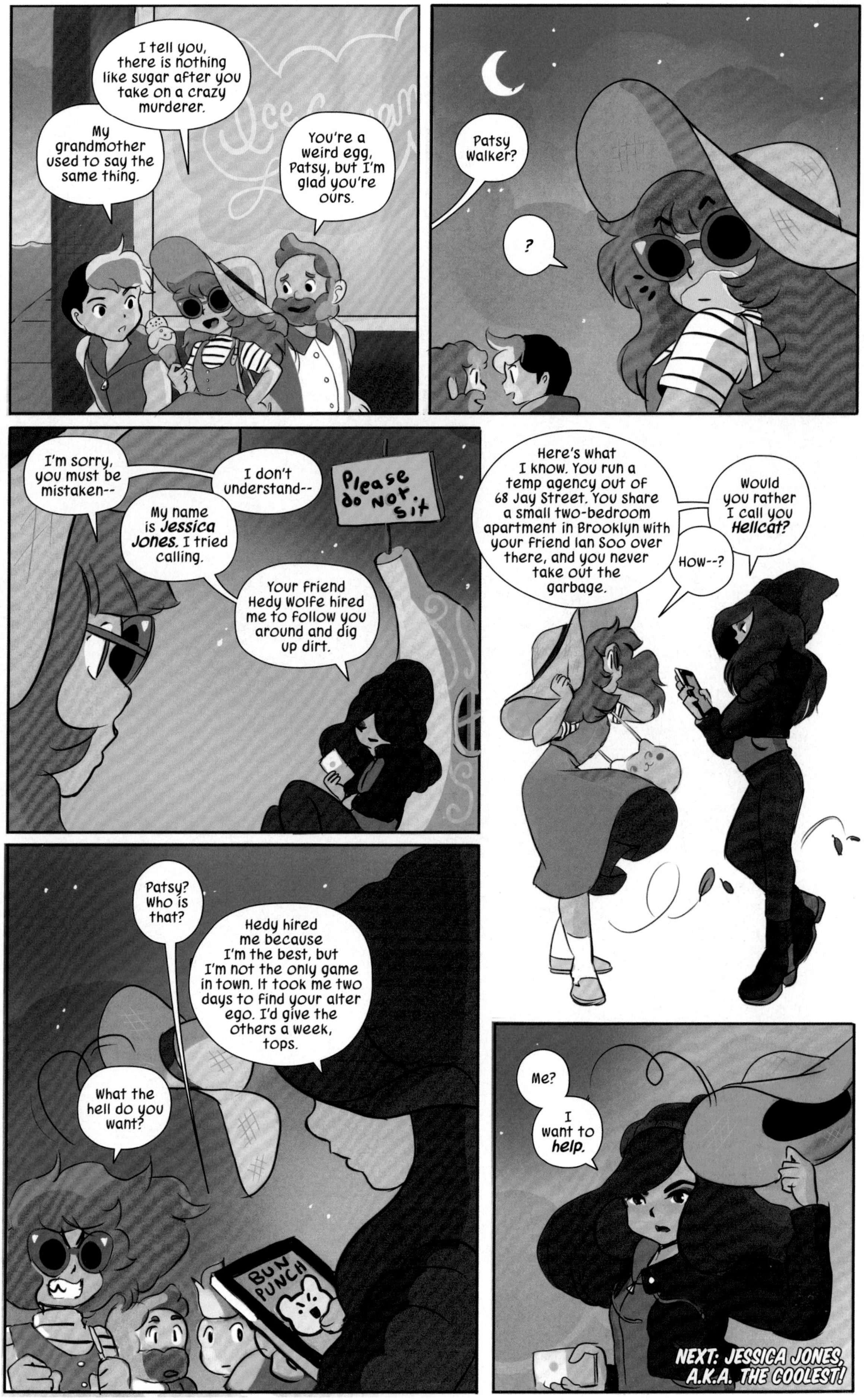
I tell you, there is nothing like sugar after you take on a crazy murderer.
My grandmother used to say the same thing.
You're a weird egg, Patsy, but I'm glad you're ours.
Patsy Walker?
?
I'm sorry, you must be mistaken--
I don't understand--
Please do not sit
My name is Jessica Jones. I tried calling.
Your friend Hedy Wolfe hired me to follow you around and dig up dirt.
Here's what I know. You run a temp agency out of 68 Jay Street. You share a small two-bedroom apartment in Brooklyn with your friend Ian Soo over there, and you never take out the garbage.
How--?
Would you rather I call you Hellcat?
Patsy? Who is that?
Hedy hired me because I'm the best, but I'm not the only game in town. It took me two days to find your alter ego. I'd give the others a week, tops.
What the hell do you want?
BUN PUNCH
Me?
I want to help.
NEXT: JESSICA JONES, A.K.A. THE COOLEST!

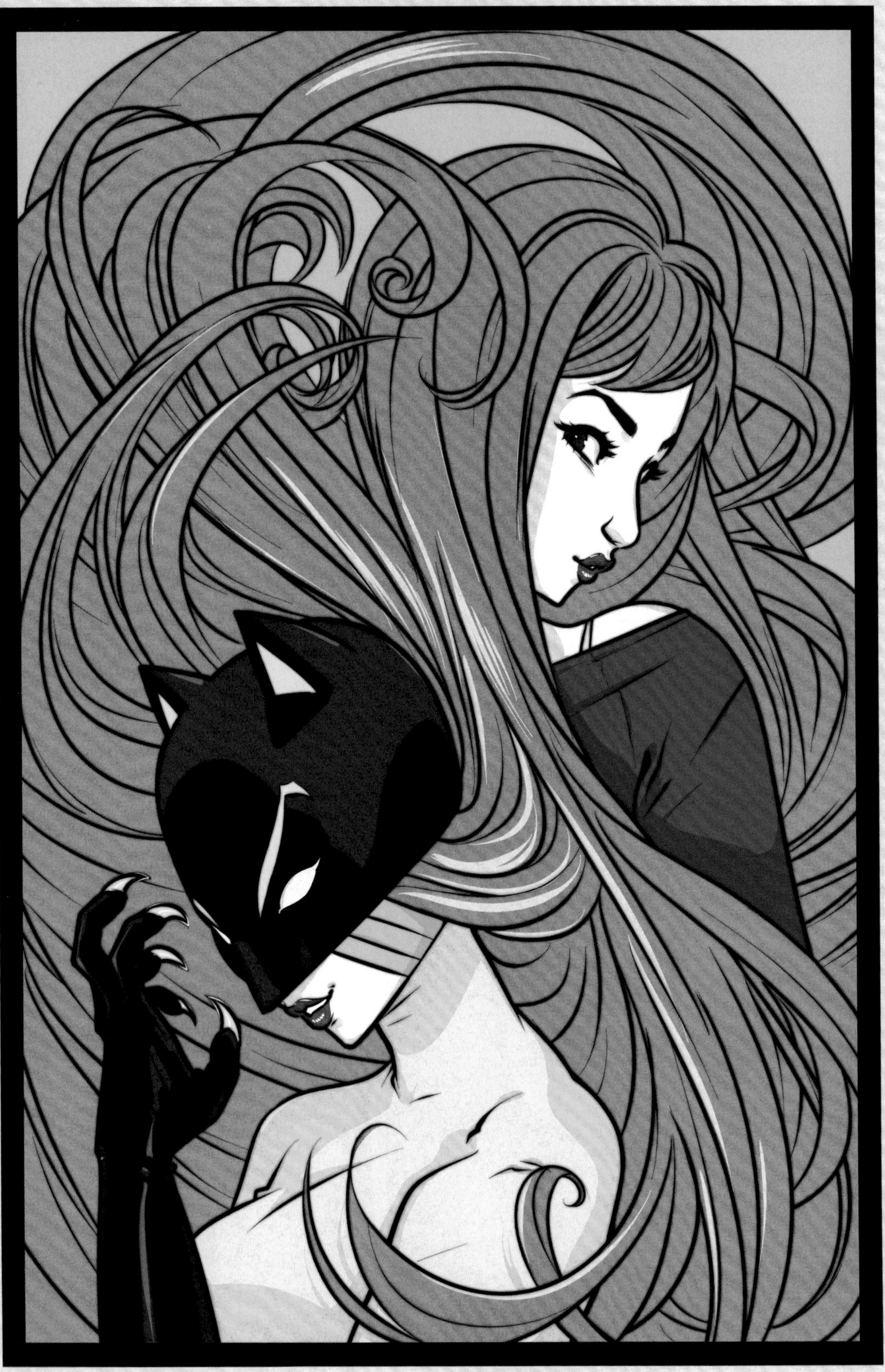

#1 ARTIST VARIANT BY **Sophie Campbell**

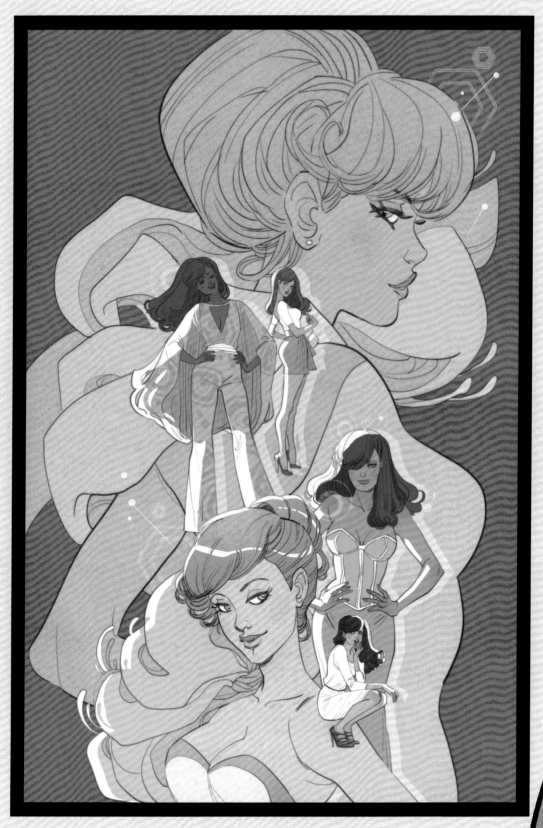

#1 FASHION VARIANT BY **Marguerite Sauvage**

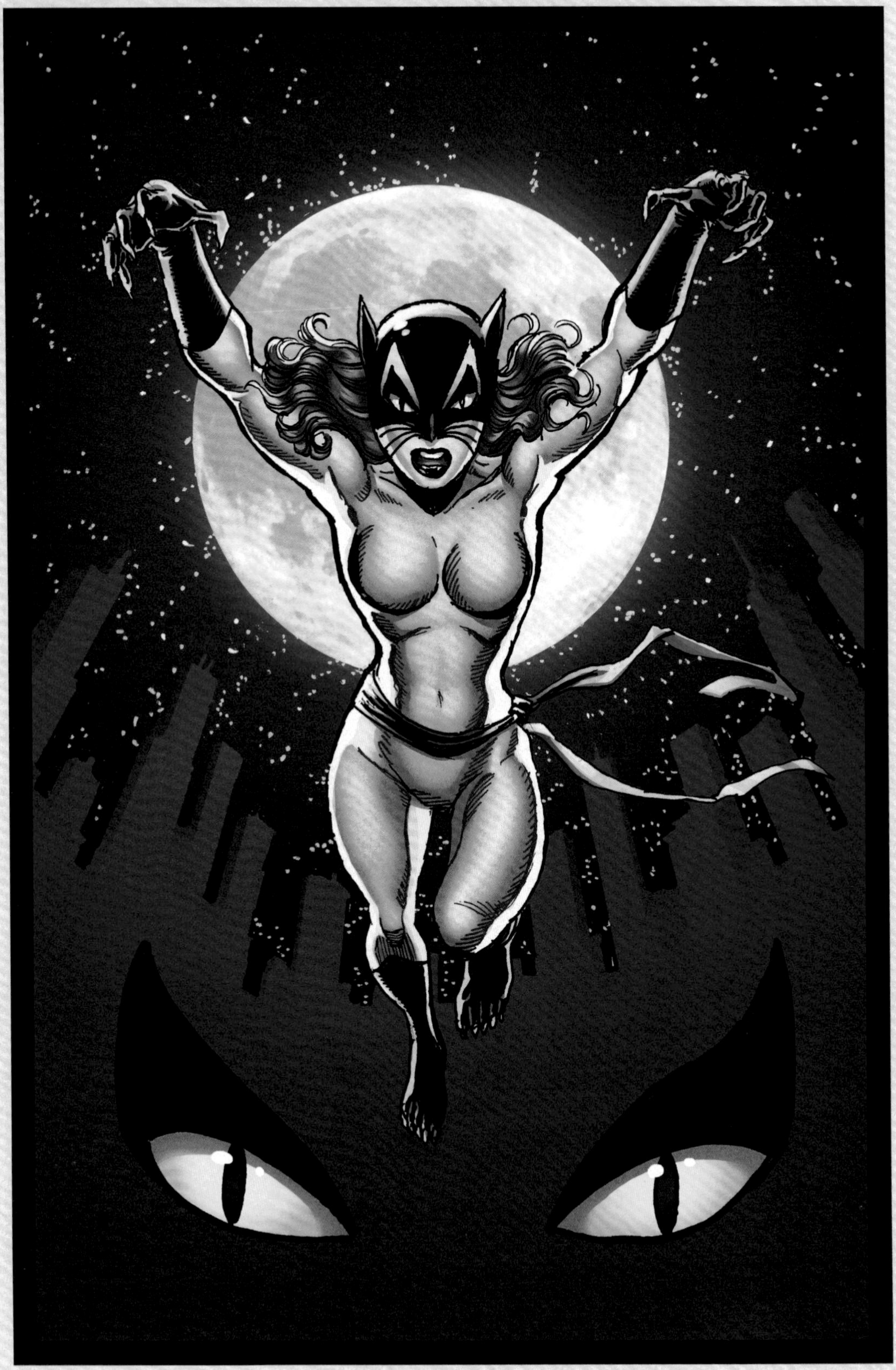

#1 CLASSIC VARIANT BY **George Perez** & **Laura Martin**

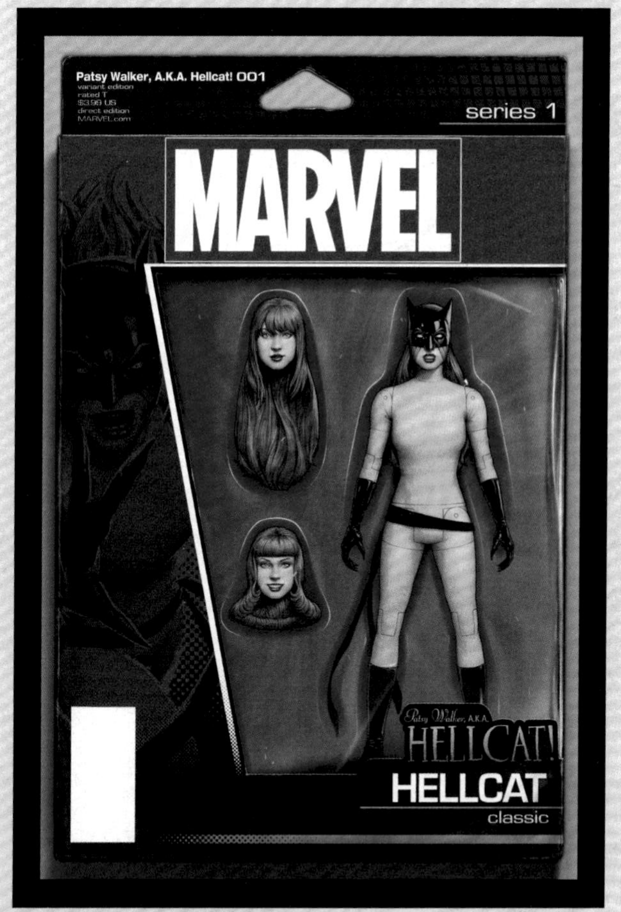
Patsy Walker, A.K.A. Hellcat! 001
variant edition
rated T
$3.99 US
direct edition
MARVEL.com
series 1
MARVEL
Patsy Walker, A.K.A.
HELLCAT!
HELLCAT
classic

#1 ACTION FIGURE VARIANT
BY **John Tyler Christopher**

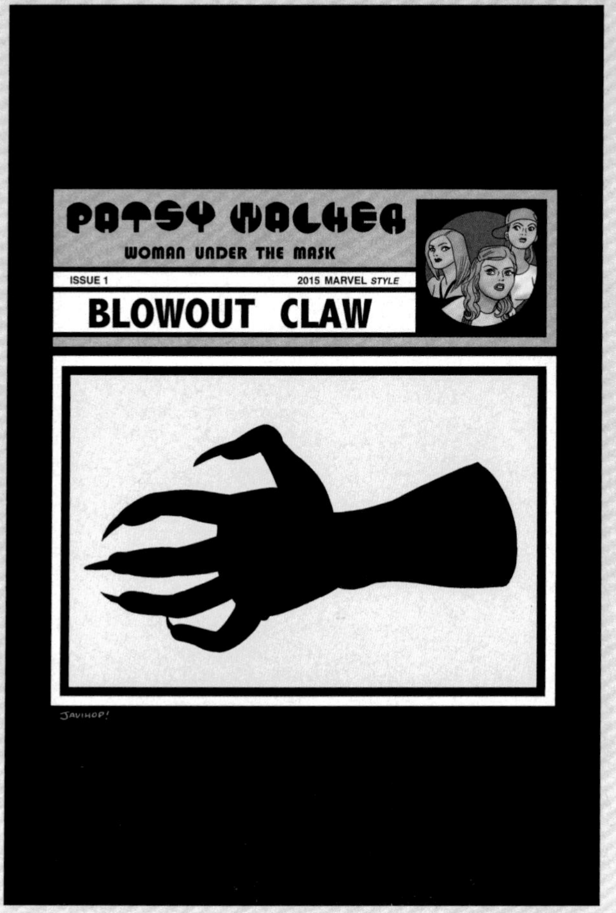
PATSY WALKER
WOMAN UNDER THE MASK
ISSUE 1
2015 MARVEL STYLE
BLOWOUT CLAW
JAVIHOP!

#1 HIP-HOP VARIANT
BY **Javier Pulido**

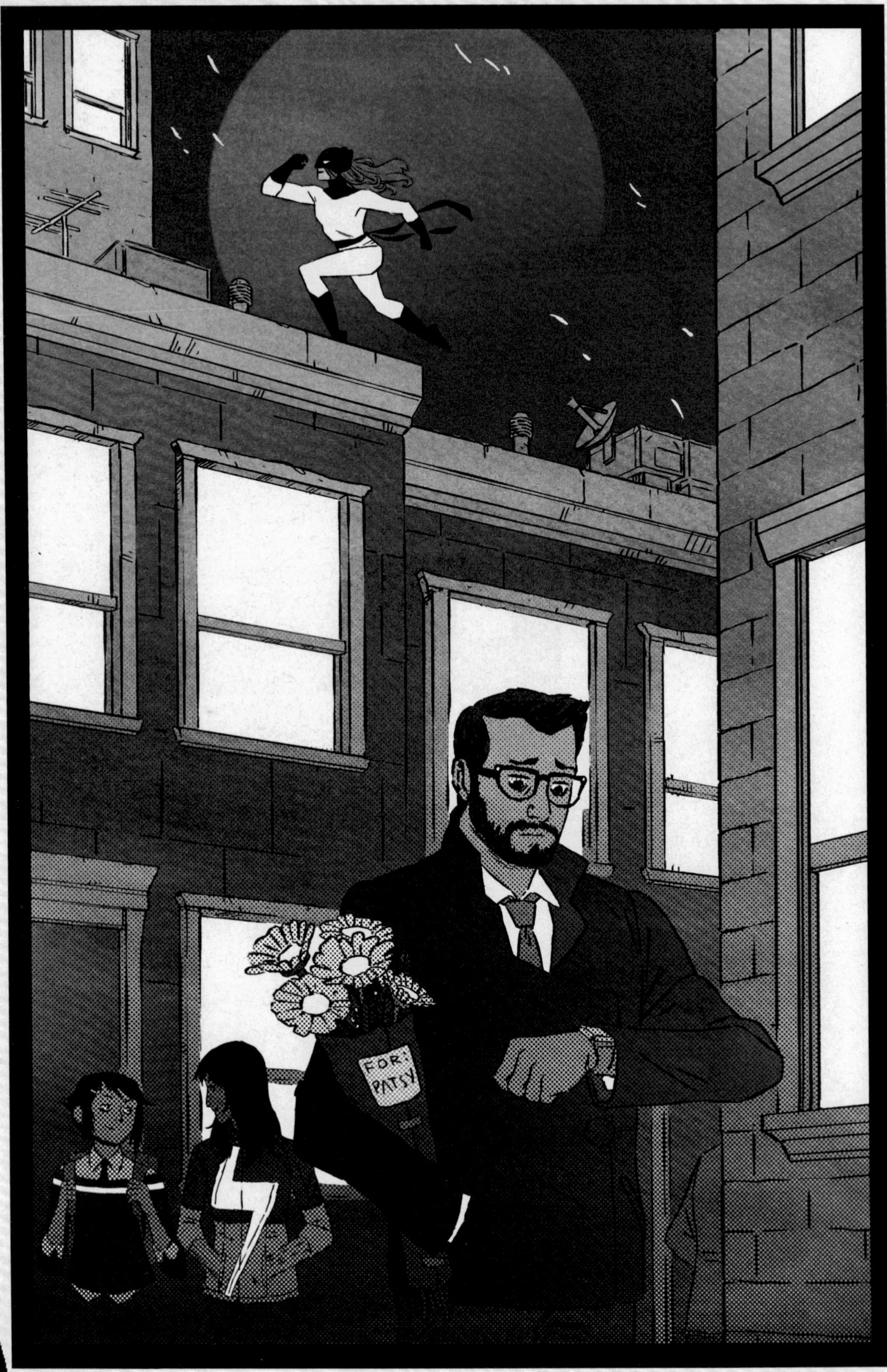
FOR: PATSY

#2 VARIANT BY **Jake Wyatt**

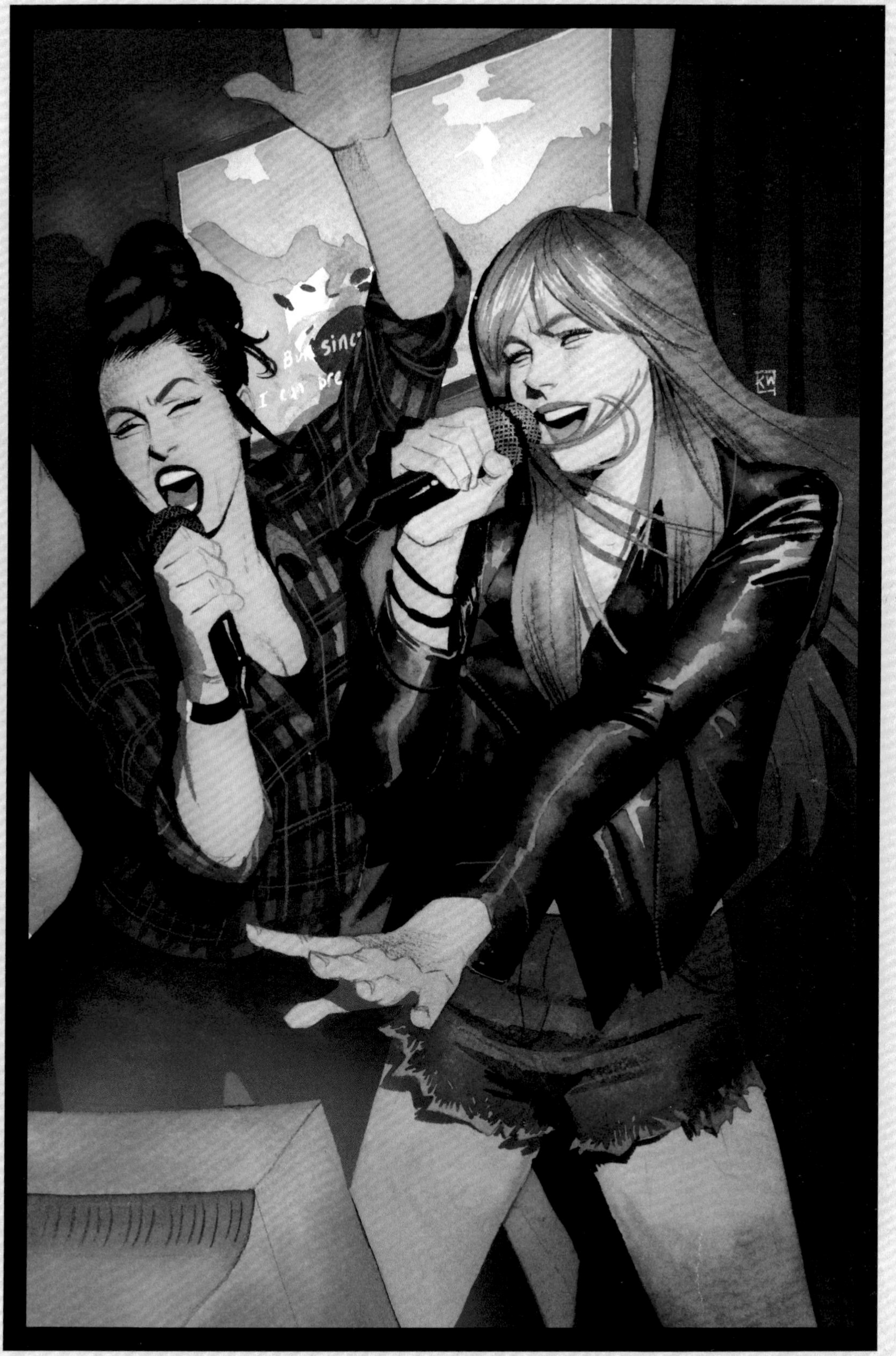

#3 VARIANT BY **Kevin Wada**

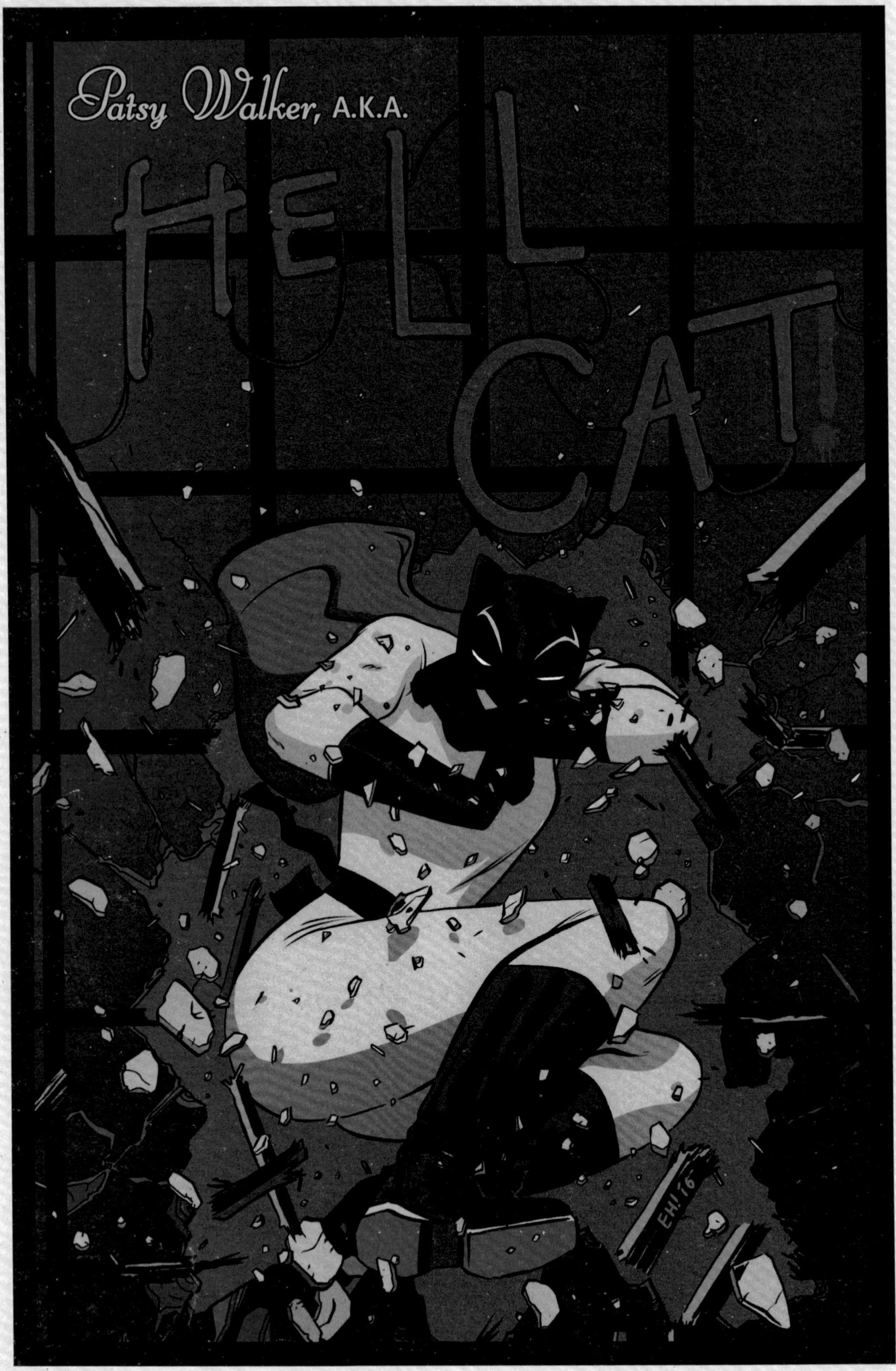
Patsy Walker, A.K.A.
HELLCAT!
EH! 16

#4 WOMEN OF POWER VARIANT BY **Erica Henderson**